Treating Sexually Abused Children and Their Nonoffending Parents

Interpersonal Violence:
The Practice Series
Jon R. Conte, Series Editor

Interpersonal Violence: The Practice Series is devoted to mental health, social service, and allied professionals who confront daily the problem of interpersonal violence. It is hoped that the knowledge, professional experience, and high standards of practice offered by the authors of these volumes may lead to the end of interpersonal violence.

In this series...

Treating Sexually Abused Children and Their Nonoffending Parents

A Cognitive Behavioral Approach

Esther Deblinger
Anne Hope Heflin

Interpersonal Violence:
The Practice Series

SAGE Publications
International Educational and Professional Publisher
Thousand Oaks   London   New Delhi

For information address:

SAGE Publications, Inc.
2455 Teller Road
Thousand Oaks, California 91320
E-mail: order@sagepub.com

SAGE Publications Ltd.
6 Bonhill Street
London EC2A 4PU
United Kingdom

SAGE Publications India Pvt. Ltd.
M-32 Market
Greater Kailash I
New Delhi 110 048 India

Printed in the United States of America

Library of Congress Cataloging-in-Publication Data

Deblinger, Esther
    Treating sexually abused children and their nonoffending parents: A cognitive behavioral approach/ authors, Esther Deblinger, Anne Hope Heflin.
        p.   cm.
    Includes bibliographical references and index.
    ISBN 0-8039-5928-1 (cloth)—ISBN 0-8039-5929-X   (pbk.).
    1. Sexually abused children. 2. Cognitive therapy for children.
  3. Parents of sexually abused children. I. Heflin, Anne Hope.
    II. Title. III. Series: Interpersonal violence ; v.16.
    RJ507.S49D43   1996
    618.92′858360651—dc00   96-9963

This book is printed on acid-free paper.

96 97 98 99   10 9 8 7 6 5 4 3 2 1

Sage Production Editor: Diana E. Axelsen
Sage Typesetter: Marion S. Warren

Contents

Foreword

The idea that sexually abused children suffer negative emotional and behavioral consequences as a result of their experiences and that therapeutic intervention will be helpful has gained wide acceptance. The evidence for this can be seen in the proliferation of specialized treatment programs and the many articles and books written on the topic. Information directed at parents of sexually abused children routinely identifies the possible effects of sexual abuse and encourages treatment as the appropriate response.

There is now a large body of literature describing sexual abuse effects in children seen shortly afterward, in clinical samples of children, adolescents and adults, and in adults in the general population. While it is now known that children have a range of difficulties following abuse experiences, with some children exhibiting few deleterious consequences, there is a belief that early, abuse-focused intervention not only will reduce symptoms but will also mitigate the development of subsequent, more serious outcomes. This has led to the formulation of an approach to sexual abuse treatment that is specifically organized around the abuse experience and directed at presumed or predicted effects of abuse experiences.

Although abuse-specific treatment appears to be widely practiced, there is as yet only modest empirical support for its effectiveness. However, scientific studies are accumulating and promise to eventually clarify the elements of a therapy regimen for these children that are beneficial in both the short and longer term. The extant studies generally find that treatment improves outcome over no treatment, and there is a suggestion that abuse-specific treatments may have superior results. How much treatment or even whether all children require formal intervention has not been established. There is much still to be learned. However, in the meantime, professionals are recommending and parents are seeking treatment.

Esther Deblinger and Anne Hope Heflin's book, *Treating Sexually Abused Children and Their Nonoffending Parents: A Cognitive Behavioral Approach,* will offer enormous guidance to practitioners who want to undertake treatment that is theoretically driven, empirically grounded, and relatively straightforward to deliver. Preliminary results of a randomized clinical trial using the approach are encouraging. The cognitive-behavioral conceptualization provides the theoretical framework for understanding commonly observed effects and suggested interventions. The great advantage of this perspective is that it makes sense and can be readily grasped by professionals and families alike. Very importantly, it draws on the many already proven therapeutic strategies that are used for other emotional and behavioral problems of children.

The field of sexual abuse treatment has not always made the best use of existing knowledge about the causes and cures for children's difficulties. There is now substantial evidence for the effectiveness of child psychotherapy, and the characteristics of more effective treatments have been at least partially identified. The data suggest that treatments that are relatively brief, cognitive-behavioral, targeted to specific problem areas, and structured produce the best results. Therefore, sexual abuse treatment models would do well to attend to these findings.

The authors have produced just what the field has needed: a treatment model that incorporates what has been learned about sexually abused children and the principles and practices of effective therapy. They go beyond simply describing problems and listing interventions. When therapists adopt a systematic, coherent, and practical approach that reflects the characteristics of effective treatments, there should be an improvement in the way treatment is organized and carried out.

A useful feature of the book is the liberal use of case examples. First, it grounds the book in the real-life experiences of children in therapy and reveals the authors' genuine appreciation of the variety of reactions that children may have. In addition, readers are provided with specific illustrations of how therapists can explain concepts and teach new skills. These examples help bridge the often difficult translation from general ideas or even specific techniques to actual and familiar case scenarios. It is likely that many readers will find themselves making use of the suggested explanations and strategies.

One of the most important contributions of this book is the emphasis on working with parents. Although all competent therapists recognize that parental involvement in child therapy is crucial, not as much has been written about this component of abuse-specific treatment. Of particular interest is the ingredient of teaching behavior management concepts and techniques and demonstrating their specific application to typical post-abuse problem behaviors. This has been an overlooked aspect of helping parents to be better helpers in their children's recovery process. Parental responses have been shown to be significant factors in moderating negative outcomes. Providing them with tools to effectively manage child behavior and information that encourages support should enhance the likelihood that the treatment experience will have lasting beneficial results.

It is certainly true that many sexually abused children and their families suffer from problems that are not specific to the abuse experience, although such problems may exacerbate abuse-related difficulties. In some cases, an abuse focus may not even be necessary or a priority. The approach recommended in this book does not require a lockstep application of a manualized treatment. It recommends assessment for potential or actual abuse related consequences and describes interventions that may be useful when problems are present. It allows for flexibility in the amount of focus on any particular problem area. In addition, many of the techniques, such as positive coping skills or behavior management, have application to other areas of dysfunction and can easily be transferred.

This book is especially welcome in these times of managed care and of emphasis on shorter treatments that are outcome based and result in demonstrable improvement. Sexual abuse treatment, like other therapies, will come under increasing scrutiny and may be even more difficult to defend. This is because sexual abuse is not a disorder but an experience that produces a range of effects. Unlike most proven treatments that focus simply on symptom amelioration, abuse-focused treatment may be initiated with children who are referred not for abuse-related problems but simply because abuse has been revealed. It also aims to be preventive. The kind of treatment approach offered in this book, one that is well supported and described, can serve as evidence that abuse-focused therapy can be justified and deserves continued support.

Esther Deblinger and Anne Hope Heflin exemplify the best of the practitioner-scientist tradition. Their concern and compassion for the circumstances of the children and families is evident throughout. They provide a conceptualization, structure, and content for effective treatment. Since most clinicians describe their approaches as eclectic, the cognitive-behavioral framework should not be incompatible with many other theoretical orientations. Even experienced clinicians will find many new and useful strategies that can be easily incorporated into a variety of treatment settings. There is every reason to believe that this book will enhance the quality of the treatment that is being delivered and hence the positive outcomes for children and families.

LUCY BERLINER, M.S.W.
Harborview Sexual Assault Center
Seattle, Washington

Preface and Acknowledgments

I would like to describe how this book developed and acknowledge the many colleagues and friends whose creative ideas and support through the years greatly contributed to its completion.

Ideas for the book began percolating back in 1987, shortly after Dr. Susan McLeer offered me the position of co-director of the Child Sexual Abuse Diagnostic and Treatment Center at the Medical College of Pennsylvania. Dr. McLeer greatly encouraged my efforts to develop a clinical service and a research program to address the needs of sexually abused children. Along with our colleagues at the Medical College of Pennsylvania, Dr. McLeer and I initially collaborated on several investigations aimed at examining the psychological sequelae suffered by the many sexually abused children referred to the center.

The studies revealed a wide array of symptomatology exhibited by sexually abused children, with the vast majority of children suffering at least partial symptoms of post-traumatic stress disorder (Deblinger, McLeer, Atkins, Ralphe, & Foa, 1989; McLeer, Deblinger, Atkins, Foa, & Ralphe, 1988; McLeer, Deblinger, Henry, & Orvaschel, 1992). Based on that finding, we began to think about developing interventions for sexually abused children suffering post-traumatic stress disorder and related symptoms. An examination of the treatment literature in the field of child sexual abuse turned up many interesting articles describing creative treatment approaches but almost no empirical data supporting their efficacy.

As a Ph.D. graduate from the State University of New York at Stony Brook, with its heavy emphasis on research, my next instinct was to identify empirically supported interventions that had been successfully used with populations suffering symptoms similar to those of sexually abused children. Fortuitously, Dr. Edna Foa, a member of the Medical College of Pennsylvania faculty, was actively engaged in treatment outcome research with adult rape victims. We prevailed upon her to allow us to sit in on her clinical research meetings as she and her staff discussed the treatment of adult rape victims suffering post-traumatic stress disorder.

I gained much inspiration and many clinical insights from these early meetings. However, the interventions discussed could not simply be applied to children. A great deal of developmental sensitivity and creativity was required to modify Dr. Foa's prolonged exposure procedures for use with children. My effort to develop and evaluate such a treatment approach was greatly supported by my colleagues at the Medical College of Pennsylvania, Caryn Lerman, Ph.D., Marc Atkins, Ph.D., and Delmina Henry, Ph.D. As a clinical researcher, Dr. Lerman was and continues to be a great role model and invaluable consultant. Dr. Atkins, who also works with children, was a wonderful mentor and a tremendous support. I was also extremely fortunate to be working on a daily basis with Dr. Henry, an extraordinarily gifted clinician. With considerable input from our clients, we began to design an exposure intervention for use with sexually abused children; we called it *gradual exposure.*

During this time, I began working on a preliminary treatment manual; it was to be submitted with a proposal for a grant that, unfortunately, was never funded. Despite this disappointment, Drs. McLeer, Henry, and I persisted; we designed and implemented a pilot treatment outcome investigation examining the effects of the proposed cognitive behavioral treatment model for sexually abused children (Deblinger, McLeer, & Henry, 1990). Although this was a simple pre-post design, the findings were very promising.

Shortly thereafter, I accepted Dr. Martin Finkel's offer to serve as the Clinical Director of a developing multidisciplinary center for the evaluation and treatment of suspected victims of child sexual abuse at the University of Medicine and Dentistry of New Jersey-School of Osteopathic Medicine (UMDNJ-SOM). The dean of the medical school, Dr. Frederick Humphrey, has been a great supporter of the Center's mission from the start. Dr. Finkel, the Medical Director of the center, demonstrates tremendous commitment to healing the psychological as well as the physical wounds of sexually abused children. He has been a great source of encouragement and has made it possible for me to continue to pursue the development of a state-of-the-art mental health service and clinical research program for sexually abused children. In fact, I collaborated with Dr. Finkel and our colleagues, Dr. Julie Lippmann and Dr. Robert Steer, on a treatment outcome proposal that was submitted to and funded by the National Center on Child Abuse and Neglect (NCCAN) (Grant #90-CA-1461).

This again gave me the opportunity to further refine and expand on the preliminary treatment manual. Over the last 5 years, the manual was used as a guide by the therapists participating in the NCCAN-funded treatment outcome investigation. This investigation is in its final stages, and the initial findings will be published in the near future (Deblinger, Lippmann, & Steer, in press). We are also hoping to collaborate with our highly respected colleagues, Drs. Judith Cohen and Tony Mannarino on a multisite treatment outcome investigation, comparing this cognitive behavioral approach to a nondirective supportive counseling format.

The treatment manual has also been applied to group formats with success (Stauffer & Deblinger, 1996). For her dissertation research, Dr. Lori Stauffer, a center faculty member and skillful clinical researcher, implemented a group treatment outcome study that served as the pilot data for a recently funded National Institute of Mental Health grant proposal to further validate the efficacy of this treatment model using an experimental design.

As indicated above, the treatment manual has been revised and refined over the years and used with clients participating in treatment outcome protocols, as well as with clients seen through the center's general mental health service. We are clearly committed to further refining the model based on the empirical data we are currently analyzing, as well as future treatment outcome research findings. However, with much appreciated encouragement from Jon Conte, Lucy Berliner, Terry Hendrix, and others, we decided to make the treatment manual more widely available in book form now.

Substantial changes in the treatment manual, however, were required to create a book that was clear, concise, and reader friendly. My coauthor, Dr. Anne Heflin, was instrumental in making this happen. She is not only an excellent writer, but, as a senior member of the center's faculty, she has made very valuable contributions to the book and to the center in general. I have tremendous respect for her clinical insights and her ability to convey the nuts and bolts of the treatment model on paper as well as in practice.

I also would like to express appreciation to other members of the center's faculty and staff, including Gwendolyn Barton, M.S.W., L.C.S.W., Marianne Clark, Psy.D., Julie Lippmann, Psy.D., Allyson Maedel, M.A., Lori Stauffer, Ph.D., and Merry Woodruff, M.S., who have generously shared their creative ideas and their successes and struggles in applying this treatment model. I would also like to thank Christina Hathaway and our many other practicum students for their contributions.

It should also be said that from the very start, our greatest contributors have been the children and parents themselves; they have taught us so much about overcoming trauma and have been the motivating force behind our efforts. We have shared some of their experiences through dialogues and case examples, but we have significantly altered identifying information and characteristics to protect their right to confidentiality.

Dr. Heflin and I also owe a great deal of thanks to Angela Ruiz and Eileen Rozelle for their secretarial support as well as their patience and perseverance in typing and retyping the numerous revisions of the treatment manual.

Finally, I thank my parents and family for their unending support and encouragement. My greatest thanks are reserved for my husband and best friend, Morty Sosland, and our daughters, Arielle and Sarah, for helping me balance my work with a life full of love and shared dreams. Dr. Heflin thanks her parents for their constant support, her children, Evan and Brynna, for being her inspiration and her husband, Paul, for the sacrifices, understanding, love, and encouragement that made her contributions to this book possible.

To our families

Morty, Arielle, and Sarah
and
Paul, Evan, and Brynna

Introduction

❏ Overview of Child Sexual Abuse

PREVALENCE

Child sexual abuse is an international problem that affects children of all ethnic, racial, and socioeconomic backgrounds (Finkelhor, 1994; Russell, 1983; Wyatt, 1985). Studies conducted to date reveal varying prevalence rates, most likely due to the different assessment procedures used across investigations (Wyatt & Peters, 1986). However, estimates based on the most sophisticated and rigorously conducted epidemiological studies suggest that at least one out of four girls and one out of six boys in the general population experience child sexual abuse by the time they are 18 years of age (Finkelhor, Hotaling, Lewis, & Smith, 1990; Martin, Anderson, Romans, Mullen, & O'Shea, 1993; Russell, 1983; Wyatt, 1985). Russell's (1983) findings suggest that most of these cases are not reported to the authorities. Furthermore, as one might expect, a history of child sexual abuse is even more common in child and

1

adolescent clinical populations (Kumar, Steer, & Deblinger, 1995; Lanktree, Briere, & Zaidi, 1991; Rohsenow, Corbett, & Devine, 1988; Sansonnet-Hayden, Haley, Marriage, & Fine, 1987).

SYMPTOMATOLOGY

Children's reactions to the experience of sexual abuse vary widely. It is well documented that whereas some sexually abused children suffer minimal effects, others suffer severe and sometimes long-lasting psychiatric symptomatology (Beitchman, Zucker, Hood, daCosta, & Akman, 1992; Browne & Finkelhor, 1986; Kendall-Tackett, Williams, & Finkelhor, 1993). The symptoms exhibited by sexually abused children appear to run the gamut. Emotional difficulties commonly reported include anxiety, sadness, anger, and shame (Conte & Schuerman, 1987; Tufts, 1984). Behavioral problems exhibited by sexually abused children include withdrawal, noncompliance, aggression, and inappropriate sexual behavior problems (Deblinger, McLeer, Atkins, Ralphe, & Foa, 1989; Friedrich, Urquiza, & Beilke, 1986; McLeer, Deblinger, Henry, & Orvaschel, 1992). Sexually abused children also may develop distorted cognitive views that lead to sexual dissatisfaction (Finkelhor, Hotaling, Lewis, & Smith, 1989), extreme distrust of others, and feelings of self-blame (Mannarino, Cohen, & Berman, in press). Finally, physiological symptoms such as headaches, stomachaches, and startle reactions are not uncommon among sexually abused children (Adams-Tucker, 1981; Anderson, Bach, & Griffith, 1981; van der Kolk, 1988).

POST-TRAUMATIC STRESS DISORDER

Although sexually abused children may exhibit a wide array of seemingly disparate symptoms, in recent years, there has been increasing recognition that many of these symptoms fall within diagnostic criteria for post-traumatic stress disorder (PTSD) (Deblinger et al., 1989; Goodwin, 1988; McLeer, Deblinger, Atkins, Foa, & Ralphe, 1988). There is, in fact, considerable evidence that a significant proportion of sexually abused children referred for mental health services suffer at least partial symptoms of PTSD (McLeer et al.,

1988). PTSD symptoms are described in terms of three general categories:

1. Reexperiencing the traumatic event, which may occur through intrusive memories or dreams of the event, flashbacks, or distress when confronted with reminders of the event.
2. Avoidance of memories and reminders of the trauma and diminished responsiveness, which may appear as reduced interest in activities, detachment from others, limited affective range, or a sense of foreshortened future.
3. Symptoms of increased anxiety or arousal, such as sleep disturbance, irritability, concentration problems, hypervigilance, or a tendency to be easily startled (American Psychiatric Association, 1994).

The treatment model to be described was originally developed for use with children who meet full criteria for the diagnosis of PTSD. Since then, the authors have recognized that the model may be tailored for effective use with children who exhibit only partial symptoms of PTSD, as well as children suffering with other related symptoms, such as generalized anxiety, depression, phobias, inappropriate sexual behaviors, and other behavioral difficulties.

MODERATING VARIABLES

Research has been conducted in an effort to identity variables that may moderate the severity of symptomatology suffered by sexually abused children. The findings suggest that abused children suffer significantly more symptomatology when the abuse is perpetrated by a father or stepfather and when the abuse involves physical force and/or more invasive contact (e.g., penile penetration) (Conte & Schuerman, 1987; Friedrich et al., 1986; McLeer et al., 1988). Although relationship to the abuser, use of physical force, and type of contact are immutable characteristics not amenable to psychological interventions, recent research suggests that the level of support children receive from nonoffending parents is a potentially modifiable variable that may be more powerful in mediating children's post-abuse adjustments. Children who receive more support from nonoffending parents appear to suffer less post-abuse symptomatology (Conte &

Schuerman, 1987; Everson, Hunter, Runyon, Edelson, & Coulter, 1989; Tufts, 1984).

Unfortunately, there is considerable evidence that nonoffending parents suffer significant levels of distress themselves following a child's disclosure of abuse (Deblinger, Hathaway, Lippmann, & Steer, 1993; Kelley, 1990). This distress may in turn impair their ability to be as supportive as possible to their children. Because nonoffending parents have great potential to play a significant role in their sexually abused children's recovery, the authors strongly encourage their involvement in treatment. Participation in treatment not only may help parents cope with their own personal distress, it may also help parents respond more supportively and effectively to their children's difficulties.

> *Parents may play a significant role in sexually abused children's recovery.*

❏ Cognitive Behavioral Therapy

The psychotherapy approach to be described in this book is based on a cognitive behavioral treatment model. This model is based on the central premise that cognitions, behaviors, and emotions are highly interdependent. Thus, an intervention that specifically targets one of these areas of human functioning is expected to indirectly affect the other aspects of human functioning and adjustment. Cognitive behavioral methods, in fact, represent an integration of newer techniques that directly target cognitions and emotions with the more well-established and demonstrably effective behavioral techniques. Cognitive behavioral interventions seem particularly suited to addressing the problems of sexually abused children and their families for a number of reasons.

- Cognitive behavioral therapy encompasses a variety of interventions that are applicable to a wide array of psychological difficulties. This broad applicability is critical due to the diversity of symptomatic responses exhibited by sexually abused children and their nonoffending parents. Moreover, cognitive behavioral therapy uses different interventions to target symptomatology in the cognitive, behavioral, and emotional realms. Because many abused children suffer difficulties in all these areas to varying degrees, it is important to have the flexibility of using cognitive strategies, behavioral procedures, and/or emotional-processing techniques, depending on the difficulties presented by the child and family.

- The rationale and strategies for implementing cognitive behavioral interventions are made explicit to clients. Rather than engaging clients in a mysterious process with the implied goal of emotional health, a cognitive behavioral therapist generally offers a treatment rationale, a clear and commonsense therapy plan, and realistic expectations for outcome. Thus, the clients are in a better position to determine if the proposed interventions will suit their personal needs. This may be particularly important to children and nonoffending parents whose abusive experiences have left them feeling that they have little control over their lives.

- Cognitive behavioral therapy requires the therapist and client to work collaboratively in designing interventions that can be used in sessions and at home. Such collaborative efforts are likely to encourage feelings of empowerment among abused children and their nonoffending parents. Although these families may have little control over the investigative and prosecutorial processes associated with the abuse, the collaborative nature of cognitive behavioral therapy promotes a greater sense of control and self-respect.

- Although cognitive behavioral therapy is generally considered to be a short-term approach, it offers clients skills for coping with their current difficulties as well as those that may arise in the future. Because the impact of sexual abuse may be felt by children through different stages of their lives, it is important to provide children and parents with skills that can be used not only during the course of therapy but also after therapy has ended.

- Because children of any racial, religious, or ethnic background may suffer sexual abuse, the therapeutic interventions used need to be acceptable and effective with culturally diverse families. Due to the active, directive, and structured nature of the approach, cognitive behavioral interventions not only appear to be effective but also seem to be preferred by minority groups including African Americans, Native Americans, Hispanics, and Asians (Paniagua, 1994).

- Cognitive behavioral therapy has its roots in scientific principles derived from research in psychology. Moreover, its growth and application continue to be closely tied to the empirical literature. Although cognitive behavioral therapists are not the only clinicians who express the need for empirical documentation of therapeutic efficacy, they do appear to have the strongest track record with regard to treatment outcome research. Many of the interventions to be described in this book have been empirically tested and have demonstrated effectiveness with populations suffering symptoms similar to those of sexually abused children. Several investigations have found cognitive behavioral interventions to be effective in treating post-traumatic stress in adult trauma victims (Foa, Rothbaum, & Ette, 1993; Foa, Rothbaum, Riggs, & Murdock, 1991). In addition, preliminary empirical evidence demonstrates the effectiveness of these interventions with sexually abused children (Cohen & Mannarino, 1996; Deblinger, 1995; Deblinger, McLeer, & Henry, 1990; Stauffer & Deblinger, 1996; Deblinger, Lippmann, & Steer, in press).

❑ Theoretical Model

To conceptualize the etiology and treatment of psychological symptoms, the cognitive behavioral theoretical model integrates learning theory, particularly the influence of conditioning, contingencies, and models in the environment, with the impact of cognitive factors (Kendall, 1985). This model is used below to explain the development and maintenance of abuse-related symptoms in sexually abused children.

MODELING

Modeling is an example of a simple learning process that can explain the development of both positive and negative behaviors in sexually abused children. Children constantly imitate what they see and hear. Thus, through observational learning, sexually abused children sometimes imitate verbalizations and behaviors exhibited by the perpetrators of their abuse. The sexually abused child, for example, may use foul language or engage in inappropriate sexual behaviors as a result of observing the offender. The development of children's cognitive views and belief systems is also significantly influenced by role models in their environment. Sex offenders, as well as nonoffending parents, may model dysfunctional attitudes regarding the abuse, sexuality, relationships, the trustworthiness of others, and so on. A nonoffending parent who acts as though the sexual abuse is the worst thing that could ever have happened to the child may unintentionally encourage the child to adopt the same catastrophic view of the experience. However, it also should be noted that in the aftermath of a sexual abuse disclosure, there are many opportunities for children to learn positive coping behaviors by observing the responses of significant others. For example, if nonoffending parents discuss the sexual abuse in a calm, open, and direct manner, the child is likely to imitate that style in communicating his or her own thoughts, feelings, and concerns regarding the abuse. Indeed, as noted earlier, nonoffending parents may be sexually abused children's most influential role models.

RESPONDENT AND INSTRUMENTAL CONDITIONING

Another learning mechanism that may explain the development of sexually abused children's symptoms is referred to as two-factor theory. Two-factor learning theory suggests that fears are acquired through respondent conditioning and maintained through instrumental conditioning (Mowrer, 1939). According to respondent conditioning principles, when neutral stimuli are paired with unconditioned fear-evoking stimuli, the neutral stimuli alone begin to elicit fear responses. For example, for children who are abused in the dark, darkness may be the previously neutral stimulus that is paired with the unconditional fear-evoking stimulus, the sexual abuse. As a result of that learned association between darkness and sexual abuse, the children learn to fear darkness.

When fear responses lead to avoidance of previously neutral stimuli, instrumental conditioning comes into play. Each time avoidance behavior occurs, it is negatively reinforced by a reduction in anxiety, thereby increasing the likelihood that the avoidance behavior will reoccur. To continue with the example provided above, children who learned to fear darkness as a result of the association between darkness and abuse now begin to avoid darkness to avoid experiencing the fear. Each time they successfully avoid the dark, they experiences a reinforcing reduction in anxiety, which increases the likelihood of future attempts to avoid the dark.

Recent revisions of classical two-factor theory suggest other mechanisms for the development and maintenance of avoidance behavior. According to approach-withdrawal theory, avoidance may be maintained as a result of the positively reinforcing qualities of relaxation and/or other safety cues that follow avoidance behavior. Thus the children's avoidance of the dark also is positively reinforced by the sense of relief they experience upon successful avoidance, as well as by any other positive consequences, such as increased parental attention in response to their verbalized fears of the dark.

Through the processes of generalization and higher order conditioning, a wider range of previously neutral stimuli may be paired with fear-evoking stimuli. Subsequently, additional previously neutral stimuli begin to elicit fear and avoidance responses. For example, the children described above initially may have feared only the darkness in their own bedrooms, because that was where the abuse occurred. However, through generalization and higher order conditioning, they learned to fear darkness in general, across different settings. Such responses then become increasingly debilitating as the innocuous stimuli that elicit them proliferate.

These conditioning principles provide a framework for understanding the development of post-trauma symptoms often suffered by sexually abused children. Many sexually abused children experience feelings of fear, anxiety, pain, sadness, or anger during the episodes of sexual abuse. Although they naturally associate these negative feelings with sexual abuse, some children, particularly those suffering PTSD, generalize these feelings of distress from the actual experience of abuse to nonthreatening abuse-related cues such as darkness, men, bathrooms, or getting undressed, as well as memories, thoughts, and/or discussion of the abuse. These cues are not in and of themselves dangerous, but because of their association with the abuse, they may trigger the emotions the children experienced during the abuse. Thus, in an effort to avoid these disturbing emotions, many sexually abused children work hard to avoid thinking, talking, or being reminded of the abuse.

> *Children work hard to avoid thinking, talking, or remembering sexual abuse.*

Moreover, many children use the same mechanisms that were seemingly adaptive in coping with the actual abuse (e.g., dissociation, denial, numbing, avoidance) to cope with innocuous abuse-related stimuli. Unfortunately, children who continue to respond to abuse-related cues with denial, avoidance, and/or dissociation may be inadvertently strengthening the inappropriate associations made between psychological distress and innocuous reminders of the abuse. For example, each time an innocuous abuse-related cue is avoided, a child experiences a reduction in distress and/or a feeling of safety that reinforces the avoidance behavior and strengthens the association between innocuous abuse reminders and emotional distress. Thus, although these coping mechanisms may have helped the child survive the abuse, their continued use once the abuse has ended may be maladaptive. Such continued avoidance may cause children to needlessly avoid innocuous situations, potentially preventing them from enjoying positive experiences.

For example, children who avoid all men with beards because their perpetrator had a beard may be hindered from participating effectively in situations with other bearded men, such as teachers, coaches, or neighbors. Furthermore, continued avoidance of abuse-related thoughts and memories may prevent these children from effectively processing and understanding their abusive experiences, potentially leaving them with misperceptions and inaccurate cognitive schemas related to the abuse. Furthermore, there is preliminary evidence that adult survivors using strategies of avoidance and suppression to cope with memories of child sexual abuse tend to be more symptomatic than those who rely on more active coping mechanisms (Leitenberg, Greenwald, & Cado, 1992).

The treatment approach described in this book includes gradual exposure and processing interventions designed to break the problematic associations sexually abused children have made between negative feelings and abuse-related cues, such as memories and innocuous reminders. In that way, the children become more comfortable confronting abuse-related thoughts and memories. Furthermore, this therapeutic work decreases children's reliance on maladaptive coping responses to innocuous abuse reminders such as avoidance and dissociative responses. This therapeutic approach also uses the modeling process described earlier as the therapist him- or herself models ways to communicate about and cope effectively with troubling abuse-related thoughts, feelings, and reminders. In addition, the therapist trains the nonoffending parent to model effective coping strategies for the child and to respond more effectively to abuse-related disclosures and behavior problems. Further information about the components of this treatment approach is provided in the following chapter.

2

Overview of Treatment Model

❏ Clients for Whom This Treatment Approach Is Most Appropriate

AGE RANGE

The treatment model as described here is usually used with children in the age range of approximately 3 to 13. Given the wide range of abilities and difficulties experienced by children in that age range, it is important that the therapist adapt the treatment model to the developmental level of each child. For example, preschool children often are not able to recall as many specific details of their abusive experiences as are older children. Thus, the therapeutic work focused on helping children become more comfortable with their thoughts and memories of the abuse is likely to be briefer for preschool children than for older children; there may not be as much material with which to work.

11

This treatment model also may be used effectively with adolescents if adaptations are made in the areas of sexuality and behavior management skills. Typically, much more work will need to be done in the area of sex education with teenagers than with younger children. Finally, the authors believe this general treatment approach also can be used successfully with children who are developmentally delayed, as long as they are functioning cognitively at a minimum 3-year-old level. Again, the therapist's style of communication and the specific therapeutic activities should be adapted to the child's developmental level.

SYMPTOMATOLOGY

The treatment model to be described is most appropriate for use with children who exhibit symptoms of PTSD and/or confusion or misconceptions about their sexual abuse experiences. The focus of the treatment approach is on alleviating PTSD symptoms, such as distress regarding memories of the abusive experience, avoidance of those memories and reminders of the abuse, and hyper-arousal symptoms; correcting any misconceptions or dysfunctional thoughts the child has regarding the abusive experience; and ameliorating any behavior problems the child has developed as a consequence of the experience.

Clearly, many children who have experienced sexual abuse have other symptoms such as depression, generalized anxiety, and oppositional behaviors. In many cases, such symptoms can be treated effectively with the techniques to be outlined in this treatment approach. For example, depression and anxiety symptoms may be treated successfully with the cognitive coping techniques to be described, and parents may learn to effectively manage their children's oppositional behaviors by learning behavior management skills. However, this treatment approach is not appropriate as an initial treatment strategy for children exhibiting psychotic symptoms or active suicidal intent. In such cases, the psychotic or suicidal symptoms should be assessed and treated before moving on to this treatment approach.

CLARITY OF ABUSE ALLEGATIONS

This treatment model is proposed for use primarily with children whose disclosures have been substantiated through an investigation by child protection or law enforcement officials. Even in such cases, however, it is recommended that clinicians formulate their own independent opinions concerning the allegations by completing a comprehensive evaluation prior to initiating treatment. Such an evaluation should include the collection of information from multiple sources (e.g., child protection and law enforcement officials, medical doctor, nonoffending parent, offending parent, when possible) as well as a carefully conducted nonleading interview(s) with the suspected victim(s).

Some of the therapeutic components of this treatment approach, such as gradual exposure and processing, cannot be used if it is unclear whether the child experienced sexual abuse. Other components, however, may be appropriately used to offer symptomatic relief. For example, behavior management may be useful in treating inappropriate sexual behavior in very young children even when the origin of such behavior is unclear. In general, however, therapists should pursue extended evaluations to clarify the validity of abuse allegations before initiating treatment focused on alleged sexual abuse.

INVOLVEMENT OF NONOFFENDING PARENTS

The treatment model proposes the involvement of not only the sexually abused child but also that child's nonoffending parent(s) or guardian(s). Children can benefit immensely from the involvement of a loving adult in their treatment, whether that adult is a nonoffending parent, another relative such as a grandparent, or a foster parent. The participation of that guardian communicates to the child how committed the adult is to the child, allows the child to develop skills for talking with the adult about the abusive experience, and offers the adult training in specific ways to help the child.

In the majority of cases, parents are adequately supportive of their child to be able to participate effectively, even if they are unsure of the veracity of the allegations or have questions about some of the details. However, if the nonoffending parents are overtly disbelieving and nonsupportive of the child, they may be unable to participate in this treatment approach productively. In that situation, it is often most effective to involve a second therapist to work individually with the parent. With parents who are initially disbelieving, a long-term goal may be to bring the child and parent together in joint sessions, after the parent has made progress in becoming appropriately supportive of the child. In situations in which it is not possible to involve a nonoffending parent or guardian, either because no such person is available or because he or she is not adequately supportive, the therapist may proceed with treatment for the child alone.

❏ **Course of Treatment**

This treatment approach is based on a short-term model (see Figure 2.1) that was originally developed for use in several treatment outcome investigations (Deblinger et al., 1990; Deblinger, in press; Stauffer & Deblinger, 1996). In the context of these investigations, we have had a great deal of success applying this model in both individual and group formats in about 12 treatment sessions following the completion of an evaluation. However, in clinical settings, treatment may extend from 12 to as many as 40 sessions, depending on the needs of the child and the complexity of the case. Treatment is generally longer in duration when children present with multiple diagnoses, when the family and/or legal circumstances are complex, and when there is potential for family reunification.

The proposed treatment typically begins with the therapist dividing treatment sessions into individual meetings with the child and parent. The number of sessions devoted to individual work with the child and parent varies considerably. Individual sessions are conducted until parents and children begin to show reduced symptomatology and improved coping skills. When such progress is evident, the therapist will begin spending at least part of the therapy sessions in joint meetings including both parent and child. Joint sessions are usually initiated about halfway through treatment. These joint therapy sessions are intended to provide the parent and

Figure 2.1. Overview of Therapeutic Model

child with skills for communicating about and processing the sexual abuse experience together so that they can continue the therapeutic process on their own.

❏ Therapeutic Components

The therapeutic work is described in terms of three different components that are similar for the child and parent treatment. Although for ease of discussion these components are described as separate and distinct focuses of treatment, in practice these components overlap, with work on one component contributing toward progress on another component. In addition, the treatment model should be viewed as fluid, with work shifting from one component to another, depending on the needs of the specific clients.

COPING SKILLS TRAINING

The initial focus of treatment for both the child and parent often is on the component entitled *coping skills training*. This component provides clients with skills for coping effectively with the emotional distress that may be generated by the sexual abuse experience. Depending on the clients' needs, this training may focus on such skills as emotional expression, cognitive coping, and relaxation training.

Emotional expression skills often are important in helping both children and parents effectively label and communicate their feelings about the abuse. Cognitive coping skills training teaches children and parents to identify and dispute dysfunctional or overly pessimistic thoughts about the abuse while replacing them with more accurate and effective coping responses. For example, parents learn to dispute overgeneralized thoughts, such as "my child will be troubled by the sexual abuse for the rest of his/her life," by citing evidence that they have reason to be more optimistic about their children's future. These skills minimize distress clients may feel as a result of dysfunctional thoughts. Relaxation skills training is particularly useful with clients who are suffering considerable physical tension and those who are very anxious about directly addressing and discussing the abusive experience(s).

GRADUAL EXPOSURE AND COGNITIVE AND AFFECTIVE PROCESSING

Gradual Exposure

As clients are able to cope with their difficult emotions more effectively, they may be better able to tolerate work in the next treatment component, titled *gradual exposure and cognitive and affective processing*. Gradual exposure is the cornerstone of this treatment approach. Gradual exposure combines elements of two cognitive-behavioral interventions designed to alleviate maladaptive fear, anxiety, and post-traumatic stress responses. These interventions are prolonged exposure and systematic desensitization. Prior empirical investigations have demonstrated the effectiveness of prolonged exposure in treating the symptoms suffered by adult PTSD sufferers (Fairbank & Keane, 1982; Foa et al., 1991); thus, initially, it seemed the treatment of choice for sexually abused children suffering PTSD symptoms. However, during early clinical trials with children, it quickly became evident that, unlike adult patients, sexually abused children were often unwilling to subject themselves to anxiety-provoking stimuli for prolonged periods in exchange for the promise of long-term therapeutic benefits. In addition, many nonoffending parents expressed concern about the high levels of anxiety associated with prolonged exposure.

Systematic desensitization, on the other hand, offered the advantage of using a gradual hierarchy of anxiety-provoking stimuli, which might be easier for children to tolerate. However, all the fears and anxieties sexually abused children experience may not be apparent at the outset of therapy, and they may not fit neatly into a hierarchy. In addition, it is sometimes difficult to engage sexually abused children, particularly young and/or developmentally delayed children, in the visualization and/or relaxation exercises required for systematic desensitization procedures.

To meet the needs of sexually abused children, the first author and her colleagues at the Medical College of Pennsylvania combined elements of systematic desensitization and prolonged exposure in designing the intervention referred to as gradual exposure. Like systematic desensitization, gradual exposure encourages children to confront feared stimuli, such as their thoughts and memories of the abuse, in a graduated fashion. A highly detailed hierarchy need not be constructed; however, when developing a treatment plan, it is important to assess the degree to which various stimuli provoke anxious or avoidant responses.

Initially, children will be encouraged to endure low-level anxiety-provoking stimuli before moving on to confront more distressing stimuli. For example, the therapist initially may ask a child to talk about child sexual abuse in the abstract because that is less anxiety provoking than discussing his or her own abusive experience. Thus, the therapist may begin by engaging the child in discussions of factual information regarding sexual abuse such as prevalence, types of children affected, and identities of sex offenders. Then over time the child may be asked to describe the least distressing of his or her own abusive experiences before moving on to discuss more anxiety-provoking memories. As is the case with prolonged exposure, gradual exposure to the anxiety-provoking stimuli should be repeated until the innocuous stimuli no longer elicit maladaptive anxiety or avoidance.

With exposure to each different anxiety-provoking stimulus, it is expected that the child's anxiety level may increase. However, that increase in anxiety seems to reflect the increased anxiety the child experiences naturally upon exposure to abuse-related stimuli outside the therapy setting, rather than being a unique consequence of the therapeutic work. It is our experience that most children and their parents are well able to tolerate this temporary increase in anxiety, if it is predicted for them in advance and they understand the long-term purpose of the work. Over time, the repeated exposures to abuse-related stimuli in a safe therapeutic setting appear to lead to a decrease in anxiety level. By the end of treatment, the child is expected to confront abuse reminders and discuss abuse-related memories without experiencing significant distress. Thus gradual exposure aims to disrupt the maladaptive associations between innocuous abuse-related cues and the more extreme negative emotions that develop as a result of respondent conditioning. Moreover, when habituation occurs, new associations may replace the old ones; that is, more adaptive responses such as feelings of control, comfort, bravery, and/or pride may become connected to previously anxiety-provoking situations, thoughts, and/or discussion.

In addition to breaking the associations between innocuous abuse-related cues and distressing emotions, the connection needs to be disrupted between avoidance of innocuous abuse-related cues and positive or negative reinforcement. Repeated experiences with reduced anxiety as a result of avoidance behaviors strengthens avoidance and escape habits. Thus, it is very important for children to endure the anxiety-provoking thoughts and/or cues until anxiety decreases naturally without the use of avoidance. In so doing, the child will learn that distress decreases without resorting to the use of escape strategies such as avoidance, dissociation, numbing, acting out, and so on, thereby resulting in decreased dependence on these maladaptive coping mechanisms. In addition, the child will learn that feelings of safety and mastery may be achieved in the face of memories, thoughts, and reminders of the abuse.

Many parents also benefit from participating in gradual exposure exercises. At the start of therapy, many parents have less information than the investigator or caseworker about their child's abuse. Moreover, parents often experience high levels of anxiety when confronted with thoughts or reminders of their child's abusive experience and thus may seek to avoid those reminders. Unfortunately, in exhibiting such avoidant behavior, they model

> *Distress can decrease without the use of escape strategies.*

ineffective coping responses for their children. Thus, parents often need to participate in gradual exposure exercises in order to become more comfortable with abuse-related stimuli, information, and discussion themselves so that they can model more successful coping strategies for their children.

Cognitive and Affective Processing

As gradual exposure proceeds, another equally important aspect of the child's treatment can begin, the cognitive and affective processing of the abusive experiences. Post-traumatic stress symptoms such as avoidance and hyper-arousal often interfere with the ability of sexually abused children to cognitively process and integrate the abusive experiences. As these symptoms diminish in response to gradual exposure, the children should be increasingly able to openly discuss their thoughts and feelings regarding the sexual abuse and its aftermath (i.e., the investigations, family disruptions, reactions of others, court proceedings). However, without the assistance of a therapist or another helping adult, it is extraordinarily difficult for sexually abused children to make sense of these experiences due to their limited knowledge base and incompletely defined belief system. Similarly, children struggling alone with their feelings may find it very difficult to sort out confusing and often conflicted emotions about the abuse and the perpetrator. Thus, children's independent efforts to process abusive experiences may be unsuccessful, resulting in repetitive traumatic play and/or reenactment that may be highly dysfunctional.

Moreover, the experience of child sexual abuse may set the stage for the development of distorted and maladaptive cognitions and feelings about sex, relationships, and the world in general. Thus, it is critical to involve children in discussions and exercises that encourage them to process the abusive experiences cognitively and affectively, while participating in educative and therapeutic discussions. This component of treatment is based on cognitive therapy approaches (Beck, 1995; Beck, Rush, Shaw, & Emery, 1979; Seligman, 1991) that encourage the identification and challenging of maladaptive cognitions and beliefs. The overall objective is to identify and correct dysfunctional assumptions sexually abused children may develop regarding self, relationships, sexuality, personal safety, and other related areas of concern.

Parents are also encouraged to process and dispute dysfunctional thoughts about the abuse in a similar way. This is particularly important given the evidence that children develop coping styles similar to those of their parents (Seligman et al., 1984). It is expected that when parents learn to think and talk about their children's abuse in less pessimistic ways, they will feel better themselves and model more effective coping responses for their children.

BEHAVIOR MANAGEMENT SKILLS TRAINING

The third therapeutic component for parents is behavior management skills training. Particularly for parents whose children have responded to the sexual abuse experience with significant behavior problems, the therapist may focus considerable time on teaching the parent behavior management skills derived from social learning theory. Parents' reactions to their children's abuse-related behavior problems may significantly influence the improvement or exacerbation of such difficulties. Well-meaning parents, for example, may model and reinforce avoidance behavior, believing that their children are better off forgetting about the abuse. Furthermore, parents may inadvertently reinforce abuse-related behavior problems by responding with increased or inappropriate attention. For example, children who begin talking excessively and inappropriately about sexual issues may continue such talk based on all the attention it generates. Cognitive behavioral interventions are used to treat these negative behavior patterns by helping parents (a) learn to model and reinforce effective coping responses in their children and (b) learn to respond to children's abuse-related behavioral difficulties with effective behavior management skills.

EDUCATION REGARDING CHILD SEXUAL ABUSE, HEALTHY SEXUALITY, AND PERSONAL SAFETY SKILLS

This therapeutic component for children is described in the chapter on child intervention, but both children and parents can benefit from education. Education may be provided at a variety of points in treatment. The first topic, education regarding child sexual abuse, includes information about what sexual abuse is, why it occurs, who it affects, who the perpetrators are, how children feel when they have been abused, and why they do not tell. Most often this education is provided at the beginning of the gradual exposure work and during cognitive coping exercises, because it is offered to assist children in disputing dysfunctional thoughts about the abuse.

The second topic included in this component is education regarding healthy sexuality. The therapist, in conjunction with the parents, should plan to provide developmentally appropriate sex education to the child, most often in the context of joint parent-child sessions. Given the evidence that sexually abused children may be at risk for developing sexual anxiety and difficulties (Cohen, 1995; Finkelhor et al., 1989), basic sex education should be combined with exercises that will help children explore and process their attitudes and feelings regarding sexuality.

The third topic, personal safety skills training, includes education regarding the continuum of OK-versus-not-OK touches, the identification of inappropriate touches, and skills for responding effectively to inappropriate sexual touches. Again, this education often can be provided during joint parent-child sessions.

❏ The Therapist's Roles

ADVOCATE

Throughout the different therapy components, the therapist will serve as an advocate, educator, role model, and coach. Therapists working with sexually abused children and their families often assume an advocacy role on behalf of their clients. Such advocacy generally takes the form of assisting clients to negotiate effectively through unfamiliar systems and agencies (e.g., criminal justice, child protection and victim witness organizations) (Deblinger & Heflin, 1994). For many parents, contact with these agencies can be overwhelming, intimidating, and frustrating. Therapists should help by providing some basic information about the agencies and their roles. In addition, therapists can offer parents guidance and direction as to who can best respond to their concerns (e.g., law enforcement vs. child protection) or, with the consent of their clients, they may directly contact the appropriate professional to clarify information, enhance communication, and/or express concerns as an advocate for the child. Therapists, however, may also find it necessary at times to highlight the limitation of their influence on the legal proceedings and suggest that therapy time may be more productively used by focusing on what can be influenced, such as the child's adjustment.

EDUCATOR

Therapists offer important educational information to children and parents regarding child sexual abuse, healthy sexual development, and behavior management and personal safety skills. However, it should be noted that providing education that will lead to significant changes in cognitions, behaviors, and emotions is no easy task. Thus, cognitive behavioral therapists must master effective educational techniques. The strategies that make an educator effective—for example, planning lessons in advance and setting students up for success—will similarly influence the success of the cognitive behavioral therapist. Some examples of effective strategies are found in Box 2.1.

BOX 2.1

Strategies of Effective Educators/Therapists

The same techniques that make educators effective can also be used by cognitive behavioral therapists. These include:

- Assessing the clients' baseline knowledge and/or skill level
- Sharing assessment data in the form of feedback
- Preparing adequately by planning the session in advance
- Respecting and tailoring the approach to the individual
- Stimulating clients to think rather than providing all of the answers
- Making the environment safe to take risks
- Pacing therapeutic exercises to set clients up for success
- Motivating clients to pay attention, collaborate, and complete assignments at home
- Offering charismatic, stimulating, and creative presentations
- Providing skills and information that have wide applicability to real life situations
- Modeling and encouraging active participation in the learning process
- Simultaneously demonstrating predictability and flexibility

---

ROLE MODEL

Throughout the therapeutic process, the therapist serves as an important role model, particularly with respect to communication skills, positive coping behaviors regarding the abuse experience, and behavior management skills. Given that one of the treatment objectives is to have the child tolerate memories and discussions of the sexual abuse calmly, without significant distress, it is crucial that the therapist demonstrate calm, matter-of-fact discussions of sexuality and sexual abuse. The significance of the therapist's role in modeling effective communication is heightened by the fact that the child may not have had any other adult communicate regarding the abuse in this way.

Therapists may begin modeling open communication during the evaluation process when they pursue a nonleading interview designed to provide an opportunity for children to discuss any sexual abuse experience they have had. In addition to demonstrating clear and open communication themselves, therapists should respond to children's disclosures with calm and empathic remarks. This is particularly important as highly emotional reactions to disclosures are likely to create anxiety in children, discouraging further disclosures. Therapists, therefore, are encouraged to process their own personal reactions to children's disclosures with supervisors and/or colleagues.

Although children often will show some anxiety or embarrassment when discussing abuse-related issues, therapists should not allow this embarrassment to alter their communication style. Thus, while a child may

Therapists should model effective communication.

choose to whisper about the abuse, the therapist should respond in a clear and normal tone of voice. Discussions of sex education provide another opportunity for therapists to model open communication regarding sexuality. When discussing sex education, it is helpful to use humor and to discuss sexuality in positive ways to encourage further communication by children.

Similarly, therapists serve as role models for parents regarding ways to cope and communicate effectively with their children regarding the sexual abuse. Initially, by pursuing therapeutic goals in a straightforward, systematic manner, therapists demonstrate that it is possible and appropriate to cope with abuse-related discussion in a calm, direct, and effective way. Similarly, therapists should model effective communication by discussing the abuse with parents in a calm, open, and explicit manner. Therapists may subsequently use role plays as opportunities to model for parents how to effectively discuss the sexual abuse and healthy sexuality with their children. Therapists will continue to model those skills for parents during the joint parent-child sessions.

Therapists also will serve as important models for parents in demonstrating behavior management skills. Therapists may use role plays to model many of the behavior management skills being taught. In addition, therapists may look for opportunities to demonstrate effective behavior management skills during interactions with children that the parents observe. For example, the therapist might demonstrate the effective use of praise by praising the child for waiting quietly while the parent is meeting with the therapist individually.

Therapists also serve as role models for healthy coping in other related areas. In general, therapists should model a view of the world that is both accurate and hopeful by talking about difficult issues in direct, honest, and optimistic terms. For example, in most cases, therapists may convey the view that with parental support and counseling, children are likely to fully recover from the abusive experience. Therapists also may model effective means of coping with specific emotions such as expressing anger through verbal, written, or artistic methods for a client who is demonstrating anger in ineffective ways.

COACH

Therapists also assume the role of coach in work with both children and parents. As coaches, therapists are responsible for planning and structuring the therapeutic activities and keeping clients focused on that work. Thus, occasionally, therapists may have to redirect clients who are discussing unrelated issues. Just as a coach might give an athlete a pep talk, the therapist motivates clients by reminding them of treatment goals and applauding their efforts in working toward those goals. Indeed, it is important that the therapist draws client attention to any progress they are making; for example, in being able to discuss the abuse more comfortably. In addition, therapists serve as coaches in reviewing client performance in role plays and homework assignments, providing praise when clients respond effectively and offering gentle suggestions as to how clients might complete a task more successfully.

3

Initiating Therapy

❏ Therapy Environment

In establishing a therapy setting, therapists should be aware that the physical environment may influence clients' feelings about therapy and possibly their responsiveness to treatment. Interestingly, there is some empirical evidence that preschoolers interviewed by friendly therapists in warm, pleasant surroundings may be more accurate in their responses to questions than preschoolers who are interviewed by less friendly (stern) therapists in more stark office environments (Goodman, Bottoms, Schwartz-Kenney, & Rudy, 1991). In designing a therapy setting, the following issues should be considered.

- The therapy setting should establish a warm, welcoming atmosphere.
- The waiting room should offer comfortable seating, quiet activities, such as crayons and paper, and/or appropriate reading materials.

- The furnishings of the therapy office should be comfortable for adults and children (e.g., small chairs and/or carpeting for sitting on the floor with children)
- The atmosphere should convey that the therapist likes and respects children (e.g., friendly, childlike wall hangings, other children's drawings).
- The setting should offer privacy with minimal distractions from external noise and interruptions.
- The setting should provide a sense of consistency and or predictability (e.g., the same office should be used each session, if possible).
- Most important, the therapy office should not be too stimulating or distracting for children due to an overabundance of toys displayed. Rather, a small selection of toys should be available so that children have some choices, without being overwhelmed. Some useful toys include paper, crayons, toy telephones, dolls, puppets, and a feeling chart depicting different emotions.

❏ Establishing Collaborative Relationships

In order to maximize the effectiveness of therapy, it is important that the therapist establish a collaborative partnership with the child's parent or guardian whenever possible. Such a relationship is important for a number of reasons: to ensure the child's consistent attendance, to access the parent's knowledge and insight about the child, and to engage the parent in the therapeutic process. This type of collaborative relationship may best be established by communicating respect for the parent's opinions and knowledge regarding the child. Furthermore, the therapist should emphasize to the parent that the parent's role with the child is much more important than the therapist's role ever can or should be, both by virtue of the amount of time the parent has with the child and by virtue of the significance of the parent-child relationship. Moreover, the parent's participation in treatment can have a great influence on the child's responsiveness to therapy. When parents believe that their contributions are truly needed and valued, they are much more likely to participate actively in treatment.

Engaging the child in the therapy process may be best accomplished by entering the child's world. Throughout the child's sessions, this may mean sitting on the floor, discussing the child's favorite activities, TV shows, and so on, and generally engaging the child in fun and appealing activities. Although the therapist may respond to difficulties with sincere concern, he or she need not maintain an overly serious atmosphere. Rather, the therapist may encourage a relationship that allows for serious discussion as well as humor and enthusiasm. Most important, the therapist-child relationship should include a sense of acceptance and collaboration. This may be accomplished by actively eliciting and using the child's ideas for achieving therapy goals and assignments. Although all of a child's suggestions may not be acceptable, some are likely to be extremely creative and productive.

> *The therapist-child relationship should include acceptance and collaboration.*

The timing of the therapy sessions also may influence the client's attendance and level of active participation. Collaboration is required to establish a day and time for weekly sessions that is both practical and consistent for all parties. For children, the therapist and parents may attempt to avoid establishing a schedule that would interfere with the child's nap time, bedtime, dinnertime, school hours, and/or favorite activity. If appointments are scheduled directly after school or at other times when children may be hungry, it may be important to arrange for them to have some type of snack so they can concentrate on therapeutic work. Although it is not always possible to offer therapy at the most ideal times, working with clients to identify the best time establishes an excellent precedent for collaborative problem solving.

❑ Setting Limits

By establishing certain rules and limits associated with the therapy sessions, therapists again can establish some sense of predictability and control. Initially, it is important for parents and children to understand the requirements for their participation in therapy in terms of both active participation in sessions and completion of assignments at home. In addition, the importance of consistent attendance should be stressed with rules established for cancellations and no-shows.

Many children do not require that limits be set on their behaviors during sessions. For those children, it is not necessary and may even be anxiety provoking to describe a series of rules and regulations for the sessions. However, other children may require some limits on their behaviors. If it becomes apparent during the first few sessions that limits are necessary, the therapist should determine exactly which behaviors require limits, always attempting to minimize the number of limits as much as possible. Having a number of different limits may be confusing to children and will make it more difficult for them to comply successfully. After deciding which limits are required, the therapist should plan how he or she will handle the situation if the child does not comply with those limits. Then those limits should be communicated clearly to both parent and child in a positive way.

For example, with a young child who has used markers to draw on the walls or table in the therapist's office, the therapist might set a limit in this way:

> Billy, in this office, we use the markers only on paper. That way you can draw me some beautiful pictures to hang on my bulletin board.

If the child breaks that rule by again drawing on the wall, the therapist might calmly put the markers away for a portion of the session, saying,

> Remember, the rule is that markers are used only on paper. Later, we'll use them again and try to remember that rule.

Later in the session, the therapist might bring the markers out again in order to give the child a chance to comply with the limit successfully. If the child does restrict his or her drawing to the paper, the therapist should praise the child for remembering the limit.

Setting limits may be particularly important with regard to physical contact between the child and therapist. Some sexually abused children may be highly fearful of the mildest physical gestures and/or may misinterpret them as sexual. Others may exhibit behavior at the other end of the spectrum, demonstrating no physical contact boundaries and engaging in highly sexualized behaviors toward the therapist. The therapist should model means of conveying warmth and affection that are socially and developmentally appropriate for that child. The therapist may need to set limits for sexual behavior in clear and simple language, using a calm and firm tone. However, the conversation around this issue need not be negative. Harsh discipline around sexual behavior would be confusing to a child who has been taught this behavior by another adult. Rather, the therapist should assist the child by teaching alternative means of expressing affection and experiencing pleasure. For example, if the child touches the therapist's breast, the therapist might say,

> That's a private part of my body. You may not touch me there. But I would be glad to hold your hand.

Often that education is adequate to change the child's behavior during sessions.

In cases in which the child continues the inappropriate touching, the therapist should respond calmly, with a consequence similar to that given for any other repeated inappropriate behavior. For example, the therapist might explain that he or she will be using time out to help the child remember which touches are appropriate and which are inappropriate. In addition, the therapist should look for opportunities to offer positive reinforcement for appropriate touches such as shaking hands, giving high fives, or holding hands.

Sexually abused children may be highly fearful of physical gestures.

By encouraging conversations and questions around the issue of touching, the therapist can facilitate further exploration and correction of the many misconceptions children may have developed as a result of their sexually abusive experiences. The treatment of inappropriate sexual behaviors is addressed in greater detail in the chapter on parent interventions.

❏ Assessment

Therapists should base the treatment plan on their own carefully conducted and comprehensive psychological evaluation. In cases of child sexual abuse, the evaluation is a complex process. Indeed, a thorough description of the evaluation process is beyond the scope of this book; however, we have included a brief discussion of the steps in an evaluation to indicate how assessment findings influence therapy plans. Readers seeking further information are encouraged to read the *Guidelines for Psychosocial Evaluation of Suspected Sexual Abuse in Young Children,* published by the American Professional Society on the Abuse of Children (1995), and *Evaluating Children Suspected of Having Been Sexually Abused,* by Kathleen Faller (1996).

The overall assessment process in child sexual abuse cases involves both an evaluation of the validity of the abuse allegations and an evaluation of the child's psychological functioning, including his or her responses to the abusive experience. The assessment findings are critical to effective treatment planning. Indeed, treatment based on incomplete findings or on someone else's evaluations and/or reports may be highly misguided. For example, when a teacher suggests that a child is hyperactive, medication would not automatically be prescribed. Nor would psychotherapy necessarily be recommended for a child whose teacher described him or her as depressed after the death of a loved one. Rather, treatment recommendations should stem from a thorough evaluation, integrating information from a variety of sources, to develop a comprehensive case conceptualization.

The development of a collaborative therapist-client relationship generally begins during the evaluation process when the therapist requests a great deal of input and assistance from the client(s) in collecting information that will result in a comprehensive and well-grounded evaluation. Cognitive behavioral therapists are particu-

larly interested in collecting information concerning the client's behaviors, emotions, cognitions, and environment as this information
will have direct implications for treatment. A variety of assessment
methods may be used, including observation; psychological
measures; interviews with the victim, perpetrator (if possible in cases
of intrafamilial abuse), and significant others; and reports from social
service agencies, medical and mental health professionals, and
teachers.

In evaluating cases of child sexual abuse, diagnosticians are often
faced with contradictory information. Thus, they must be undaunted
by contradictions, while continuing to search for more consistent
information. In conceptualizing a case, therapists not only gather
information but also integrate this information with their knowledge
of psychopathology, developmental psychology, and the empirical
data relating to child sexual abuse. Ultimately, in the initial conceptualization of a case, therapists attempt to offer the most logical and
parsimonious explanation for the client's difficulties. Because social
service and law enforcement agencies are often the initial referents
in cases of suspected child sexual abuse, they may at times attempt
to suggest diagnoses or direct the course of treatment. Although it is
important for therapists to cooperate, to the extent possible, with
these agencies' investigations, diagnostic and therapeutic recommendations should be developed by therapists independently.

EVALUATION OF ABUSE ALLEGATIONS

In order to evaluate the validity of the abuse allegations, the
therapist should pursue a nonleading individual interview with the
child. This interview also can be valuable for treatment purposes, in
establishing a baseline for the child's level of distress and avoidance
as he or she discusses the abuse experience. Faller (1996) suggests
that the therapist initially should pose general, open-ended, nonleading questions that provide an opportunity for the child to disclose
any abusive experiences. An example of such a question is "Why did
your mom bring you here today?" The objective is to use such
questions to elicit a free narrative from the child, in which the abusive
experiences are described spontaneously.

If the child does not disclose in response to general questions, Faller (1996) suggests that the therapist may ask more focused but still nonleading questions, which might focus on the private parts of the body, the possible circumstances of the alleged abuse, or the person who may have abused the child. For example, when interviewing a child allegedly abused by her father during a weekend visit, the therapist might ask,

What do you like to do with your dad when you go to visit him?

Subsequently, the therapist might ask,

Is there anything you don't like to do with your dad during visits?

If the child responds to the focused questions with information about the alleged abuse, the therapist may resume asking more open-ended questions, that is,

Tell me more about that.

or

What happened next?

Therapists are generally discouraged from asking multiple-choice questions, as such questions may elicit socially desirable responses or may be leading, particularly with young children who may choose a response without really understanding the question. Similarly, therapists should refrain from asking any leading questions that might put words in the child's mouth. An example of a nonleading interview is provided in Box 3.1.

The therapist should carefully note the child's level of anxiety and avoidance as the interview progresses. This information will assist the therapist in developing the hierarchy of abuse-related stimuli for the gradual exposure process. For example, if the child cries throughout the interview, gives minimal responses to questions, and attempts to end the interview, the therapist should plan to pursue the

---

BOX 3.1

Case Example: Interview Regarding Abuse History

Here's how a therapist might begin an interview with a child, in an effort to evaluate the abuse history.

Therapist: Sharon, what do you understand about why you're here today?

Sharon: I don't know.

Therapist: Did your mom tell you anything about why you were coming?

Sharon: No, she just said we were going to a doctor's office.

Therapist: Well, that's right. But do you remember what kind of doctor I said I am?

Sharon: Yeah, you're a talking doctor.

Therapist: Good job! You were really listening when I explained that. One of the things I talk to kids about is things that make them feel worried or upset. Can you think of anything that has made you feel upset?

Sharon: When my mom yells at me.

Therapist: What does she yell at you about?

---

gradual exposure process slowly, beginning with topics that are only minimally anxiety provoking. On the other hand, if the child discloses an abuse experience fairly easily, with significant detail, the therapist can expect that the gradual exposure process will move more rapidly. The therapist also should use this interview to generate plans for future topics for discussion and questioning later in the therapeutic process.

ASSESSMENT OF OVERALL PSYCHOLOGICAL FUNCTIONING

In addition to evaluating the validity of the abuse allegations, the therapist should complete an overall assessment of the child's psychological functioning. The initial purpose of this assessment is

---

Sharon: If I don't get my homework done or I don't get in bed when she tells me to.

Therapist: Does anyone else ever do anything that makes you feel worried or upset?

Sharon: Only Eddie.

Therapist: Who is Eddie?

Sharon: My next door neighbor. He's 15.

Therapist: What does Eddie do that makes you upset?

Sharon: He touched me, and I didn't like it.

Therapist: Can you tell me more about that?

Sharon: [long pause] Well, he touched my private, down there.

Therapist: What did he touch your private with?

Sharon: His finger. He stuck his finger all the way in.

Therapist: Then what happened?

Sharon: He told me I'd better shut up or he'd cut me. I was crying.

Therapist: So what happened?

Sharon: I tried to stop crying, but I couldn't because he was squeezing my arm too tight. Then I heard my mom calling me to come in. I think he heard her too because he let me go, but he told me I'd better not tell anybody.

Therapist: What happened next?

[Sharon continued with a description of her disclosure to her mother.]

---

to screen out any children for whom this treatment program is not appropriate. Children who are actively suicidal; engage in dangerous acting out behaviors, such as excessive drug or alcohol use; or are actively psychotic should receive other therapeutic interventions before participating in this treatment program. Therapists should be careful to distinguish between true psychotic hallucinations or delusions and the flashbacks of abuse experiences that may be experienced as a symptom of PTSD. The second purpose of this stage of the evaluation is to identify any areas of general psychological distress that should be targeted as a focus of therapy.

This portion of the evaluation may be pursued with semistructured interviews with both children and their parent(s) regarding any symptoms of psychological distress the child is exhibiting. The therapist also should consider using standardized psychological measures to assess the child's psychological functioning so that the child's level of symptomatology can be compared with that of other children of the same age and sex. Although specific assessment measures to be administered will vary from case to case, the authors have found the following measures to be helpful in assessing sexually abused children's general level of functioning.

The Child Behavior Checklist (CBCL) (Achenbach, 1991a) is completed by a parent or guardian and provides information about a wide range of internalizing and externalizing symptoms that may be exhibited by the child. With parental permission, the child's teacher may be asked to respond to a similar measure, called the Teacher Report Form (TRF) (Achenbach, 1991b), thus providing a view of the child's behavior in another setting as observed by a different person. The CBCL and the TRF are particularly useful in providing an assessment of the child's externalizing behaviors, which the child himself or herself, may not readily acknowledge. In the event that significant externalizing behaviors, such as angry, aggressive, oppositional behaviors, are described, the therapist can expect to devote considerable time to behavior management training with the parent(s).

Children themselves are usually the best reporters of internalizing symptoms.

Although parents and teachers often are the best source of information regarding externalizing symptoms, children themselves are usually the best reporters of internalizing symptoms. Thus, the therapist should consider administering self-report measures to the child, if he or she is old enough to respond appropriately (i.e., 7 to 8 years old and up). Two well-standardized and widely used measures of children's depression and anxiety are the Child Depression Inventory (Kovacs, 1985) and the State-Trait Anxiety Inventory for Children (Spielberger, 1973). If the child is exhibiting an elevated level of depression or anxiety, the therapist should plan to devote more time to cognitive coping skills training, with an emphasis on identifying the dysfunctional thoughts that may be contributing to the child's anxious/depressive symptomatology.

ASSESSMENT OF ABUSE-SPECIFIC SYMPTOMS

The final, and a very important, aspect of the evaluation process is the assessment of symptoms specific to the sexual abuse experience. Three measures that are useful in measuring abuse-specific symptoms are the Children's Impact of Traumatic Events Scales (CITES) (Wolfe, Gentile, & Wolfe, 1989), the Trauma Symptom Checklist for Children (TSC-C) (Lanktree & Briere, 1992), and the Child Sexual Behavior Inventory (CSBI) (Friedrich et al., 1992). The CITES is a measure of children's abuse-related perceptions. It offers an empirically derived model for examining the impact of child sexual abuse along four dimensions: PTSD (intrusive thoughts, avoidance, hyper-arousal, sexual anxiety), abuse attributions (self-blame and guilt, empowerment, vulnerability, and dangerous world), social reactions (negative reactions from others and social support), and eroticism. The CITES is particularly useful for identifying areas of dysfunctional thoughts regarding the abuse. For example, the child might endorse items indicating that he or she has very negative views of sexuality or anticipates critical responses from others regarding the abuse. If areas of cognitive distortion become apparent in the child's responses to the CITES, the therapist should plan to address those distortions during the child's cognitive processing work.

The TSC-C also measures symptoms related to the abuse experience; however, it does not refer specifically to an experience of sexual abuse and thus may be particularly useful with children who have experienced multiple types of abuse. The TSC-C has scales measuring anxiety, depression, post-traumatic stress, sexual concerns, dissociation, and anger. Its scales for dissociative symptoms and anger are particularly useful, because those symptom areas are not frequently assessed by other measures. Again, this measure is helpful in identifying specific symptoms that may be addressed in treatment.

The CSBI is an inventory completed by parents; it assesses sexual behaviors, ranging from normal behaviors to explicit sexual activity. It is the only available standardized measure that assesses sexualized behaviors in children. Given that a significant proportion of sexually abused children exhibit inappropriate sexual behaviors (Deblinger et al., 1989; Friedrich et al., 1992), it is important to evaluate the presence of such behaviors.

❏ Presenting Evaluation Findings

PROVIDING FINDINGS TO PARENTS

It is critically important to offer a verbal presentation of the evaluation findings to the nonoffending parent(s). This presentation, of course, is much broader than a psychiatric diagnosis. Therapists should present in clear nonjargon terms those salient factors that led them to the conclusions and therapeutic recommendations offered. For example, rather than reporting that the child's score on the Child Depression Inventory was significantly elevated, the therapist might describe how the child was acknowledging feelings of significant sadness and depression. The clinical meaning of the scores and diagnoses obtained should be shared. Visual presentations such as the child behavior profile derived from the Child Behavior Checklist (Achenbach, 1991a) can be particularly helpful when presenting findings to parents. The information and logic that led to the evaluation findings should be clearly explained. In turn, the therapy recommendations should be presented in terms of how they stem from the evaluation findings.

Diagnostic conclusions, as well as rationales and expectations for treatment, should be summarized by the therapist. This information will assist the client in making an informed choice regarding the appropriateness of this type of therapy at this time. By presenting findings and therapy recommendations in this manner, the therapist encourages a collaborative attitude, while also inspiring confidence in the foundation of the therapeutic approach.

PROVIDING FINDINGS TO THE CHILD

Generally, the child should not be present during the therapist's presentation of evaluation findings to the parent(s), so that the therapist and parent(s) can talk freely and openly regarding any symptoms the child is exhibiting. However, depending on the child's age, the therapist may choose to present evaluation findings to the child in a separate meeting. Older children may have questions or concerns about what the therapist learned during the assessment process and may benefit from some explanation of the findings. An explanation of evaluation findings is less likely to be valuable for younger children.

Any findings presented to the child must be described simply and concretely. Caution must be used to avoid overwhelming the child with too much information or with frightening information about emotional or behavioral problems. Typically, the findings can be summarized, with a focus on the child's own experience of any symptoms. For example, the therapist might say,

> Remember last week when you told me that thoughts about the abuse bother you, sometimes interrupting you during school and at bedtime, that you sometimes have bad dreams about the abuse, and that you try not to think about the abuse and to stay away from things that remind you of it? Well, it sounds like your thoughts and memories of the abuse are getting in your way and bothering you. I know of some things we can work on together to stop those thoughts from bothering you so much.

Subsequently, the therapist might explain how the treatment plan would address those specific symptoms.

❏ Presenting Treatment Rationales

TREATMENT RATIONALES FOR PARENTS

Following a discussion of the evaluation findings with the parent(s), the therapy objectives, treatment rationales, and realistic expectations for outcome should be provided. Clients who have had prior therapy experiences may be encouraged to talk about the perceived differences between the proposed therapy plan and their previous therapy experiences. Therapists should be prepared to field questions about the therapy process and expected outcomes. At this juncture, it is particularly important to inspire the confidence of the clients. Indeed, a therapist's ability to inspire confidence is critical to the effective implementation of cognitive behavioral techniques because a client who does not have confidence in the therapist and the interventions proposed will not be likely to practice the techniques and thus will not reap the benefits of the suggested interventions. When presenting the treatment rationale, the therapist may enhance the parents' motivation to actively participate in therapy in the following ways:

- Demonstrating knowledge and understanding of the experiences suffered by the child and his or her nonoffending parent(s)
- Offering a clear conceptualization of the development of the child's abuse-related difficulties
- Demonstrating how the interventions will serve to ameliorate and prevent abuse-related difficulties in the future
- Discussing the dangers of avoidance and minimization with respect to the long-term adjustment of the sexually abused child
- Sharing data on the adult survivors of sexual abuse who did not receive support as children
- Describing interventions and their respective rationales in clear concrete terms
- Emphasizing the powerful role of the nonoffending parent(s) in terms of the child's post-abuse adjustment.

The therapist should explain the different components of therapy to the parent(s), including parent sessions, child sessions, and joint parent-child sessions. When discussing the parent sessions, the therapist should explain that these sessions provide information and skills training to assist parents in coping with their emotional reactions, as well as their child's emotional and behavioral responses. It may be emphasized that the nonoffending parent will ultimately be the child's most important therapeutic resource, now and long after therapy ends. The therapist may further explain that the healing process will only be initiated during the child's individual sessions and will continue during joint parent-child sessions and even after formal therapy sessions end. As the parents become more comfortable with abuse-related discussion, they will be encouraged to participate as cotherapists in joint sessions with the child.

Rationales for the treatment techniques (e.g., coping skills training, gradual exposure, cognitive and affective processing of memories of the abuse, and education) to be used in the child's sessions should also be provided. It should be indicated that therapy may be difficult for the child, because the processing of sexually abusive experiences can be painful. However, suppressing abuse-related thoughts and memories could lead to even more damaging long-term consequences, including destructive thought patterns and post-traumatic stress symptoms that could interfere with the child's development. It is critical to forewarn parent(s) that they will need to encourage the child's continued attendance, even if the child complains that the sessions are distressing. Box 3.2 provides a case example, outlining how the treatment rationale might be presented to parent(s), explaining the use of gradual exposure with sexually abused children.

(text continued on p. 45)

BOX 3.2

Case Example: Treatment Rationale for Parent(s)

The following dialogue shows how a therapist might present a treatment rationale to parents and explain how gradual exposure is used with sexually abused children.

Therapist: Child sexual abuse and the investigation that follows can be highly traumatic for a child. In response to this experience, sexually abused children may experience many different emotions. Often when children remember the abuse experience, they feel some of same distressing emotions, such as fear, anger, sadness, or shame, that they experienced at the time of the abuse. In fact, children may experience those same emotions whenever they are confronted with anything that reminds them of the abuse.

(continued)

BOX 3.2 *Continued*

For example, a girl who was abused by a man with a beard may become frightened whenever she sees a man with a beard. Can you think of any things that your child may be avoiding because they remind her of the sexual abuse?

Mother: Well, ever since the abuse started, Mary won't sleep in her room without a light on. I didn't understand why at first, but maybe it's because the abuse happened in the dark.

Therapist: I think you may be right. That's not an unusual fear for children to develop if they were abused in the dark. You can see that distressing memories of the abuse can be a problem for Mary, causing her to be upset in situations when she should not have to be distressed. Over time, many children learn to avoid becoming upset by trying to avoid any thoughts or reminders of the abuse, just as Mary tries to avoid becoming upset by avoiding the dark, which makes her remember the abuse. Unfortunately, this may cause children to avoid harmless situations that might actually be positive, if these uncomfortable associations were not getting in the way. Mary should not have to always be afraid of the dark because of this unfortunate experience she had as a child. Avoidance can lead to other types of problems, as well. For example, a child may avoid any type of physical contact because it reminds her of the abuse, causing her to develop problems with sexual relationships in the future.

Mother: Do you think Mary will have problems with relationships?

Therapist: The fact that Mary has a loving, supportive mom and that both of you are participating in counseling will greatly reduce her chances of developing any significant abuse-related difficulties. What we're doing now is identifying the possible problems that can arise out of a pattern of avoidance so that we can work together to prevent those types of problems from developing.

Mother: I see.

Therapist: Often, well-meaning adults may unintentionally encourage the avoidance of disturbing memories by saying "Forget about it, it will never happen again, put it in the past." Some parents may feel uncomfortable with the discussion of sexual abuse themselves and may subtly influence the child not to talk about it.

BOX 3.2 *Continued*

Mother: Oh gosh, I think I've done that myself. I told her not to worry about it, that it's all over now, and she doesn't ever have to think about it again.

Therapist: Many parents respond that way at first. After all, most parents never expected to have to handle a situation of child sexual abuse, and they haven't been trained in how to respond to such situations. That's why you're here, so that we can figure out together how we can best help Mary. Unfortunately, with highly traumatic events, ignoring disturbing memories and feelings doesn't make them go away. These memories may continue to pop up for years, disrupting the child's life. Avoidance of these distressing thoughts is understandable, but it simply does not work very well. In fact, attempts to suppress memories and avoid feelings may result in serious and long-term symptoms, such as post-traumatic stress symptoms, depression, anxiety, and sexual dysfunction. We've already talked about some symptoms that Mary seems to be currently experiencing because she is trying to avoid thinking of the abuse.

Mother: Like her nightmares and her problems concentrating at school?

Therapist: Exactly. It is unlikely that Mary will ever completely forget the abusive experience. Continuing to try to avoid thoughts of the experience takes a great deal of effort and will cause Mary to avoid potentially positive situations and experiences unnecessarily. Because Mary probably will always have memories of the abuse experience, it is important that she become as comfortable with those memories as possible.

Mother: Oh, I was hoping that she would be able to just forget about this eventually.

Therapist: I don't think that is very likely, particularly given that Mary is 10 years old. She probably will always remember something about what happened. In order to be more comfortable with her memories, she needs to be able to process the sexual abuse experience and her associated emotions. It is important for her to remember and understand what has happened so that she can learn to comprehend the abuse and put it in perspective as she develops cognitively and emotionally. In that way, we can neutralize those memories so that they no longer have the

---

(continued)

BOX 3.2 *Continued*

power to be so upsetting for Mary. I hope to help Mary process the experience by doing the opposite of avoiding memories, discussion, and discomfort. I will encourage her to process the experience by exposing herself to the anxiety-provoking memories, images, and discussion in a gradual way. We will start by discussing topics that are not too upsetting for her, and as she gets more comfortable, we will move onto more difficult topics. At each step, we will stay with the discussion until she becomes more comfortable with that abuse reminder. Many children allow themselves to think or talk about the abuse in short spurts but stop thinking of those memories when the anxiety or emotions become too uncomfortable. My goal is to help Mary to talk about the abuse, experience the emotions, even see cues associated with the abuse for longer periods of time until her anxiety diminishes. I believe this exposure and processing can lead to reductions in nightmares, phobias, concentration problems, and avoidance behaviors. In order to help Mary become more comfortable with her thoughts and memories of the abuse, we will be talking about the experience quite a bit, until she becomes used to these discussions.

Mother: I'm afraid Mary won't like that very much. She doesn't ever talk about the abuse with me.

Therapist: For many children, this process is uncomfortable, especially at first. It will require courage on Mary's part, and she'll need lots of praise and encouragement to complete this hard work. Don't be surprised if at some point she complains about coming and says she doesn't like the work. That means we're approaching difficult issues she isn't comfortable discussing. At those times in particular, you'll need to be encouraging, telling her how important this work is to help her feel better in the long run. I will try to make our work as pleasant as possible by using a variety of techniques such as talking, drawing, writing stories or poems, or even making tapes in order to help Mary explore abuse-related thoughts. In the long run, I believe the gradual exposure process is the best way to help her live comfortably with her memories of the abuse experience.

TREATMENT RATIONALES FOR THE CHILD

Similarly, treatment objectives and rationales should be presented to the child, although in an abbreviated and simpler fashion. For all but the youngest children, it is appropriate to outline the major components of the child's treatment plan (i.e., coping skills training, gradual exposure, and education regarding sexual abuse, healthy sexuality, and personal safety skills).

The dialogue provided in Box 3.3 illustrates the presentation of the treatment rationale to an 8-year-old girl. Note that the therapist attempts to be clear, simple, and interactive in her discussion with the child. Portions of this treatment rationale often need to be repeated

(text continued on p. 47)

BOX 3.3

Case Example: Treatment Rationale for Child

The following dialogue shows how a therapist might present a treatment rationale to an 8-year-old girl in an interactive way, using clear and simple language.

Therapist: I'd like to tell you something about my plans for the work we will do together.

Mary: OK.

Therapist: First of all, I want to teach you what we know about sexual abuse.

Mary: Yuck!

Therapist: Yuck?

Mary: I hate talking about that.

Therapist: Well, I think that usually we feel better about things that we really understand. I'd like to teach you so much about child sexual abuse that you'll be an expert. Once you know all I have to teach you, I think you'll understand more about it and won't feel as confused.

Mary: I guess that would be good.

Therapist: I know that it is hard sometimes to talk about what happened with your dad, so I'd also like to teach you some ways to handle those upsetting feelings.

(continued)

BOX 3.3 *Continued*

Mary: Like what?

Therapist: Well, sometimes when you're feeling nervous and upset, it helps to relax like you're a wet noodle. Then you don't feel so nervous.

Mary: [laughing] A wet noodle?

Therapist: Yeah, it seems like it would be pretty hard to be a nervous wet noodle, doesn't it?

Mary: Yeah. What else will we do?

Therapist: Remember how you told me that when you think about what your dad did, you get scared and upset?

Mary: Yeah, I just try not to ever think about it.

Therapist: Are you able to keep those thoughts out of your head all the time?

Mary: Well no, sometimes they pop in anyway, mostly when I'm doing my schoolwork and when I'm going to sleep. I try to forget about them though.

Therapist: Well, I don't want those thoughts to keep on bothering you. If I had some kind of magic laser and could just zap them out of your brain so you could forget about them forever, we might try that. But we don't have that magic laser. I don't think that you can forget about them forever because you're too smart and too old to do that. The next best thing is to find a way for you to be more comfortable with remembering what happened.

Mary: How can I do that?

Therapist: In order to get more comfortable thinking about the abuse, we need to have you think about it and talk about it so much that you really get used to remembering it.

Mary: You want me to talk about it?

Therapist: Yes, I do. I know that may seem hard at first, but it will get easier and easier. It's like getting into a cold swimming pool. When you first stick your toe in, it feels like an iceberg. Then you wade in up to your knees and you're still shivering. Once you get your tummy wet, you're starting to get used to it. And after a few minutes, the water feels great and you're not cold at all. Have you ever done that?

Mary: Yeah, lots of times. I love to swim!

Therapist: Well, getting used to talking about the abuse is sort of like getting used to the water in a swimming pool. At

---

BOX 3.3 *Continued*

first it seems hard to talk about, but every time you talk about it, it gets easier and easier until you're used to it.

Mary: I don't know. That sounds kind of hard.

Therapist: It may make you uncomfortable at first, but it's the best way for you to get used to thinking about the abuse so that those memories of what happened won't pop into your head and bother you anymore. We can start by talking about some of the easier things so that you can get used to that before we talk about anything more difficult.

Mary: Do we have to talk about it a lot?

Therapist: Yes. In fact we'll talk about it so much that talking about it won't upset you anymore, you'll just get bored with it! I'll try to find ways to make it more fun though. We don't have to just talk. We can also draw pictures, write a book or poems, or even make up a song about what happened.

Mary: My teacher says I'm really good at drawing.

Therapist: Terrific! We can start with drawing then if you like.

Mary: Yeah. That would be good. Can I show my mom the drawings?

---

throughout the course of therapy as encouragement for the child to overcome her avoidance and continue the work of gradual exposure.

With both parents and children, after offering the overall rationale for treatment, the therapist may describe the specific interventions, highlighting some of the therapy exercises planned. It also is useful to emphasize the importance of doing the work of therapy at home as well as during sessions. In addition, when presenting the treatment plan, it is helpful to provide some general expectation for the duration of therapy. Providing some indication of length of treatment may assure both parent and child that the process is not endless and that there is a clear plan with a finite end. In most cases of child sexual abuse, treatment can be completed in 3 months to 1 year. Of course, it is not possible to provide an absolute termination date early in treatment; however, it is helpful to provide an estimate based upon the client's situation. The therapist may offer an estimated duration for treatment, saying that at the end of that period, the progress made in treatment may be assessed. The decision to terminate or continue in counseling may then be based on the assessment of the client's current psychosocial functioning, as well as other factors that might indicate a need for ongoing support (e.g., upcoming court involvement, etc.). When therapy is open-ended, clients may feel a lack of control as they are more dependent on the therapist to determine when the intervention will end. In general, parents may be more amenable to a time-limited treatment commitment because it offers them a greater sense of clarity, closure, and accomplishment.

4

Child Intervention: Therapeutic Components

❑ **Overview**

The child intervention consists of several cognitive behavioral methods, including modeling; coping skills training; gradual exposure; cognitive and affective processing; and education regarding sexual abuse, healthy sexuality, and personal safety skills. Gradual exposure and cognitive and affective processing are the principal components of this intervention. Initially, gradual exposure aims to assist the sexually abused child in disconnecting the associations frequently made between emotional distress and abuse-related memories, thoughts, discussion, and other reminders. This connection is often maintained by adults who attempt to minimize the sexually abused child's distress by shielding him or her from abuse-related stimuli or discussion. Although well-meaning, the parents of sexually abused children often inadvertently strengthen the association between abuse-related cues and emotional distress by avoiding abuse-related discussion, thereby signaling that the associated thoughts and memories are too horrible to confront and process openly (Lyons, 1987).

In the security of the therapeutic environment, gradual exposure slowly but repeatedly exposes children to abuse-related thoughts, discussion, and/or stimuli until anxiety or other forms of emotional distress decrease. With repeated exposures, children's emotional responses diminish through a process referred to as habituation. When this occurs, relaxed or neutral responses may become connected with previously feared abuse-related memories and/or discussion. The resulting overall reduction in emotional distress frees sexually abused children to process their abusive experiences cognitively and affectively.

Following successful gradual exposure, therapists may help children understand more about what happened, correct any misconceptions they may have, and put the experience in perspective. Similarly, therapists may help children process the experience affectively, as they are encouraged to sort out their feelings about the experience and about the perpetrator with the goal of achieving a greater sense of emotional equilibrium.

The child's individual therapy sessions may be structured as follows. The initial sessions typically are spent building rapport, completing the evaluation, and presenting assessment findings and treatment rationale. Subsequently, the child's therapeutic work begins. This work may be described in terms of the following components:

1. Coping skills training (i.e., emotional expression, cognitive coping skills training, relaxation training)
2. Gradual exposure and cognitive and affective processing
3. Education regarding child sexual abuse, healthy sexuality, and personal safety skills

The number of sessions devoted to each of these components and the order of implementation are flexible so that the therapist may tailor the therapy to best meet the child's needs. Often, work may be pursued involving more than one component during the same sessions. For example, the first portion of a session may be devoted to reviewing coping skills training, while the second portion of the session may be reserved for gradual exposure and processing exercises. Following the completion of the therapy components, the final therapy sessions are reserved for evaluating treatment progress, reviewing skills developed, and discussing ways to continue the therapeutic process at home. The basic therapy components are described in detail below in the order in which they are most commonly implemented.

❏ Coping Skills Training

The coping skills training (e.g., emotional expression, cognitive coping skills, relaxation training) focuses on providing skills that may help children cope with the wide array of emotions they may experience in response to abuse. For many children, the trauma of abuse leads to emotions that are difficult and more intense than any feelings they have experienced before. Thus, it is not surprising that sexually abused children often need assistance in sharing these feelings and coping with them effectively. Coping skills training encourages the development of skills that will enhance children's ability to get in touch with and share the feelings, thoughts, and sensations they experienced during and after the abuse.

Typically, some work in this area should be completed early in the therapeutic process as these skills help to maximize the benefits of the gradual exposure and processing exercises. Children also may be encouraged to apply the coping skills learned in treatment to the individual difficulties they face in their daily lives. This component of therapy focuses primarily on training in emotional expression, cognitive coping, and relaxation because these skills may be particularly useful in coping with thoughts and feelings that may have been experienced during the course of the abuse. However, depending on a child's needs, therapists may choose to incorporate other skill-building interventions into these sessions as well (e.g., problem solving and/or social skills training).

EMOTIONAL EXPRESSION SKILLS

Early in treatment, therapists may help children to develop a vocabulary for emotions, accurately identify emotions in themselves as well as in others, and appropriately express emotions. Typically, younger children will need more education regarding emotions than will older children. However, even older children who are intellectually informed about emotions may benefit from work on emotional expression, particularly if they are uncomfortable or unaccustomed to discussing their own feelings.

Developing a Vocabulary for Emotions

Therapists may initiate work on emotional expression skills by first eliciting and expanding a child's emotional vocabulary. Although sexually abused children often experience a wide range of emotions, they may not have the words to label those emotions. When teaching appropriate labels for emotions, the therapist may encourage a child to list as many feelings as he or she can, saying,

> People have lots of different feelings. What are some ways that you feel sometimes?

Children also may identify feelings that they like and feelings they do not like. With children who lack an adequate vocabulary for emotions, therapists may elicit or provide those labels by using a chart illustrating a variety of feelings. Such "feelings" charts or posters are widely available commercially (e.g., through Childswork /Childsplay, Inc.).

Identifying Other People's Emotions

After the therapist has determined that the child has a basic vocabulary for emotions, the therapist may focus on developing skills for accurately identifying different emotions. The therapist might begin this work by saying,

> When people are feeling happy or sad or mad, you can sometimes tell how they feel by the sound of their voices or the look on their

faces. Have you seen someone who was very sad? How did he [or she] look? How could you tell that he [or she] was sad?

The therapist may continue this discussion of physical and verbal clues regarding a variety of different emotions. In addition, the therapist may introduce an exercise in which the child can practice identifying how a person is feeling.

This exercise can be conducted in a variety of ways. Younger children may learn to identify facial clues for emotions by guessing which feelings the therapist is depicting when drawing a series of faces. Photographs, pictures, and puppets also may be used to identify and label emotions. Some children may enjoy reading a story about other children expressing their feelings. *Ellie's Day,* by Susan Conlin and Susan Levine Friedman (1989), and *Feelings Inside You and Outloud Too,* by Barbara Kay Polland (1975), Ph.D., are good choices for discussing feelings.

When teaching children to identify emotions in other people, the therapist may teach the phrase, "Look, listen, ask." The therapist can explain that the first steps in learning how someone else is feeling are to look at their face and listen to their voice and words. However, it is possible to misperceive someone else's emotions based only on those observations. Thus, to be accurate in understanding another's emotions, it is best to ask that person how he or she is feeling. The therapist may reinforce the lesson of look, listen, ask by playing charades with the child. Each person can take turns acting out a scene that displays certain emotions. The observer can be asked to guess the feeling being depicted by looking, listening, and asking questions. Ultimately during joint sessions, children may ask nonoffending parent(s) to clarify any emotions displayed by the parent that were confusing to the child. This is particularly important because sexually abused children sometimes misperceive the emotions expressed by nonoffending parent(s) and others when they first disclosed the abuse.

> *Children may misperceive emotions expressed by nonoffending parents.*

Identifying the Child's Own Emotions

The therapist also should focus attention on the child's awareness and identification of his or her own emotions. This is particularly important because sexually abused children may have a tendency to distance themselves from emotions. During these exercises, it is important to emphasize that there are no right or wrong feelings. The therapist may enhance the child's awareness and identification of emotions by encouraging the child to discuss real and personal (although not necessarily abuse-related) situations that have led to a variety of different emotions. For example, the therapist might say,

> Tell me about a time when you felt excited. What were you excited about? Could anyone else tell that you were excited?

A similar conversation might be pursued regarding a variety of other feelings such as being happy, mad, sad, scared, proud, worried, ashamed, excited, confused, and so on.

Developing Effective Means Of Expressing Emotions

As a child becomes more aware of his or her own emotions and more comfortable discussing them, the therapist may shift the focus of work onto developing appropriate means of expressing emotions. Initially, the therapist may elicit from the child means of expressing various emotions such as sadness, happiness, anger, fear, love, worry, and so on. For example, the therapist might ask,

> What do you do when you feel sad?

For younger children, it may be helpful to ask more specific and concrete questions such as,

> When was the last time you felt sad? What did you do then?

Children may describe both adaptive and maladaptive ways of responding to different feelings. The therapist may encourage the child who offers maladaptive methods of coping to consider alternative coping responses. For example, if a child described coping with sadness by sitting alone and not talking to anyone, the therapist might respond in these ways:

> If you do sit by yourself, without talking, how do you feel? Does that help you feel better?

> What does make you feel happy/OK again?

> What do you do to make someone else feel better when they are sad?

> Some things you can try to feel better are: talking with parents/friends/teachers about how you feel [ask children for a list of people they could talk to]; listening to music; drawing or painting a picture; writing a poem, song, story about your feelings and/or problems.

It is important for children to understand that it is OK to feel sad, mad, scared, and so on. The therapist may say,

> You know, everybody feels sad sometimes. It does not help to hide those sad feelings because it does not make them go away. Instead it is better to express your feelings, and there are many different ways to do that.

The therapist may continue to talk with the child about ways of expressing a variety of other feelings, focusing on those emotions that are particularly relevant for a specific child. It is preferable for the therapist to elicit the child's individual methods for sharing feelings or making himself or herself feel better before making suggestions. In that way, the therapist is more likely to hear about any ineffective means of expressing emotions and also is able to encourage the continued use of any appropriate means of expressing emotions.

When teaching means of expressing emotions, it can be helpful to have the child role-play or use puppets and/or dolls to depict a situation illustrating a specific emotion. After using a role play to illustrate the child's specific emotion and current strategies for expressing that feeling, another role play may be used, if needed, to illustrate more adaptive coping strategies.

After discussing the child's own strategies for coping with various emotions, the therapist may emphasize the importance of sharing feelings with someone. The therapist may say,

> There are lots of things you can do when you have different feelings, but remember that it always helps to talk to someone about how you feel. Who are people that you can talk to?

It may be useful to have the child draw a picture or write a paragraph about one person he or she can talk to about any kind of problem. Role plays may be used again to allow the child to act out how he or she could talk about specific feelings with another person.

Coping With Anger Effectively

When discussing emotional expression, it often is useful to spend some time discussing anger, both because it is a commonly experienced emotion and because inappropriate expressions of anger can be particularly problematic. With a child who offers maladaptive responses to anger, the therapist may help the child think through to the probable negative outcome of that ineffective response. For example,

> Well, if you were really, really mad and you did hit your brother, then what would happen?

Although mental health professionals used to encourage the venting of anger through means such as hitting a pillow or a "bobo doll," current research indicates that such exercises or prolonged discussions focused on the anger only maintain that emotional state and the unhealthy physiological responses associated with it (Tavris, 1989). Thus, it is more appropriate to encourage children to work toward appropriate resolution of the anger-provoking situation. In situations in which such resolution is not possible (i.e., it may not be possible to "right the wrong" the child experienced in being abused), therapists may encourage children to explore and express their anger through a variety of therapeutic activities. The therapist, for example, may encourage a child to discuss, write, or draw a picture to communicate anger as well as other associated emotions. The purpose of that exercise is to allow the child to gain insight into his or her own feelings, not to allow the child to brood over anger.

Some children focus excessively on their anger as a means of distancing themselves from other painful emotions or because they lack awareness of those other emotions. Therapists should encourage such children to identify and express the full range of emotions they are experiencing. Some children will benefit from writing a letter to the perpetrator, expressing all their feelings. Typically such a letter should not be mailed, as the perpetrator's response may not be anticipated and may be harmful. Having clarified the basis for their feelings and having expressed the anger, it is time for them to move on and stop focusing on that emotion.

Children may be encouraged to use cognitive coping strategies (described in the next section) to replace anger-provoking thoughts with anger-reducing thoughts such as, "I'm not going to let him (the perpetrator) upset me anymore," or "I'm going to focus on having a great life ahead of me." Children also may be taught to control their anger by breathing deeply, using relaxation techniques, exercising, or distracting themselves with other activities. It is important for children and parents to understand that the objective is not to eliminate appropriate anger, but to prevent it from becoming all consuming and/or being expressed in ways that may be damaging to the child. Readers are referred to *Anger, The Misunderstood Emotion* (Tavris, 1989) for further information about the development, maintenance, and management of anger.

Therapists may summarize the training regarding appropriate expression of emotions by teaching children the phrase, "show and tell." They may explain that children can most effectively cope with emotions by "showing" them through appropriate behaviors and by "telling" other people about them. For young children in particular, this phrase may help them remember and use the emotional expression training.

Discussing Abuse-Related Emotions

Gradually but deliberately, the therapist can move the discussion from feelings about a variety of issues to feelings about the sexual abuse experience. For example, the therapist might say,

> We've talked a lot about feelings. Now, I want to talk about how it feels to be sexually abused. Kids usually have a lot of different feelings about that. What kinds of things did you feel?

The therapist may help the child generate feelings he or she experienced during the abuse, after the abuse, during the investigation, and currently when he or she thinks about the abuse.

It is particularly important to encourage a discussion of confusing or mixed-up feelings because many sexually abused children experience this. The therapist may ask,

> Did you ever feel confused, like you're not sure how you should feel or like you have different feelings all at the same time? When a child feels all mixed up like that, it is hard to know what to do. What do you think you should do if you are feeling all mixed up about something?

Depending upon the child's response, the therapist may need to offer the following information:

> One great thing you can do when you are feeling confused about anything is to talk to someone. When you are feeling confused about a touching problem, it is very important to talk to someone so that he or she can help you. Who can you talk to about a confusing problem?

Then the therapist may help the child generate a list of available people.

> There are lots of people you can talk to. The important thing is that you talk to someone, and if the first person you talk to doesn't help you, you can talk to someone else. You did that. You told someone what was happening to you and you got help. You did a great job!

COGNITIVE COPING SKILLS

Children's efforts to make sense of their experiences are reflected in their thoughts. These thoughts ultimately provide the foundation for their developing views and belief systems. Sexually abused children often have very little information and experience to call upon in their attempts to make sense of their abuse. As a result, their thoughts about the abuse may be very confused, inaccurate, and dysfunctional. It is, therefore, essential to help sexually abused children become aware of and share their abuse-related thoughts. Once the children have done this, therapists can help them use cognitive coping skills to identify and alter negative or inaccurate thoughts that may be contributing to emotional and behavioral difficulties.

Because sexually abused children often exhibit considerable avoidance to abuse reminders in the early stages of therapy, it usually is preferable to present these skills in terms of their general use before applying them specifically to the abuse experience. These techniques may be more easily used by older children. However, by slowing down the pace and offering many concrete examples, children as young as 7 may benefit. Readers interested in further information regarding the empirical development and use of these techniques are referred to *The Optimistic Child* (Seligman, Reivich, Jaycox, & Gillham, 1995).

Interrelationships of Thoughts, Feelings, and Behaviors

The therapist should begin the cognitive coping treatment component by explaining the interrelated nature of thoughts, feelings, and behaviors. When discussing these interrelationships and presenting examples, the therapist may use the problem triangle depicted in Figure 4.1 to illustrate the connections between thoughts, feelings, and behaviors. To explain how thoughts, feelings, and behaviors can influence each other, a therapist might follow the method outlined in Box 4.1.

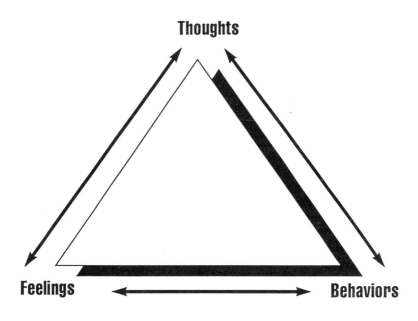

Figure 4.1. Cognitive Coping Triangle

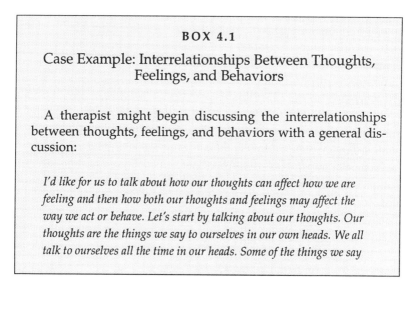

BOX 4.1

Case Example: Interrelationships Between Thoughts,
Feelings, and Behaviors

A therapist might begin discussing the interrelationships
between thoughts, feelings, and behaviors with a general discussion:

*I'd like for us to talk about how our thoughts can affect how we are
feeling and then how both our thoughts and feelings may affect the
way we act or behave. Let's start by talking about our thoughts. Our
thoughts are the things we say to ourselves in our own heads. We all
talk to ourselves all the time in our heads. Some of the things we say*

BOX 4.1 *Continued*

*to ourselves are helpful or make us feel good while other things we
say make us feel unhappy.*

*For example, when we walk past a mirror, most of us look in it and
say something to ourselves about how we look. A person might think
to herself, "I really like this new skirt, it looks really nice." Those
thoughts probably make that girl feel happy, confident, maybe proud.
On the other hand, another person might say, "I hate this new
haircut! It makes me look like a dork!" How do you think those
thoughts would make the person feel?*

The therapist should continue this work by having the child
identify the emotions generated by thoughts:

*Billy wasn't invited to a classmate's birthday party. Billy thinks,
"Nobody likes me. That's why I don't get invited to birthdays." How
do these thoughts make Billy feel? Then how does Billy behave
toward other kids?*

The therapist should be prepared to offer further fictitious
examples until the child seems to have caught on to the problem
triangle concept, particularly with respect to the influence
thoughts have on our feelings and behaviors. As this work
continues, the therapist may shift from having the child identify
the emotions depicted in an example to having the child identify the thoughts underlying the emotions. For most children,
identifying underlying thoughts may be somewhat more difficult than identifying emotions. The therapist should provide
examples that describe the fictitious child's problem and his or
her emotional reaction while asking the client to identify the
thoughts that triggered the feelings. The following example
requires the client to identify the underlying thoughts.

*On Tuesday, Kathy's mother said they might go to the movies during
the weekend, but on Saturday her mother says they are too busy with
other activities to go. Kathy is really angry. What might she be
thinking to cause her to feel so angry?*

Different Thoughts Result in Different Emotions

As the child begins to grasp the relationships between thoughts, feelings, and behaviors, the therapist should explain that to a large extent we can control our thoughts and thus ultimately our feelings. We can choose to think about a particular situation in positive, optimistic ways, and then those thoughts will generate positive feelings.

To illustrate that possibility, the therapist may provide the child with developmentally appropriate examples of how one can have different thoughts about the exact same problem, resulting in different emotions. An example is provided in Box 4.2. The therapist may use different examples to elicit from the child the various feelings that might result when someone thinks about a problem in different ways. Visual presentation of different examples using paper and pencil or the chalkboard can be very helpful in teaching children these concepts.

After modeling the process for the child, the therapist may ask the child to work through an example, demonstrating how different thoughts about the same situation can result in different feelings. The therapist should continue practicing with a child until he or she is consistently able to identify the positive (optimistic) or negative (pessimistic) thoughts that underlie different feelings in various examples. Again, the therapist can explain to the child that there are many different ways to think about the same problem. Furthermore, the therapist may say,

> When we think about a problem in a way that leads to OK or good feelings, we call those thoughts positive, hopeful, or optimistic thoughts. On the other hand, when we think about a problem in ways that lead to bad feelings, we call those thoughts negative or pessimistic thoughts.

Disputing Negative Thoughts

Once the child understands how it is possible to think about the same situation in different ways, the therapist should begin to teach the child how we can change negative, unproductive thoughts to more optimistic thoughts that result in more positive

---

BOX 4.2

Case Example: Different Thoughts Result in Different Emotions

A therapist might use the following story to help a child learn how different thoughts result in different emotions.

Sally and Jennifer are in the same third-grade class. They both failed their first math test of the year, each receiving a score of 55. When Sally got her test back, she thought, "I must be the stupidest kid in the school. I failed this test, now I'll get an F in math on my report card, and I'll end up flunking the third grade! This kind of thinking made Sally feel [have the child fill in the blank].

Jennifer received the same grade, but she had different thoughts about it. She thought, "Well, I didn't really study very hard because I went to my friend's birthday party. Now I know what kind of tests Mrs. Smith gives and what I need to do to get ready for the next test. Next time I'm going to start studying a week in advance and I'm sure I will pull this grade up." These thoughts made Jennifer feel [have child fill in the blank].

---

emotions. The therapist should emphasize that negative thoughts are not necessarily true or permanent (no matter how much we believe them). We can change our negative thoughts and help ourselves to feel better. The therapist may further explain that the process of changing thoughts and emotions is a skill that must be practiced to be used effectively. Furthermore, the change in thoughts and emotions often does not occur quickly and completely, particularly if the problematic thoughts and emotions are ones that have been experienced on a repeated basis. However, with practice it is possible to change both the thoughts and feelings that have been distressing. Using fictitious examples, the therapist can teach the child to formulate positive replacement thoughts to substitute for negative, dysfunctional thoughts. An example of this process is provided in Box 4.3.

BOX 4.3

Case Example: Disputing Negative Thoughts

A therapist might help a child learn about disputing negative thoughts, by telling the following story:

Sarah was the first student through the lunch line and sat down at a
table in the corner. When her friends, Kathy and Nicole, came
through the line, they sat at another table. Sarah thinks, "They don't
like me anymore. Nobody likes me. I'm the least popular girl at
school." Those thoughts cause Sarah to feel sad and hurt. How can
she replace those negative thoughts with more optimistic thoughts
that will help her feel better?

If the child has difficulty generating a positive replacement thought, the therapist might suggest the following: "They must not have seen me over here. I am sort of hard to notice in this corner. I'll go over and sit with them."

The therapist should continue having the child generate replacement thoughts for fictitious examples until the child is adept at that process.

Applying the Model to the Child's Own Negative Thoughts

Once the child has a good grasp of the concepts presented, the therapist may encourage him or her to dispute his or her own negative (although not necessarily abused-related) thoughts, replacing them with more positive, hopeful thoughts. When encouraged to do so, some children can challenge their negative thoughts quite readily.

The therapist may begin teaching the child the process of disputing negative thoughts using relatively minor difficulties, but ultimately the child should be encouraged to dispute negative abuse-related thoughts in this manner. At times, eliciting abuse-related thoughts may be difficult, particularly with children who are suffering post-traumatic stress symptoms and are avoidant. Many sexually abused children, in fact, are not ready to practice disputing abuse-related thoughts until after they have participated in some gradual exposure exercises. Prior to gradual exposure, it may be preferable just to have children work at identifying and expressing underlying negative thoughts regarding other issues. Because thoughts are often automatic, habitual, and/or fleeting in nature, helping children bring their thoughts to awareness sometimes requires considerable practice. Once the child has developed some skill in identifying and acknowledging thoughts in general and has become more comfortable confronting memories of the abuse, the therapist may begin to elicit abuse-related thoughts. This is often best done in the context of gradual exposure when the child may be gently encouraged to identify abuse-related feelings and the thoughts underlying them. The accuracy and usefulness of the thoughts may be best assessed later during processing exercises. The therapist can then teach the child to dispute negative abuse-related thoughts. The example in Box 4.4 illustrates how the therapist can teach the child to dispute

---

BOX 4.4

Case Example: Disputing Abuse-Related Thoughts

The following dialogue shows how a therapist might help a child learn how to dispute dysfunctional abuse-related thoughts.

Therapist: Michelle, you said that you feel guilty about the abuse. What are the thoughts going through your head when you are feeling guilty?

Michelle: I just keep thinking that my dad couldn't help doing that to me because I was wearing such short, baby-doll pajamas. He told me that was why he did it.

Therapist: Well, let's try to figure out how accurate that thought is. Do any of your friends wear that style of pajamas?

Michelle: Yeah, lots of them do. My sister does too.

Therapist: And were they sexually abused because they wear those pajamas?

Michelle: No, I don't think so. At least I know my sister wasn't.

(continued)

BOX 4.4 *Continued*

Therapist: Do you remember what we learned from the information sheet about why sexual abuse occurs?

Michelle: I remember that it's never the kid's fault, even if she asks for the abuse to happen. The grown-up is always responsible.

Therapist: Great! You were really paying attention to that. So do you think that wearing your baby-doll pajamas really caused the abuse to happen?

Michelle: No. I guess my Dad just said that so it wouldn't seem like his fault.

Therapist: I think you may be right. So how can you replace that thought so that you don't have to feel guilty?

Michelle: I can say to myself that what you wear does not cause abuse. Abuse is caused by the person who does it.

Therapist: Great job! Let's practice using that in some role plays.

---

negative abuse-related thoughts. Other examples follow in the sections on cognitive and affective processing.

Best Friend Role Play

Another means of encouraging children to dispute negative thoughts is to use what we refer to as "best friend" role plays (similar to "Mr. Puppet game" described by Seligman, 1991). In these role plays, children are asked to imagine that their best friend is having certain negative thoughts, and they need to convince the best friend (played by the therapist, puppet, empty chair, etc.) that these negative thoughts are not true. It is generally a good idea to encourage children to give it a try before modeling the process of disputing negative thoughts for them. Again, this provides some information about the child's baseline abilities.

When using the best friend role play to help a child dispute dysfunctional abuse-related thoughts, it is extremely important to remind the child frequently that these are not the therapist's own thoughts. Rather, the thoughts you will be expressing are thoughts that the child may have expressed previously. With younger children, it helps to use a puppet, thereby reinforcing the message that this is an exercise or game, not the therapist's real thoughts or feelings. It also helps to use the negative thoughts the child actually shared. Going beyond those thoughts may cause the child to wonder if the therapist is expressing the child's negative thoughts or the therapist's own personal thoughts. The example provided in Box 4.5 illustrates how the therapist might introduce and pursue the best friend role play with a 10-year-old boy named Tony.

As indicated earlier, although the therapist may spend the early therapy sessions teaching these coping skills, they may be practiced, when clinically appropriate, throughout the course of therapy. The process may seem artificial at first, but as children continue to practice challenging their negative thoughts, it will naturally become part of their coping repertoire. More time should be devoted to cognitive coping exercises for those children who have obtained high scores on depression or pessimism measures as they are likely to be less able to cope effectively with traumatic events due to their dysfunctional cognitive styles.

Cognitive Coping Skills Training With Young Children

Children who are younger or developmentally delayed may have difficulty comprehending the process of identifying and disputing dysfunctional thoughts. For these children, the therapist may teach a series of positive self-statements that can replace dysfunctional thoughts. These self-statements should be tailored to the child's particular difficulties. Thus, for example, a child who seems to have a poor self-image might be encouraged to say, "I am special because . . . " or "I am just as good as other kids." A child who seems to be withdrawn and/or fearful might learn to say, "Trying new things can be fun" or "I can be very brave sometimes." Other positive self-statements specific to abuse-related fears and worries are discussed in greater detail in the section on gradual exposure and processing.

Children's learning and retention of new skills may be greatly enhanced through the use of behavioral rehearsal. Thus, rather than relying on verbal instruction to teach positive self-statements, children may be engaged in role plays in which they are encouraged

BOX 4.5

Case Example: Best Friend Role Play

Here's how a therapist might use the "best friend" role play
with a 10-year-old boy named Tony.

Therapist: We've been getting together for several weeks now,
and you shared with me some of your feelings and
thoughts about the sexual abuse. Some of the things that
you say to yourself about the abuse are pretty mean. In fact,
if you had a best friend who was sexually abused, I don't
think you would say those things to him. So what I would
like to do is a role play in which I will play you. In fact,
maybe I can wear your hat to get into your character if
that's OK. Then I will share with you some of the things
you seem to say to yourself. I would like you to be my very
best friend and try to help me feel better. In fact, you can
use all the information you learned in counseling so far to
convince me that some of the thoughts I have are not
correct. What do you think?

Tony: Well, I don't know.

Therapist: Let's give it a try. I think you'll be great!

Tony: OK.

Therapist: Which of your friends do you want to be?

Tony: I guess I'll be Matthew. He's a good friend.

Therapist: OK, I'll be you and you be Matthew. Ready?

Tony: Yeah.

Therapist [in role of Tony, the client]: Hey, Matthew, can we
talk for a minute?

Tony [in role of Matthew]: Yeah, what's going on?

Therapist: Remember when I told you what happened with me
and our neighbor, Wayne, how he touched me and stuff?

Tony: Yeah, what a creep!

Therapist: I want you to swear you won't tell anyone about it.
And I'm never going to talk about it again, OK?

Tony: Why?

Therapist: Because I'm afraid if I talk about it, more and more
people will find out about it.

BOX 4.5 *Continued*

Tony: Well, I won't tell anyone about it if you don't want me to.

Therapist: Thanks, you're a really good friend, but I'm still worried that people will find out.

Tony: How do you think everyone will find out?

Therapist: Well, I had to tell so many people about it—a police officer, a child protection person, and this counselor who keeps bugging me to talk about it.

Tony: [smiles] Yeah, she's a real pain.

Therapist: I just don't want to talk about it. I'm really afraid it's going to get out. Do you think the counselor or the officer will tell anybody?

Tony: I don't think they are allowed to—they're supposed to keep this stuff, what do you call it, confidential.

Therapist: Yeah, I think you're right. The counselor did say something about that. But still if one kid finds out—then *everyone* in the whole school will be talking about it. Don't you think *everyone* will think I'm disgusting?

Tony: I don't think you're disgusting, and I know other kids who like you a lot and would stick up for you.

Therapist: But what about all the other kids?

Tony: If one kid finds out, they may talk about it with a couple of kids for a little bit, but not everyone. Besides I think they'll think Wayne's the creep, not you.

Therapist: You really think so? Maybe you're right, but it will still bother me to think that everyone is talking about it *all the time.*

Tony: [long pause] They may talk about it a little, they might even have some questions about it. But they're not going to keep talking about it all the time.

Therapist: Are you sure? It's pretty bizarre stuff.

Tony: Honestly, Matthew, the kids probably have better things to talk about.

Therapist: Like what?

Tony: Well, the playoffs and girls.

Therapist: Yeah. I guess you're right. That helps me feel a lot better. Thanks!

to incorporate positive self-statements into the scenes as frequently as possible. The therapist may assist the children in transferring these skills from the therapy office to real situations by reenacting interactions that they have, in fact, experienced or anticipate experiencing. Through role plays, children can also learn to distinguish when positive self-statements may be more appropriately said to themselves or out loud.

RELAXATION SKILLS TRAINING

Children who are highly anxious and who avoid discussions of their abusive experiences may benefit from relaxation skills training. These skills may give children a greater sense of control over the anxiety they fear they may experience when confronted with abuse reminders.

Children may benefit from learning to use relaxation skills.

In addition, the relaxation training may be pleasant, thus facilitating a positive association between therapy and this pleasant activity and possibly mitigating against a negative association between therapy and the aversive experience of recalling the abusive experience. In actuality, however, most children are able to tolerate discussions of their abuse, as long as the increasingly anxiety-provoking discussions are encouraged in a carefully paced, gradual manner.

However, if relaxation training is needed, it should be geared to the child's developmental stage. Older children (i.e., those above 10 years of age) may be taught progressive relaxation including guided tension-releasing exercises. However, they may not have the attention span to work through all of the muscle groups in one session. Thus, the therapist may want to teach head, torso, and leg exercises separately or identify and focus on the most problematic muscle groups. Younger children may be more responsive to image-induced relaxation. They may be taught to distinguish states of tension and relaxation respectively by standing like a "tin soldier" and collapsing into a chair like a "wet noodle." The child may then learn to elicit the wet noodle feelings in the face of anxiety through personalized self-instructions such as relax, hang loose, lighten up, or calm down.

In general, children should be encouraged to practice the relaxation exercises twice daily at home. In addition, children should be instructed not to practice relaxation exercises as a prelude to sleeping, as the goal is to help children achieve a conscious state of relaxation when they are awake and confronting fears. After children are consistently able to achieve a state of relaxation, therapists may encourage them to use this skill in several different situations. Initially, children may be encouraged to use relaxation skills outside of therapy when they are confronting highly distressing memories or reminders of the abuse.

The therapist also may have the child use relaxation skills at the beginning of a gradual exposure session that the child is anticipating with great anxiety. Alternatively, relaxation skills may be used in a paradigm more similar to systematic desensitization, with a state of relaxation being induced and paired with a particularly anxiety-provoking image of the abusive experience. However, therapists should be aware of the possibility that children may use relaxation skills as a means of avoiding the gradual exposure work. Thus, it is preferable not to interrupt gradual exposure work to implement relaxation exercises except when there seems to be no other way of pursuing the work of gradual exposure. For further information regarding the techniques of relaxation training, readers are referred to *Relaxation: A Comprehensive Manual for Adults, Children, and Children with Special Needs*, by Cautela and Groden (1978).

❏ Gradual Exposure and Cognitive and Affective Processing

As indicated earlier, gradual exposure is perhaps the cornerstone of this therapy approach. The purpose of gradual exposure is to gradually expose children to thoughts, memories, and other innocuous reminders of the abusive experience until they can tolerate those memories without significant emotional distress and no longer need to avoid them. Many children resist this work initially because of the discomfort it generates. It is important to forewarn parents that sexually abused children may initially resist this approach and/or may experience some increased symptoms early on. If not appropriately forewarned, the child's resistance may undermine parental motivation and confidence in the therapy approach.

After becoming more comfortable with discussions of the abuse, children will be able to pursue cognitive and affective processing, during which the therapist will help them correct any misconceptions regarding the abuse, enhance their cognitive understanding of the abuse, and clarify their emotional responses to the abuse. For some children, remembering and discussing the abuse itself is not particularly difficult. Such children will require less time for gradual exposure proper, although they may still need significant time spent on cognitive and affective processing of the abuse.

Most sexually abused children may be engaged in gradual exposure exercises without the use of relaxation skills to combat distressing feelings. In fact, it is preferable for sexually abused children to reexperience and endure the distressing emotions elicited during gradual exposure until the emotions diminish naturally. This powerfully demonstrates to them that there is no need to fear the negative emotions associated with the abuse. Many children find that they are more than capable of coping with these emotions. In addition, they learn that the feelings often diminish during the session in a surprisingly brief period of time. However, relaxation skills training may be used to jump-start the gradual exposure process with children whose extreme anxiety and/or avoidance is interfering with their ability to participate in even the mildest gradual exposure exercises. In such a case, relaxation and/or cognitive coping skills training may heighten the child's sense of control or preparedness, thereby enhancing his or her receptivity to the gradual exposure exercises planned.

THERAPIST ISSUES

Although gradual exposure may appear to be a relatively straightforward procedure, it is actually quite difficult for many therapists to implement. Typically, a mental health professional's objective is to help individuals feel better. However, for gradual exposure to be successful, children must be encouraged to endure some anxiety and distress before reaching the goal of feeling better. As a child begins to show signs of distress, the therapist's natural instinct may be to back off or to give the child a break for several sessions. Clearly, this is an empathic response; however, it is counterproductive for the gradual exposure process. By backing off, the therapist is not only reinforcing avoidance, but he or she is modeling it. Thus, it is important to be aware of the tendency as a therapist to avoid distressing abuse-related issues. When the child begins to exhibit some distress during the course of gradual exposure, the therapist may view this as progress and continue to move forward gradually.

PREPARING FOR GRADUAL EXPOSURE

During the course of the evaluation, including the initial interview regarding the abuse allegations, the therapist should gather information regarding the child's fears of abuse-related stimuli and avoidance patterns. Through conversations with the child and the parent and through personal observation, the therapist will collect information about specific situations or objects the child avoids or feels distressed about, such as darkness, bathrooms, bedtime, being alone with men, inadvertent touches, and so on. Similarly, the therapist should gather information regarding the child's thoughts or memories that seem to be distressing, resulting in patterns of avoidance. Furthermore, the therapist may learn that the child is anxious about possible consequences of the abuse or the resulting investigation, such as peers finding out about the abuse, family disruption as a result of the child's disclosures, feared negative perceptions by other people, fears that the offender will carry out physical threats to the child, or anxieties about going to court.

This information regarding the child's pattern of avoidance and anxiety will guide the development of a gradual exposure treatment plan for the child, allowing the therapist to begin the gradual exposure process with the least feared cues and move on to increasingly difficult stimuli over the course of treatment. For example, during the evaluation, the therapist may find that the child seems to be increasingly distressed as the conversation moves from general discussion about family members to more focused discussion about the abusive family member and the abusive behavior. Thus the

BOX 4.6

Sample Gradual Exposure Hierarchy

Here is a sample hierarchy of topics to be used with a child who experienced multiple episodes of abuse. A hierarchy should be treated as a useful guide that can be modified to reflect new information gathered in the course of therapy. The child may be engaged in gradual exposure by drawing, discussing, or writing about the topics listed below. Later in the therapy process, some of these steps may be repeated in joint sessions with nonoffending parents.

1. General information about child sexual abuse.
2. Nonabusive interactions with the offender.
3. The disclosure and resulting investigation.
4. The first episode of abuse.
5. Additional types of abusive contacts.
6. Other specific episodes of abuse (associated with special events such as holidays, birthdays, beginning or ending of school year).
7. The most disturbing or embarrassing abusive episodes.

therapist might begin gradual exposure by talking with the child about the entire family before moving on to discuss the child's relationships with the offender in general and then eventually focusing on the actual abusive behavior. Box 4.6 provides a sample hierarchy of topics for gradual exposure with a child who experienced multiple episodes of abuse. Such a hierarchy is a useful guide, but it need not be rigidly adhered to, as information gathered during the course of therapy may alter or add further steps to the hierarchical ordering.

During the evaluation sessions, the therapist also may identify the child's play preferences (e.g., drawing, doll playing, puppeteering) and may determine the level of the child's imagery skills. This information will be useful in planning the exposure sessions.

Although it is important to provide parents and children with a general treatment plan, in most cases, it is not necessary or useful to describe the specific items on the therapist's tentative hierarchy to a young child. Such details may only heighten the child's anxiety and impede the gathering of additional details regarding the abusive experiences. Moreover, the specifics of the plan may change in response to the child's initial reactions and progress during the early exposure sessions.

Occasionally, in work with older and less avoidant children, it may be beneficial to involve children in the development of a general hierarchy for gradual exposure as that involvement may afford the child a greater sense of control and collaboration. Therapists should use their clinical judgment to identify when that involvement might be helpful.

However, in virtually all cases the general plan for the gradual exposure sessions should be explained to children, as was described earlier in the section on treatment rationale. Children should be informed that therapy is hard work and sometimes they may be asked to talk about things that are upsetting. In addition, the therapist should emphasize that the child's hard work will pay off because it will help the child to feel better, so that he or she will not feel as much distress when confronted with reminders of the abuse. It is important that parents know to encourage their children's participation even if the children do not feel a need for therapy. Many sexually abused children deny and/or suppress abuse-related memories and thoughts so successfully that they initially have difficulty acknowledging worries or problems associated with the abuse. With such a child, it may be helpful to explain,

> Sometimes we don't know that something bothers us, but it stays in our memory and causes us problems in the future. That is why it is very important to talk about your thoughts about the abuse now so that we can prevent them from becoming worries or problems later on.

INITIATING GRADUAL EXPOSURE

During gradual exposure sessions, therapists should work in a structured, directive manner to aid children in reexperiencing and processing their thoughts, memories, and emotional responses to the abuse. Children should be encouraged to confront abuse-related cues and memories, while experiencing and sharing the sensations, thoughts, and feelings they elicit. The therapist will need to repeatedly remind the child that it is better to let his or her feelings show than to keep them bottled up inside. Thus, while crying and other emotional responses may be encouraged, the therapist will repeat exposures to abuse-related cues until the emotional responses diminish. By disconnecting abuse-related reminders from the associated distress, the child will be able to store the abusive experiences in his or her conscious memory with greater clarity and perspective. Some children may respond to the gradual exposure work with flat affect rather than with heightened emotional distress. Such children may be avoiding the emotions associated with the abuse more than the memories of the actual events experienced. The goal of gradual exposure with such children is to help them recall, confront, and become comfortable with the emotions they experienced at the time of the abuse as well as the emotions that are generated by abuse-related thoughts and other reminders.

Children often have more information than we realize.

Education Regarding Child Sexual Abuse

Many sexually abused children experience generalized avoidance and distress in response to all abuse-related cues and may benefit from an initial exposure to discussion of sexual abuse issues in general. Sexually abused children often seem to find it easier to talk about sexual abuse in the abstract than to talk about their personal experience of abuse. In such cases, it is helpful to begin gradual exposure with a series of questions and answers regarding sexual abuse, as a means of providing general educational material. Some questions that might be included are

What is child sexual abuse?
How do children feel when they have been sexually abused?
Who is sexually abused?
Who sexually abuses children?
Why does sexual abuse happen?
Why don't children tell?

It is important to elicit answers from the children before providing answers to these and other questions. Children often have more information and a better understanding of sexual abuse than we realize. It can be encouraging to them to receive affirmation of their thoughts and beliefs. In cases in which they do not have accurate information, it is important to elicit their responses so that their misconceptions can be identified. These misconceptions may be corrected by offering children an example that may help them rethink their responses and come to a more appropriate conclusion. For example, if a child believes that this happens only to girls, the therapist may point out the pictures in the office that were clearly drawn by sexually abused boys.

The process of discussing this educational information regarding sexual abuse also allows the child to further process his or her own experience of abuse. For example, when asking how children feel when they have been sexually abused, the therapist might add,

Let's start by talking about how you felt when you were touched by
_____.

Thus, this educational information can be used to educate the child regarding sexual abuse, to pursue gradual exposure, and to assist in cognitive processing, depending on the point in therapy when it is provided. Because children learn through repetition, these educational points may be reviewed throughout the course of therapy.

Another means of providing general information regarding child sexual abuse while exploring a child's thoughts and beliefs about his or her own abuse experience is to read books about sexual abuse with the child. As is true for the educational information described above, books about sexual abuse should be viewed as a tool for initiating discussions about the child's own abusive experiences. When using books in this way, it is preferable to read the book out loud during sessions, either with the therapist reading to a young child, or with an older child reading aloud himself or herself or alternating reading with the therapist. The therapist should interrupt the reading frequently to pose questions and initiate dialogue about the book and about the child's own experiences. For example, after reading an account of a child being sexually abused, the therapist might pause and ask the client how he or she believes the child in the book is feeling and how the client felt at a similar point in his or her abusive experiences. At other points, the therapist might ask the child how the abusive experience described in the book is similar or dissimilar to the child's own experience. Two books we have found to be useful in this way are *I Can't Talk About It* and *Something Must Be Wrong With Me*, both by Doris Sanford (1986, 1993). These books do not contain explicit descriptions of sexually abusive interactions and thus are appropriate for use early in the gradual exposure process.

THE PROCESS OF GRADUAL EXPOSURE

When the child demonstrates some success with the initial gradual exposure exercises (i.e., general discussions about child sexual abuse or the offender), it is time to move on to more specific discussions of the child's own abusive experiences. Again, this work should be pursued in a gradual fashion, moving from discussions of the least to the most distressing experiences. For many children, this more personalized work may begin with discussion of their disclosure experience. From that point, the discussion may move to the least distressing abusive episode.

The therapist will use information gathered during the evaluation process, input from the child, and his or her own clinical judgment to continue to move the work forward in a general way. The therapist's goal is to help the child become more comfortable discussing details of the abuse, so that he or she no longer needs to actively avoid memories and other reminders of the abuse. Caution must always be used not to move beyond the child's own memories of the abuse. The therapist should not suggest details or memories that the child has not provided. The exposure exercises should not encourage fantasy play but the sharing of real experiences. In an effort to gain mastery over their abusive experience, young children sometimes end their description of an abusive experience with a statement about an aggressive act like, "then I threw him out the window." To help children remain as reality-based as possible, sometimes it is useful to gently pose a question such as:

> Is that what really happened or is that what you would like to have done?

Many children will seek to avoid distressing issues, but the therapist should be prepared to gently but repeatedly direct the child's attention back to the gradual exposure exercise. For example, when asking a child to describe a distressing memory of sexual abuse, the therapist should help the child focus on that specific abusive episode as long as possible. The therapist may do this by simply repeating the child's verbal description of the sexual abuse and, if needed, by asking open-ended questions. These questions should elicit information about the sensations, emotions, and thoughts experienced by the child during the course of the episode described. Therapists, however, should avoid distracting the child from focusing on the experience of the sexual abuse by asking too many specific questions. The objective is not to interrogate the child about the episode, but rather to assist the child to confront the traumatic memory as fully as possible while enduring the associated emotions and sensations.

The extent to which the child will have clear, specific, detailed memories of the abuse will depend on a number of factors, including the child's age, the length of time since the abuse occurred, and the number of episodes of abuse. For example, preschool children should not be expected to remember as many specific details of their abusive experiences as older children. Young children also may be particularly vulnerable to the suggestive effects of repeated questioning. That is, repeated questions regarding the same issue may cause the child to feel pressured to make up details to satisfy the therapist, even if the child cannot remember the details being requested. Thus, therapists working with preschool children should be very careful not to push a child to provide details beyond those that the child readily remembers. Typically, the gradual exposure work will take less time with very young children than with older children as there will be fewer details to discuss.

Children who experienced multiple episodes of abuse may have difficulty remembering specific details clearly because they tend to merge the episodes together. In such a case, a child may describe the abuse in general ways, such as "He always took me in his bedroom and then he would rub my private with his hand." Such a generalized discussion may not help the child to reexperience the emotions associated with specific episodes. Thus, the therapist might help the child move beyond such generalized discussions by focusing on specific episodes such as the first and last episodes of abuse; episodes associated with specific occasions such as holidays, birthdays, trips, visitors in the home, or school events; or episodes in which different types of sexual contact were pursued. In cases involving multiple episodes, it often is not realistic to expect the child to remember specific details of all the episodes. In determining whether or not to continue to pursue gradual exposure regarding specific memories, the critical question is whether or not there remain memories that are distressing to the child. Any such memories should be identified, described, and processed until they no longer have the capacity to cause significant distress or avoidance.

In all the gradual exposure sessions, therapists should assist children in identifying and communicating the sensations, thoughts, and feelings they experienced during episodes of abuse. As the exposure sessions reduce discomfort with abuse-related discussion, children should be encouraged to describe their memories and express any concerns more openly and in greater detail. It is often useful to unobtrusively take notes regarding some of a child's expressed thoughts and feelings, particularly those that seem to be dysfunctional. The therapist, however, should not disrupt the gradual exposure process to dispute thoughts but should address them sometime later during processing exercises.

MODES OF GRADUAL EXPOSURE

Although the exposure sessions should be directive and structured, therapists may offer a variety of exposure methods from which
children may choose. Verbal discussions of the abusive experiences
typically remain the primary mode of gradual exposure; however,
alternative modes of gradual exposure can be very useful in eliciting
children's cooperation, breaking through resistance and avoidance,
providing children with a sense of control, and making the
therapeutic work more fun. During these sessions, it is important to
limit the therapy materials to those toys and props that may encourage play and/or talk around abuse-related issues. More detailed
information follows regarding several different modes of gradual
exposure.

Reenactment With Play Materials

Young children may be asked to reenact their abusive experiences
with dolls or puppets. The child may be asked to assign the different
characters to selected dolls or puppets. The therapist should encourage the child to act out the real experiences. If the child has
trouble understanding the instructions, the therapist may initiate
the reenactment for the child on the basis of the information the child
has already provided. The therapist should avoid using the words
"pretend" or "make-believe" as these words may encourage fantasy
play. Rather, the objective is to encourage the use of creative props to
assist the child in describing and/or demonstrating the abusive
interactions actually experienced. This method may be particularly
useful for younger children, who think concretely, do not
demonstrate good visualization skills, and cannot tolerate lengthy
discussions. Here is how a therapist might introduce this exercise.

> Jennifer, last week you told me about what happened with your
> Uncle Louis. Today, I brought some dolls so that you can show me
> exactly what happened. You may have dolls at home that you pre-
> tend with, but my dolls are not for playing make-believe games,
> Jennifer. We use these dolls so you can show me exactly what hap-
> pened. This doll can be Uncle Louis and this can be the Jennifer doll.
> Now can you show me everything that happened that first time?

Creative Products Depicting the Abuse

Older children may prefer to describe their abusive experiences using other creative outlets such as drawing, painting, or writing about their thoughts and experiences in the form of a book, poem, or song. These techniques are particularly useful as they allow children to document abusive experiences with a tangible creation of which they are proud and that may be shared with supportive family members. With many children, it is helpful to engage them in writing a book describing the abusive episode(s), the disclosure process, and their successes in coping with the aftermath of the abuse. In some cases, it is possible to provide additional motivation for the child by asking permission from both the parent and the child to share an anonymous version of their poem or book with other children or children who may be having greater difficulty communicating about the abuse. Many children experience a sense of pride and accomplishment in being able to help other children. Of course, the therapist should always obtain parental permission before talking with the child about that possibility. In addition, the therapist should obtain appropriate consents and be careful to ensure that all identifying information has been altered on any products that will be shared with other people.

Visualization

In this treatment model, visualization is conceptualized as exercises in which the child is asked to recall specific sensory details, focusing on visual memories of the abuse experience(s). This work does not involve the use of fantasy in creating memories and should not be confused with hypnotic suggestion or guided imagery. This method may be used with older children who demonstrate good visualization skills. The therapist might engage a child in this work with the following instructions.

> I am going to ask you to picture a scene of the abuse. It may be a little uncomfortable, but getting used to thinking about it will help you feel better. I will ask you to close your eyes if you like so you won't be distracted. [Some children prefer to keep their eyes open, perhaps to maintain a greater sense of control. The therapist should allow the

child that control.] Try to recall the sceene as clearly as you can, as if you were really there.

The child should then be asked to concentrate on and describe one particular abuse-related scene. The therapist may pose some specific questions initially to help the child return to the scene of the abuse. For example, the therapist might say,

> I want you to remember everything you can about the very first time your Pop-pop touched you in a "not OK" way. Can you tell me where you were when that happened? Describe the room you were in and what it looked like. Was it daytime or nighttime, light or dark?

After the child has answered these questions, the therapist might continue as follows.

> As you describe what happened, I'd like you to remember any sounds you heard while you were there and any smells you smelled. Remember how your body felt; what you were thinking; and how you were feeling inside.

The therapist will continue to encourage the child in recalling all the details of that specific episode by asking brief questions periodically, including What were you thinking? What were you feeling? and What happened next? However, the questions should be asked only as necessary to assist the child in visualizing the abuse experience. Too many questions can actually interfere with the visualization experience, distracting the child from the image that is the focus.

Similarly, during the visualization process, the therapist should not encourage the child to engage in intellectual discussions or respond to numerous questions; that would disrupt the child's focus on the memory. However, following this exposure exercise, the therapist may ask the child additional questions about what the child was recalling and how the child is feeling. At that time, the therapist may ask the child to describe more sensory details related to the scene the child was recalling. As always, the session should not end until the child's anxiety level has naturally diminished or coping skills are employed to help the child regain his or her composure.

In Vivo Exposure

This technique is most often useful in the later stages of the exposure process. The following instructions might be given to begin an in vivo session with a child who has a fear of darkness.

> I understand that you are afraid of the dark, even in places that are really pretty safe. I would like to help you feel more comfortable in the dark. At one point, I will ask you to turn off the light in this office. While we sit in the dark, we can talk, listen to music, or just sit quietly; it is your choice. After a short while I will ask you to turn on the light, and we will talk about how you felt and what you were thinking. Are you ready to try it?

Other in vivo exposure exercises may need to be assigned for homework. When possible, it is preferable to involve nonoffending parents in such homework assignments so that they can offer support, encouragement, and words of praise for their children's efforts. Some sexually abused children, for example, get into the habit of wearing several layers of clothes to bed in an effort to protect themselves from abuse. Unfortunately, although the actual threat of abuse may cease because the perpetrator is no longer in the home, the child's fear and associated behavior may remain. With the help of the therapist, the child and nonoffending parent may develop a series of hierarchical steps that may be taken toward the goal of wearing a nightgown or pajamas to bed. The gradual exposure process may begin with a low-level anxiety-provoking assignment such as having the child take off her coat when she is indoors. Eventually the child may be asked to remove more and more of the unnecessary clothes until he or she is able to tolerate wearing a nightgown or pajamas.

Although the threat of abuse may cease, the child's fear may remain.

MANAGING AVOIDANCE BEHAVIORS

Sexually abused children vary considerably in terms of their willingness to cooperate with gradual exposure. Whereas some children are quite responsive, others may be highly anxious and avoidant. There are several steps therapists may take to overcome children's resistance to the gradual exposure process.

1. Offer choice in terms of mode, timing, or length of presentation/discussion. For example, if a child simply will not tolerate further discussion of an abusive experience, the therapist might shift to a different mode of gradual exposure by giving the child a choice of drawing a picture of what occurred during the episode or writing about what happened. In that way, the child is given some control over the therapy session but is not allowed to avoid the work of gradual exposure.

2. Present abuse-related stimuli that are slightly less anxiety provoking. The therapist may need to move one step back up the gradual exposure hierarchy to discuss an episode or aspect of the abuse experience that is less difficult.

3. Encourage use of coping skills to jump-start the gradual exposure process. With a highly avoidant child, the therapist might ask the child to identify the thoughts and emotions he or she experiences when discussing the abuse. Often the child's thoughts are contributing to the emotional distress that underlies the avoidance behavior. In such a case, learning to dispute the negative thoughts may allow the child to participate more fully in the gradual exposure exercises. For example, a child who thinks, "He told me he knows what I'm doing even when he's not there. And he doesn't want me to talk about it," may be too anxious to discuss the abusive experience initially. Once the child can successfully dispute those thoughts, he or she may be much better able to talk about the abusive episodes. Alternatively, relaxation exercises may be used to help a highly anxious child become calm enough to participate in gradual exposure work.

4. Offer reminders regarding the treatment rationale. The following therapist statements may be helpful:

BOX 4.7

Case Example: Engaging an Avoidant Resistant Child

Here's how a therapist might engage an avoidant resistant child. Notice that the therapist offers a choice in the mode of gradual exposure and moves down the hierarchy to less anxiety-provoking stimuli.

Therapist: Greg, last week you did a great job of telling me about the first time that Scott touched you. Today I thought we'd continue by talking about the next time that Scott abused you.

Greg: I don't want to talk about Scott anymore. I hate this. The whole thing is stupid.

Therapist: I'm sorry, Greg. I know this may be hard at times. I'm so proud of the great work you've done because I know it isn't easy. It's really important that we continue talking about what happened so that you can become more comfortable with your memories, and they won't be able to bother you anymore.

Greg: This is making me feel worse, not better. I don't want to talk anymore.

Therapist: Well, I think it's important that we keep working on the sexual abuse, but maybe we could find another way to do it that would be easier right now.

Greg: Like what?

Therapist: We could draw a picture of what happened or—

Greg: I hate drawing!

Therapist: Well, another possibility would be to write about what happened, like writing a book, or I remember that you said you like music. We could even make up a song about what happened and record it on my tape recorder.

Greg: You mean I could use the microphone?

Therapist: Sure. And we could let your parents hear it if you'd like when you've finished it. You can even keep the tape.

Greg: What would I sing about?

BOX 4.7 *Continued*

Therapist: Anything that has to do with your feelings about Scott and the sexual abuse. You can decide exactly what it would be about. But try to make the lyrics detailed and clear so children really understand what you're singing about.

Greg: I guess I could talk about how mad I am at him and how he tricked me by acting like he was my friend. Hey, and I could warn other kids not to believe older guys like him if they act real friendly all of a sudden.

Therapist: Great! I think you've already got a good start. Would you like to work on the lyrics by dictating them to me or writing them out yourself?

It is good to share feelings.

It is OK to cry.

Sometimes children feel shaky when talking about upsetting things. That's OK.

Every time we talk about the abuse it will get a little easier.

Facing those memories is hard work, but you can do it.

The more you share your feelings, the better you will feel in the long run.

The dialogue in Box 4.7 illustrates how a therapist might engage an avoidant resistant child by offering choice in the mode of gradual exposure and by moving down the hierarchy to slightly less anxiety-provoking stimuli.

When working with a child who is highly avoidant and resistant to gradual exposure efforts, the therapist should focus on maintaining a working relationship with the child while continuing to work on gradual exposure in one form or another. In the example in Box 4.7, the therapist successfully kept the therapeutic focus on gradual exposure while maintaining a positive working relationship with the child by respecting his wish to not simply discuss another abusive episode. Sometimes it may be necessary to detour in the gradual exposure process to focus on different aspects of the abusive experience. Such a detour is not problematic as long as the child is not allowed to avoid all exposure to thoughts and memories of the abuse.

THE STRUCTURE OF GRADUAL EXPOSURE SESSIONS

During all gradual exposure sessions, exposure should continue until some anxiety reduction is evident (i.e., the child reports feeling no more than a little upset). If insufficient reduction of anxiety is evident, the therapist may introduce coping strategies, such as relaxation, cognitive coping statements, or images that deal success-fully with the feared situation. Every effort should be made to prevent the child from using avoidant or disassociative coping mechanisms prior to or during exposure sessions.

If anxiety has been decreasing within the exposure session, the therapist should call that to the child's attention by making a com-ment such as the following:

You are doing fine, continue talking and stay with the memory.

I want you to notice that you are much less upset than you were in the beginning of the session.

I can see that even though these things were really upsetting at first, you became less upset as we talked or played.

It took some courage to stick it out even though you were afraid. I bet you are feeling better now.

Following exposure, the remainder of the session may be devoted to discussing the child's reactions to the exposure session (see processing below) and reviewing the homework assignment. Parents may be asked to join the session when the homework is being discussed. For older children, homework may consist of listening to taped scenarios from that session; creating new tapes in which they discuss their abusive experiences; or writing about their experiences in journal, letter, or poetry form. Younger children (i.e., less than 9 years old) may be asked to read child abuse prevention books and/or draw pictures of their abusive experiences. Parents who are coping effectively themselves may be asked to participate and encourage discussion, reading, writing, and/or play that furthers the process of gradual exposure.

Each exposure session should offer some sense of closure. The therapist should review the progress made during treatment and solicit information about the degree to which the child's distress has decreased. The therapist may also inquire about the degree to which the child is now engaging in previously avoided situations. If the child's progress has been limited, the therapist should praise and highlight his or her general efforts to follow through. It is important to end the exposure sessions with positive, enjoyable activities and discussions. It is important not only to reward the child's hard work but also to demonstrate again that the feared pain or stress need not be enduring.

COGNITIVE AND AFFECTIVE PROCESSING

Successful cognitive and affective processing of the abuse experience is a crucial factor in the child's post-abuse adjustment. This processing may occur throughout the therapy experience, but it is most likely to happen following some success in gradual exposure. As a result of the exposure exercises, children are frequently more comfortable sharing their innermost thoughts and feelings about the abuse. The sharing of these thoughts and feelings is therapeutic in and of itself. However, processing also provides sexually abused children with an opportunity to further explore, clarify, and correct dysfunctional thoughts about the abuse. In addition, processing allows children to clarify and resolve their often conflicting and confusing feelings regarding the abuse. Thoughts and feelings about the sexual abuse and its aftermath may significantly influence a child's developing self-image and cognitive coping style. The child's cognitive schema for understanding the trauma, in fact, may become a template for cognitively processing problems in the future. For example, a girl who believes she "deserved" the abuse because she was bad may later believe she deserves any subsequent maltreatment that she receives. Thus, it is important to identify and correct maladaptive cognitions as early as possible. While listening to the child's discussions of the abuse, the therapist should be on the alert for thoughts that characterize the problem as permanent, pervasive, and personal; these may reflect a developing pessimistic style of thinking (Seligman, 1990). Children may be encouraged to dispute such thoughts, replacing them with more accurate and optimistic thoughts.

Cognitive and affective processing discussions and exercises also provide a means for addressing sexually abused children's questions and concerns. Therapists may encourage children to share concerns by consistently asking if they have any questions or worries so that the children can begin to anticipate that they will have an opportunity to ask questions each session. It is preferable to engage children in processing discussions before or after gradual exposure exercises rather than during the exposure itself. This will allow children to deeply experience the emotional reactions elicited by the abuse-related cues during exposure without the interruption of more intellectual discussion. However, it is important that children feel questions are encouraged; thus, the therapist should use good clinical judgment in deciding whether to respond immediately to a question posed during exposure or delay the response to the end of the exposure session.

Using Role Plays In Cognitive And Affective Processing

The thoughts, feelings, and sensations elicited during gradual exposure may be processed in a number of ways, through cognitive coping skills exercises, education regarding child sexual abuse, and role plays. During role plays, children may choose to play themselves or the role of someone else. For example, a child may play a friend, teacher, or therapist who is helping other sexually abused children. In this way, the child may rehearse positive statements disputing dysfunctional thoughts while the therapist can assess the child's progress in processing the abuse. A favorite type of role play for many children allows them to assume the role of a psychologist who is the host of a radio talk show. The therapist and/or the child's parent can assume the roles of different children who are calling in to the psychologist for advice regarding their own sexual abuse experiences. The therapist may write brief paragraphs in advance outlining the specific concerns of the different children calling in for advice. The concerns should reflect, at least in part, the concerns that have been voiced by the child in therapy. In responding to the concerns, the child demonstrates how effectively he or she has been able to address the issues in his or her own life. Role plays also may be used to depict scenes involving the offender and/or the nonoffending parent(s). For example, in processing emotional responses to the abuse, the child may role-play telling the offender how he or she feels about the offender and the abuse.

Using Cognitive Coping Skills In Cognitive And Affective Processing

Cognitive strategies such as disputing dysfunctional thoughts may be used with older children during processing sessions, whereas younger children may be encouraged to use positive self-statements to replace their negative thoughts. These statements, however, should be tailored to the child's particular circumstances and concerns. With older children, it is preferable to elicit statements such as these using the Socratic method (i.e., questioning designed to elicit certain responses). This approach allows children to learn a process of thinking that will help them counteract negative thoughts. The example in Box 4.8 illustrates the use of the Socratic method in teaching children to dispute negative thoughts.

Areas Of Maladaptive Cognitions

In the sections that follow, we describe some of the more common areas of maladaptive cognitions that should be identified and addressed in therapy.

Abuse Attributions. Many children experience confusion, both cognitively and affectively, regarding the causes of the abuse and the responsibility for it. The child may also have a confused or distorted understanding of why the offender abused the child. These inaccurate explanations for the abuse may also contribute to confused

---

BOX 4.8

Case Example: Use of Socratic Method in Disputing Negative Thoughts

Here's how a therapist might use the Socratic method in teaching children to dispute negative thoughts.

Tommy: I should have stopped him! I should not have let him do it to me.

Therapist: Tommy, let's think about this for a minute. I'm going to draw a stick figure here. Let's say that is you. Now we'll draw Al. How big should I make him?

Tommy: Up to here.

Therapist: So, who is the bigger of you two?

Tommy: Al is.

Therapist: Who would you guess is stronger?

Tommy: Well, Al is, of course. I'm just 10 and he's about 30-something.

Therapist: So how often do you think a 10-year-old who is this big can stop a man who is 30-something from doing something he really wants to do.

Tommy: Not very often.

Therapist: No, I think you probably could not have stopped him then no matter how hard you tried. But is he going to abuse anyone now?

Tommy: No! I stopped him from doing that. He's in jail because I told what happened.

Therapist: That's right. What is really important is that you stopped him from abusing you again or anyone else by telling.

---

feelings by the child toward the perpetrator of the abuse. It is important that the therapist address the issues of responsibility for and explanations of the abuse and of the child's feelings toward the offender.

Responsibility for the Abuse. Many children inappropriately attribute responsibility for the abuse, either to themselves or to another innocent person, such as a nonoffending parent. It is important that such misunderstandings and confusion be clarified so that the child does not continue to attribute responsibility inappropriately. In general, it is important to make clear that sexual abuse is always the offender's responsibility rather than the child's. In fact, the therapist might state that even if a child asks an older person for sexual contact, it is the older person's responsibility to say no and set the limits. It also may help children to understand that adults are held responsible for the abuse regardless of the child's behavior because the adults are bigger, more knowledgeable, and more mature, and have more options and resources than children (Berliner & Wheeler, 1987).

However, the message of "It's not your fault" should not be routinely presented to all children without respect for their individual situation and circumstances. Indiscriminately providing such messages may, in fact, be confusing to children who never considered themselves responsible in the first place. Furthermore, when working with children who do inaccurately assume some responsibility for the abuse, a general message of "It's not your fault" is not likely to address each child's specific areas of concern. It is more helpful to elicit the child's own thoughts about responsibility for the abuse so that any dysfunctional or inaccurate thoughts can be addressed specifically. For example, some children may have overpersonalized explanations such as "He abused me because I was bad."

It is particularly important to correct such personalized distortions. Indeed, recent empirical evidence suggests that adolescents who attribute the abuse to something they did as opposed to attributing the abuse to factors external to themselves were more likely to suffer depression and low self-esteem (Morrow, 1991). However, the literature suggests that some recognition of behaviors that may have contributed to the occurrence of trauma may positively influence the recovery process of victims (Janoff-Bulman, 1986). For example, if a girl was abused while at a neighbor's home her parents had forbidden her to visit, she may understandably feel responsible for having broken her parent's rule. To simply tell her, "It's not your fault," will not address her concerns regarding her violation of the rule and may increase her confusion. Instead, it may help children to identify the control they did exert or could have exerted to influence the abusive situation, while also acknowledging the limits of their control. Thus, in the example given above, the therapist might help the girl acknowledge that she made a mistake in visiting that home without permission, while explaining that her mistake did not give the perpetrator license to sexually abuse her. In addition to accurately identifying their level of control, abused children may be encouraged to practice personal safety skills as described later in this chapter. These skills may lessen children's feelings of vulnerability, while also reducing their risk of revictimization.

Distorted explanations for abuse should be corrected.

Explanations for the Abuse. While discussing responsibility for the abuse, the therapist should elicit the child's explanation for why the offender abused the child. The child's explanation should be explored before offering a "professional" explanation. This gives the therapist an opportunity to applaud and encourage a child's efforts to process the experience. Moreover, some children may have developed explanations that are accurate and more age appropriate than the explanation the therapist could offer. Other children's explanations may contain dysfunctional thoughts that should be identified and addressed in treatment. Many children may carry with them and internalize the distorted explanations provided by the offenders themselves. Some offenders may encourage children to view the abuse as sex education or as an act of love. Other offenders may blame their behavior on the nonoffending parent for not satisfying their sexual needs. By offering such an explanation to a child, the offender may set up a dynamic that allows the abusive relationship to thrive, while the child's anger is inappropriately directed toward the unsuspecting nonoffending parent. It is important to correct this distortion even after the abuse has stopped in order to encourage more positive and open communication between the child and his or her nonoffending parent.

There is some evidence that post-trauma adjustment is more positive when victims' search for meaning leads to a greater understanding or mastery over the traumatic event (Silver, Boon, & Stones, 1983). Thus, if children offer no explanation or a dysfunctional explanation, the therapist should provide an age-appropriate explanation for the offender's behavior. Highly elaborate conceptualizations may be both inaccurate and incomprehensible to children. A simple explanation that conforms to what is currently known about offenders is preferable. Berliner and Wheeler (1987) suggest the following explanation:

> The offender has a problem, he wants to be sexual with children, something which most grown-ups don't want. And he tells himself it's OK even though he knows it's wrong.

These authors discourage the use of explanations that suggest that the offender is sick, confused, or misguided, as these explanations may diminish the intentionality of the behavior and may encourage children to feel sympathy for the offender as well as guilt for feeling angry.

The Child's Feelings Toward the Offender. When the perpetrator is a parent or trusted adult, children may experience a great deal of confusion with regard to their feelings toward this person. A child may ask, "Will my father ever love me again?" or "If my father is so bad, why do I still love him?" Therapists may respond to these questions by helping children separate their feelings about the abuse from other feelings they have toward the offender. For example, the therapist might say,

> You've said that you hate your dad for abusing you, but that
> you still love him because he is your father. I think that makes
> sense because although you're angry with your dad about the abuse,
> there are probably some things about your father that are really lov-
> able.

Thus, therapists may also help children distinguish between the offender's overall character and his abusive behavior. The therapist's explanation may be along the following lines:

> What your father did was wrong, and as an adult he is responsible
> for that wrong behavior, but he may not be a bad person in general.

This explanation may have to be given repeatedly. It is very important to remain consistent in the message that although the perpetrator
may have done things that are not OK, his character may not be all
bad. Being excessively negative about a loved perpetrator may be
confusing to a child who has seen positive aspects of the
perpetrator's character, and it also may alienate the child from the
therapist. On the other hand, the therapist must be clear in communicating that the perpetrator's abusive behavior was wrong and
should not be tolerated. The perpetrator, in fact, may need to suffer
negative consequences as a result of his abusive behavior.

As mentioned previously, young children may have difficulty
identifying and disputing their own thoughts regarding responsibility and explanations for the abuse. Thus, the therapist might
provide self-statements, such as the following examples, that clarify
abuse attributions.

> The offender is responsible for the abuse.
> The abuse happened because the offender has a problem with not-OK
>   touching.
> Now I know what I can do if someone gives me a not-OK touch.
> I can still love my father even though I am mad about what he did.
> Sexual abuse can happen to anyone.

Social Reactions. Sexually abused children's perceptions of others'
reactions to the discovery or disclosure of the abuse is another
important area to explore during cognitive processing. There is
growing evidence that the reactions of nonoffending family members powerfully influence the post-abuse adjustment of sexually
abused children (Conte & Schuerman, 1987; Everson et al., 1989;
Tufts, 1984). Thus, it is important to elicit children's observations and
perceptions of others' reactions. Unfortunately, many children are
exposed to highly emotional reactions, disbelief, or both when they
disclose sexual abuse. Children's interpretations of these reactions
may significantly influence their understanding of the abuse, their
self-image, and their ability to trust others.

Sexually abused children's perceptions of others' reactions may influence their thoughts about the abuse in different ways. A child may perceive a parent's negative emotional reactions to mean that the abuse was much worse than he or she realized. Such a child may develop permanent or pervasive thoughts about the abuse that may be both distressing and dysfunctional. For example, a child may interpret Mom's extreme distress to mean that the abuse caused permanent bodily damage or destroyed the entire family. Other children may be so shaken by disbelieving responses that they may begin to question the reality of their own experience, or they may be tempted to make false recantations.

Children's perceptions of others' reactions also may influence their thoughts about themselves. Young children may be particularly prone to believing that anger or upset exhibited by others is directed toward them. These overpersonalized thoughts may lead children to experience increased guilt and diminished self-worth. Cognitive coping exercises, like the one illustrated in Box 4.9, may be used to help children process thoughts and feelings about the reactions of others. Again, therapists can use the Socratic method to stimulate children to assess the accuracy of their perceptions regarding their parents' responses and feelings toward them. Rather than offering evidence that contradicts children's dysfunctional thoughts, therapists use questions and exaggerated statements to encourage children to dispute their own dysfunctional thoughts.

Children's perceptions of others' reactions to the disclosure of child sexual abuse also may influence their ability to achieve an adaptive balance between trust versus mistrust of others. For example, a child who is sexually abused by one parent and not supported by the other may be particularly prone to developing a pervasive mistrust of others. Such a child may have difficulty trusting or depending on anyone. Although this reaction may seem reasonable, it is highly dysfunctional in terms of developing healthier family relationships in the future. Thus, it is important to elicit, process, and help children correct maladaptive thoughts such as "No one can be trusted; people will desert you when you're in trouble; people you love will betray you." Again, with a young child, the therapist may need to help the child develop positive self-statements such as these:

BOX 4.9

Case Example: Disputing Dysfunctional Thoughts Regarding Others' Responses

In the following dialogue, the therapist uses questions and exaggerated statements to help the child dispute her own dysfunctional thoughts.

Therapist: You know, Jan, we've talked a number of times about how sad or worried you are about your mom. When was the last time you were feeling really worried about her?

Jan: Just last night. She looked really upset and sad.

Therapist: What did you do when you saw her like that?

Jan: I went into my room. I figured she didn't want to see my face.

Therapist: So when you went to your room, you were thinking she didn't want to see your face. What else were you saying to yourself?

Jan: You mean what else was I thinking?

Therapist: Yes.

Jan: I was thinking that I ruined my mom's life. She'll never be happy again. My dad shouldn't have sexually abused me like that.

Therapist: What else were you thinking?

Jan: I don't know.

Therapist: Were you in your room for a while?

Jan: Yes.

Many people are proud of me for telling about the abuse.

Some people got upset when I told about the abuse because they care about me.

Some people didn't believe me at first because they didn't understand about sexual abuse, but now they believe me.

Sometimes my mom cries, but she is glad I told about the abuse.

I was brave to tell about the abuse.

There are many people who don't abuse children and can be trusted.

BOX 4.9 *Continued*

Therapist: Then you probably had a lot to say to yourself. Can you think of anything else?

Jan: Well, I was thinking that my mom hates me. She's probably disgusted by me. I was really feeling down.

Therapist: I'm not surprised that you were feeling really sad. These thoughts would probably make anyone feel pretty down. But I think some of these thoughts may not be that accurate. I've written them all on the board. Can you pick out one that might not be all that accurate and tell me why?

Jan: Well, it is true that my father should not have sexually abused me.

Therapist: You're right. That thought is very accurate and healthy too. What about the others?

Jan: I'm not sure if my mother really hates me.

Therapist: What makes you think it is true?

Jan: Well, she never talks to me about the sexual abuse. She doesn't want anyone to know about it.

Therapist: Can you think of other reasons why she may act this way?

Jan: [long pause] Maybe she's uncomfortable talking about it like I was at the beginning of therapy. And maybe she thinks other people won't understand about sexual abuse.

Therapist: Those sound like good possibilities. Now is there any evidence that your mother doesn't hate you, that your mother, in fact, loves you?

With gentle but persistent prodding the therapist challenges Jan to come up with as long a list as possible of indicators that her mother loves her.

Sexuality. Nonabused children generally develop an understanding of sex and sexuality gradually as a result of experience and information obtained from a variety of sources, including parents, peers, television, magazines, school, and so on. Although the information obtained may not always be accurate, most children absorb and integrate the information as their interest and cognitive abilities develop. Sexually abused children, on the other hand, are often bombarded with distorted information about sex and sexuality in a manner that may be premature and traumatic. In fact, sexual abuse may significantly disrupt the normal process of psychosexual development. Thus, sexually abused children may need the help of a therapist and/or nonoffending parent to get back on track toward developing a healthy sexuality. There are a number of different times in treatment when it may be appropriate to focus specifically on the development of positive views of healthy sexuality. Most often, sex education is included toward the end of treatment, often as an initial topic of joint parent-child sessions. However, with highly anxious and avoidant children, it may be useful to include sex education earlier, as a component of gradual exposure. Throughout therapy with all children, it is important that therapists assist children in identifying, expressing, and processing their thoughts and feelings regarding sexuality.

Encouraging Open Communication About Sexuality. As indicated earlier, it is important to provide children with education about child sexual abuse and personal safety skills. However, in light of the high rate of sexual dissatisfaction among adult survivors of child sexual abuse (Finkelhor et al., 1989), it is equally important to discuss sex and sexuality that is not abusive in nature. In fact, we may inadvertently encourage a sexual aversion by simply and repeatedly teaching children that what they experienced was "bad." This may be avoided by encouraging a more open, well-rounded, and accurate discussion of sex, both in abusive and nonabusive circumstances. Thus, in addition to encouraging the sharing and processing of thoughts and feelings about the abuse, the therapist may encourage the exploration of thoughts and feelings about body image, body parts, hugging, kissing, dating, sex, and sexuality in general.

Collaborating With Parents. Because parents' attitudes toward sexuality and sex education may vary considerably, it is important to elicit their views and collaborate with them when planning these sessions. Any material or books, for example, that may be used for purposes of sex education should be provided to parents beforehand for their review. Some parents may object to the discussion of certain sexual issues, or they may fear that sex education is being introduced prematurely. A clear presentation of the rationale for providing sex education to abused children may alter some of these parents' opinions; the wishes of those parents who continue to object should be respected. In these cases, the therapist may attempt to readdress the issue later in treatment when the parents have gained more confidence in the therapy process.

After obtaining parental consent, the therapist may begin to model open communication about sex and sexuality during cognitive processing discussions. Sexually abused children's thoughts and concerns about their abusive experiences will change as they grow increasingly sophisticated in their understanding of sex. Thus, perhaps the most important message to convey to sexually abused children is that it is good to talk about sex and that it helps to ask lots of questions now and in the future.

Eliciting and Disputing Dysfunctional Thoughts About Sexuality and Body Image. During processing discussions, the therapist's objective is to elicit, identify, and correct cognitive distortions about sex that the child may have developed as a result of the abuse. Some sexually abused children, for example, may view all sexual acts as bad, disgusting, scary, or dirty. The therapist may begin to correct these misconceptions by conveying the joy associated with sexual behavior when it is age appropriate and nonabusive in nature. Books such as *Where Did I Come From?,* by Peter Mayle (1995), and *A Very Touching Book,* by Jan Hindman (1985), may be particularly useful in this regard as they provide clear, accurate information about sexuality in a positive and humorous manner.

Sexually abused children also may harbor dysfunctional thoughts about their bodies, their physiological responses, and their sexual identities. Again, it is important to elicit and explore these thoughts. Sometimes children believe that others can tell they have been abused just by looking at them. Some children worry that their bodies have been infected or damaged by the abuse, whereas others may fear they will be unable to have children. Another common concern among girls who have been sexually abused is that they may be pregnant. Clearly, a complete medical exam is essential to allay some of these concerns. However, by reviewing and discussing the medical

---

BOX 4.10

Case Example: Disputing Dysfunctional Thoughts
About Sexual Arousal

Here's how a therapist might help dispute the dysfunctional thoughts of Denise, a 12-year-old girl who experienced arousal while she was being abused by her 18-year-old brother.

Therapist: Denise, we've been talking about how sexual touches can make your body feel good. I remember you telling me before that it sometimes felt good when your brother touched you. How do you feel now when you think about that?

Denise: [head down, no response]

Therapist: Denise, can you tell me how you're feeling now?

Denise: [begins crying, then speaks in a quiet voice] I feel so ashamed.

Therapist: What are you ashamed about?

Denise: I must be sick. He's my own brother, and it felt good when he touched me.

Therapist: You think you're sick because it sometimes felt good when he touched you?

Denise: Yeah.

Therapist: I think you're being pretty hard on yourself. Can you remember what we learned about the sexual parts of the body and why they are so sensitive?

Denise: Well, the book said that there are lots of nerve endings down there. That's why those parts are so sensitive.

---

exam findings, the therapist may help children dispute dysfunctional or distorted thoughts about their bodies.

Sexually abused children also may suffer guilt regarding any pleasurable physiological responses they experienced during the abuse. Again, by facilitating an open discussion regarding sexual arousal and orgasm, the therapist may help these children to acknowledge and accept their physical responses as natural and healthy. The example in Box 4.10 illustrates how a therapist would

BOX 4.10 *Continued*

Therapist: Good, you were really listening. So why do you think it felt good when your brother touched you?

Denise: I guess because he touched me gently in a sensitive spot with lots of nerve endings.

Therapist: I think you're right. Let's see if we can replace the thought that is making you feel ashamed with a more accurate thought that will help you feel better.

Denise: OK.

Therapist: The thought that made you feel ashamed was, "I must be sick because it felt good when my brother touched me." Can you think of a more accurate thought to replace that?

Denise: Well, I could say that it felt good because he touched a sensitive spot with lots of nerve endings.

Therapist: Great!

During the remainder of that session, the therapist would continue to help Denise identify and dispute her dysfunctional thoughts regarding the physiological arousal she had experienced. Subsequently, the therapist would ask Denise to practice disputing those thoughts for homework. Her progress in being able to dispute effectively would be reviewed over the next several sessions.

begin helping a 12-year-old girl, Denise, to identify and dispute her dysfunctional thoughts regarding the physiological arousal she experienced while being sexually abused by her 18-year-old brother.

Discussions about healthy sexuality and sexual arousal also may help alleviate the confusion some children experience regarding their sexual identity. Sexually abused boys may be particularly prone to questions regarding their sexual orientation if they experienced arousal during interactions with male offenders. By providing educational feedback, the therapist may correct children's misconceptions regarding heterosexual and homosexual orientations. Young children may be encouraged to use positive self-statements, such as these, to address concerns regarding sexuality.

The doctor said my body was OK.

When I am an adult, I can enjoy sex with someone I love.

My body is special because it belongs to only me.

It is OK to have sexual feelings.

Sex can be positive, loving, and fun.

❏ **Education Regarding Child Sexual Abuse, Healthy Sexuality, and Personal Safety Skills**

The final therapeutic component for children focuses on education. This education should be provided throughout the child's treatment at points when the child can most effectively use it.

BASIC FACTS REGARDING CHILD SEXUAL ABUSE

It is important that children be provided basic factual information regarding child sexual abuse so that they can better understand their experiences and can correct any misconceptions they may have. Much of this information has been described earlier and includes education regarding the definition and prevalence of sexual abuse, who is affected and who is responsible, why sexual abuse occurs, and how children may respond. As was described earlier, this information often can be provided as an introduction to the gradual exposure work. In addition, education regarding child sexual abuse should be provided as needed to dispute dysfunctional thoughts during cognitive coping exercises. Finally, basic information regarding child sexual abuse should be reviewed again when training is provided regarding personal safety skills aimed at helping children identify and respond effectively to inappropriate sexual touches.

Children should be taught that anyone can engage a child in not-OK touching. They need to know that sometimes it is a stranger, but more often it is someone they know. The therapist should explain that often a sexual offender will initiate the sexual abuse with a touch that is confusing to the child but not clearly inappropriate. Over time, the offender may escalate the touches to include clearly inappropriate sexual touches. Thus, the child should be encouraged to talk to a trusted adult about the confusing touch without waiting to be sure whether or not it was inappropriate. Furthermore, the therapist should emphasize that no matter who the person is, children need to tell—even if the person is their favorite uncle, family friend, brother, sister, mother, father, or grandfather.

In addition, it is important to emphasize to children that no matter how long the not-OK touching has been happening, it is never the child's fault. Adults know that this kind of touching is not OK. Thus, no matter who starts the not-OK touching, it is always the adult's responsibility to stop it. Sometimes adults know not-OK touching is wrong, but they choose to do it anyway. It is, therefore, important for children to tell about not-OK touching so that these individuals stop touching children in this way.

The therapist should be honest with children about the outcome. The offender may have to suffer negative consequences just as they would if they did something wrong. However, children also should be informed that by telling they may be helping the offender to get therapy for his or her problems.

EDUCATION REGARDING HEALTHY SEXUALITY

In addition to learning about inappropriate sexual touches, it is crucial that the child be taught about healthy sexuality and appropriate sexual touches. This education should be planned with the parents to be appropriate for the child's developmental level. Whenever possible, it is helpful to present this information in conjunction with the parent during joint parent-child sessions. Further discussions of education regarding healthy sexuality are found in Chapter 5, Nonoffending Parent Intervention, and Chapter 6, Joint Parent-Child Sessions.

PERSONAL SAFETY SKILLS

The third focus of education for children is personal safety skills training designed to help children identify and respond effectively to inappropriate sexual touches in the future. However, therapists should be aware and should communicate to parents that personal safety skills cannot be assumed to offer absolute protection from child sexual abuse. Indeed, regardless of children's skills, some offenders may overcome children's resistance through a variety of positive (e.g., gifts) and negative (e.g., verbal threats) inducements.

In spite of the fact that teaching children personal safety skills does not guarantee the prevention of sexual abuse, it appears worthwhile to provide this information. In fact, there is some evidence that when victimized or threatened, children who have received this type of training are more likely to use self-protection strategies and to disclose the victimization attempt (Finkelhor, Asdigian, & Dziuba-Leatherman, 1995). In addition, children may feel more confident and in control of interpersonal interactions when they have some knowledge and skills for responding to inappropriate touches.

Again, this education might be included at a number of different points in therapy. For some highly anxious children, this educational component may be included fairly early in treatment as it is often relatively easy for children to tolerate, without creating excessive anxiety. However, for many children, it is preferable to postpone the teaching of personal safety skills until gradual exposure has given them the opportunity to fully acknowledge what they did and did not do in response to the actual abuse. When personal safety skills are discussed too early, children may feel they need to distort what really happened in order to appear as if they used the personal safety skills, or they may feel guilty because they did not use the skills. In many cases, this education can be included in early joint parent-child sessions. Indeed, many children and parents may be able to pursue much of this education fairly independently in the context of homework assignments, with the guidance of the therapist. There is, in fact, some evidence that when parents (as compared to teachers) teach these skills, children may retain and use the skills more effectively in response to victimization attempts (Finkelhor et al., 1995; Wurtele, Kast, & Melzer, 1992).

Many tools are available to assist in providing this education to children at a developmentally appropriate level. These include storybooks, coloring books, videotapes, games, puppets, and dolls. Empirical research suggests that children retain these skills best when shaping, repetition, and, most important, behavior rehearsal are used to teach them (Wurtele et al., 1986; Wurtele, Marrs, & Miller-Perrin, 1987). Thus, role-play exercises should be encouraged during these sessions. In addition, the information should be presented in as clear and specific a manner as possible. What follows are some of the main points that may be covered in education regarding OK versus not-OK touches and personal safety skills.

Communication Skills

In order to discuss and disclose sexual abuse if it occurs, children need to have the vocabulary and the communication skills to do so. Thus, it is important for children to learn words for all their body parts, including the sex organs. Sexual body parts, in fact, should be taught with all other body parts, so as to avoid drawing undue attention and concern regarding the sex organs.

Therapists may point out to parents that we naturally seem to teach our children body part names including nose, eyes, mouth, and so on, while ignoring the body parts between the waist and the knees. In addition, it is important to identify with children those parts of their bodies that are considered private. With young children, it may be helpful to identify private parts as those parts that go under a bathing suit.

Body Ownership

Children should learn that their bodies belong to them. They need to learn that all parts of their bodies are important, and no one has a right to hurt any part of their body. In conjunction with teaching the child about body parts, the therapist may begin teaching the child basic information about body ownership. For example, the therapist might say,

> Your body is your very own, and you can decide how you like or do not like being touched.

OK Versus Not-OK Touches

Children should be helped to differentiate between OK touches and not-OK touches. The therapist might initiate this conversation with a focus on OK touches, as follows:

> Today we are going to talk about OK touches, not-OK touches, and confusing touches. Can you think of some touches that you like?

The therapist might help the child identify what will be defined later as OK touches. OK touches may include appropriate hugs, kisses, handshakes, pats on the back, and so on. Other OK touches that are important to talk about include: adults touching each other's private parts when that is what they both want to do, touching your own private parts, and a doctor or parent touching your private parts when you are hurt. To demonstrate an OK touch, the therapist might encourage the child to shake hands. This exercise will provide the therapist with some diagnostic information regarding the child's avoidance of OK touch. It is important to agree on the language to be used, so the therapist can communicate with the child effectively. Thus, the therapist might end this discussion with the agreement that we call these touches OK touches.

Next the therapist can focus the discussion on inappropriate touches by asking,

> Can you think of some touches that you don't like?

Again the therapist might encourage children to brainstorm and come up with their own thoughts and ideas about not-OK touches, including hitting and punching, as well as the sexual touching of a child by an older child or adult. This is a good opportunity to introduce terms such as *sexual abuse, molestation,* or *sexual assault,* if the child is not already aware of those terms. The therapist can further clarify the term *not-OK touch* by explaining that it is how a child may feel when an adult or older child touches a child's private parts.

It is important to emphasize that sometimes it is not clear if the touch is OK or not-OK, and that can be quite confusing. Thus, it is particularly important to talk to adults not only about not-OK touches but also about confusing touches. The therapist could ask the child,

> Can you think of a time when you were touched in a way that made you feel confused?

In this discussion, it is useful to talk with the child about the fact that sexual touching, including sexual abuse, may feel good to your body even though in your mind you may believe that it is not OK or you may be confused by it.

Then the therapist can initiate a conversation about personal safety skills by discussing ways the child might respond if touched in an inappropriate way. During this discussion, it is important to avoid making the child feel bad if the child did not respond in the most effective way during his or her experience of sexual abuse. For example, the therapist might say,

> Most kids aren't really sure what they should do if someone touches them in a not-OK way because no one has ever taught them what to do. Do you have any ideas about things you might try to do if anyone touched you again in a way that is not OK?

After having elicited the child's ideas about how to respond to inappropriate touches, the therapist can begin providing information regarding personal safety skills.

Right to Say No

It is useful to begin a discussion of personal safety skills by teaching children that they have the right to say no if they are being touched in a not-OK way. Children should be taught that they can say no even to an adult, if the adult is doing something that they think is wrong. Then the therapist and the child can practice saying no in a forceful way that communicates that the child means what he or she is saying. Many children will need encouragement to speak loudly and make eye contact when asserting themselves.

Getting Away

The next safety skill to be taught is to leave the situation. Therapists should encourage children to leave the person doing the inappropriate touching and go to an area where there are other people, if that is possible. Often when asked how they would respond to inappropriate touching, children answer with aggressive strategies such as "I'd kick him or I'd punch him." Although those strategies should not be labeled as wrong or inappropriate, therapists should emphasize that the most important thing to do is to get away from the perpetrator and that sometimes more aggressive responses may prolong contact with the perpetrator. Children should be encouraged to leave an uncomfortable situation, but the therapist should acknowledge that it may not always be possible for children to get away. The therapist should emphasize that even if it is not possible to get away immediately, whenever the child has the opportunity, he or she should take the next step of telling someone about the experience.

Telling Someone

An important aspect of personal safety skills training is teaching children to tell someone as soon as possible when something troubling has occurred. Children need to understand that they will not always be able to prevent sexual abuse from occurring. Children should be encouraged to identify individuals whom they can tell when something troubling happens. In discussing this skill, it is important to help children identify family members, as well as non-family members, with whom they could talk if not-OK touching occurs. This is particularly important, as many instances of child sexual abuse occur within the family. The therapist and the child might create a list of all the people the child could tell including parents, teachers, relatives, neighbors, coaches, and police officers. The child should be encouraged to keep on telling until someone understands and helps.

Keeping Secrets

Older children generally can understand the difference between appropriate and inappropriate secrets. Thus, the importance of telling inappropriate secrets can be easily stressed. With younger children, it may be preferable to explain the distinction between surprises and secrets. Children can be taught that pleasant surprises, such as birthday presents, are OK because the person will learn what the surprise is shortly. However, secrets you are asked never to tell are not OK. Furthermore, children should be told that they do not need to keep such secrets, even if someone else says that they should or must, and even if they promised to keep the secret. Again, it is important to emphasize to children that if someone does not believe or understand them when they tell a secret that is troubling, they should keep telling until someone does believe them.

Preparing for Further Contact With the Offender

When working with children who may have contact with the offender again, it is critical to prepare the child with personal safety skills training specifically focused on that perpetrator. The possibility of further contact between the perpetrator and the child is greatest when the perpetrator is a family member. In such a case, the child should be educated about the fact that many perpetrators do offend again, although we cannot predict whether or not a perpetrator involved in a specific case will reoffend. Next, the child should be given a clear definition as to what constitutes appropriate versus inappropriate touch by the offender. Finally, the child should be prepared to respond effectively to any possible inappropriate interactions or touches by the offender.

Role plays can be very effective in providing this training. The therapist should plan any role plays carefully to depict as accurately as possible how the perpetrator might interact with the child. One group of role plays may focus on confusing touches that might occur in the early stages of seduction. For example, the therapist might describe the perpetrator as cuddling with the child on the couch, watching TV, with his hand on the child's buttock. The child would then be encouraged to evaluate whether that was an OK or not-OK touch and to plan an appropriate response. In another role play, the therapist might assume the role of a perpetrator who has reoffended the child, saying,

> Please, please, don't tell about this. Don't tell your mom I touched you. You know if you tell, your mom will be so upset. I'll have to go to jail and I might never get out. And if I go to jail, what will happen to you guys? Your mom can't afford the mortgage on her own. You'll lose the house. You can't tell. I promise I'll never touch you like that again.

A number of role plays might be used depicting a variety of different scenes. In addition to this personal safety skills training, much more therapeutic work is required before family reunification should be considered. The topic of family reunification is discussed again briefly in Chapter 6 of this book.

5

Nonoffending Parent Intervention: Therapeutic Components

❑ **Overview**

As noted in the introduction, the findings of numerous empirical investigations suggest that the ability of nonoffending parent(s) to provide support following a child's disclosure of sexual abuse may be the most critical factor influencing that child's post-abuse psychological adjustment (Adams-Tucker, 1981; Conte & Schuerman, 1987; Everson et al., 1989). Nonoffending parents, however, do not always receive a great deal of support themselves. In fact, the professional community historically has not been sympathetic toward nonoffending mothers of sexually abused children. Rather, mothers, particularly of incest victims, have been portrayed in the literature as collusive, denying, and indirectly responsible for the abuse of their children (Cormier, Kennedy, & Sangowicz, 1962; Sarles,

1975; Sgroi & Dana, 1982). Although the empirical evidence indicates that most mothers do not fit these negative stereotypes (Conte & Berliner, 1988; Deblinger et al., 1993; Sirles & Franke, 1989), it is likely that some parents may have encountered these harsh attitudes in their interactions with investigating professionals as well as others. In addition, many nonoffending parents may be unable to provide adequate support to their children due to their own emotional distress as well as their limited knowledge and skills in responding to abuse-related disclosures and difficulties. The individual sessions with nonoffending parent(s), therefore, aim to provide support, as well as information and skills that will assist parents in coping with their own emotional reactions and their child's potential difficulties.

Like the child intervention, the nonoffending parent intervention can be described in terms of three major components. The initial component is coping skills training, to provide parents with skills for coping with their own thoughts and emotions effectively. During this component, parents are generally provided with educational information about child sexual abuse. The second component is gradual exposure. This component provides gradual exposure for the parent, as well as training designed to teach the parent how to help the child with gradual exposure. Included in this component is training regarding how to present sex education and personal safety skills information to the child. The third component focuses on behavior management skills that may be used in managing behavioral problems, particularly any problems that may develop in response to the child's sexual abuse experience. As was true for the child treatment components, the amount of time devoted to each of the parent treatment components and the order in which they are presented should be based on the parent's needs as well as the sexually abused child's particular symptom patterns.

❑ **Coping Skills Training**

This treatment component is devoted to assisting parents in their efforts to cope with their own emotional responses to the discovery that their child has been sexually abused. Coping skills training for parents may be initiated with work on emotional expression skills, as parents may have difficulty identifying and appropriately expressing their emotions much as children do. However, the largest component of coping skills training typically consists of cognitive coping skills and education. In addition, parents who are particularly anxious may benefit from relaxation training. In most cases, it is useful to provide coping skills training at the beginning of therapy in order to enhance the parents' ability to cope with both the stress of the immediate crisis and the emotions aroused in the gradual exposure process. The development of effective coping skills will in turn increase the parents' capacity to respond most appropriately to their child. The skills and information, however, may be reinforced and strengthened throughout the course of therapy.

EMOTIONAL EXPRESSION SKILLS

Aside from the victims themselves, there are probably no others who suffer the trauma of child sexual abuse more than the nonoffending parents. Several studies have demonstrated that nonoffending parents suffer highly significant levels of psychological distress upon discovery that their child may have been sexually abused (Deblinger et al, 1993; Kelley, 1990). Unfortunately, however, parental emotional reactions often are not acknowledged or addressed by the professional community as the focus tends to be on the sexually abused child. Therapists should begin the process of helping parents cope with their personal reactions by encouraging parents to explore and express the wide range of emotions they may be experiencing. Therapists might ask the parents to describe how they currently feel about the child's abuse experience, as well as how they felt at the time of the initial disclosure. Parents may need to be pushed to list as many emotions experienced as possible. This gives parents an opportunity to explore and clarify their own feelings.

Some parents may already have well-developed skills for identifying and expressing their emotions. However, other parents may need considerable assistance in being able to sort out confusing and conflicted emotions. Such clarification of their emotions is important in enabling parents to respond to the child in well-thought-out and effective ways and preventing parents from responding based on their own emotional distress. Furthermore, these discussions of emotions allow therapists to validate parents' feelings by demonstrating acceptance of whatever they may be expressing.

This may be particularly important for parents whose children were abused by other family members, such as parents, grandparents, and siblings. Some parents may express feelings that could be considered unsupportive of the child (e.g., disbelief, anger toward the child, concern for the perpetrator). It has been our experience that even these "nonsupportive" feelings need to be acknowledged and accepted. Taking a judgmental and/or confrontational stance at this early stage in therapy tends to be counterproductive and may hinder the development of a therapeutic relationship. Indeed, parents who are actively confronted about their disbelief of the allegations or their positive feelings toward the offender often seem to respond with an entrenched position of support for the offender.

Moreover, a confrontation frequently turns out to be unnecessary as parents' thoughts and feelings often change dramatically as they develop a greater understanding of the impact and circumstances of the sexual abuse. A positive change in maternal attitude also may occur naturally as the legal intervention creates some distance and forced separation between the nonoffending parent and the perpetrator. Over time, the therapist may gently encourage the parent to explore and discuss his or her feelings about the offender and about the parents' ability to trust and continue a relationship with that person. Often as time progresses and parents realize that they are capable of coping with life without the offender, they are better able to acknowledge that the abuse occurred and to offer the child the support he or she needs.

In the early stages of therapy, it is generally not appropriate for parents to share their feelings with their children because the intensity and volatility of the emotions expressed may be quite troubling and may interfere with the children's ability to develop and express their own beliefs and emotions regarding the abuse and the perpetrator. Thus, the therapist should encourage parents to carefully monitor and contain their expression of emotions regarding the abuse when in the presence of their children. Not only should parents be advised to avoid sharing their intense emotions directly with their children, but also they should be encouraged to carefully monitor any expression of emotions that the child might inadvertently over-hear, such as telephone conversations or discussions of the abuse with other people.

Simultaneously, the therapist should encourage parents to identify other adults with whom they can share their feelings regarding the abuse without exposing the children to those conversations. It should be noted that in the later stages of therapy, after the parents have had an opportunity to process their own emotional responses to the abuse and develop effective means of expressing those emotions, the therapist may guide the parents in sharing some of those emotions with the child in appropriate ways. It often is particularly important for the parents to clarify any intense emotional response the child may have observed at the disclosure of the abuse. For example, if the parent responded with intense anger to the child's disclosure, the parent may need to clarify that he or she was angry with the per-petrator, rather than with the child.

COGNITIVE COPING SKILLS

After encouraging the nonoffending parents to share the emotions experienced in reaction to the discovery of their child's sexual abuse, the therapist may introduce cognitive coping skills training as a means of identifying and challenging any dysfunctional thoughts underlying parents' distressing emotions. These thoughts can be disputed both in terms of content and style by offering parents new information as well as new ways of thinking about the problems they are facing. For example, the therapist should highlight educational information that corrects parents' dysfunctional thoughts about the abuse in order to reduce parental distress arising from those miscon-ceptions. In addition, the therapist may assist parents in examining and enhancing their coping styles, particularly with respect to their responses to abuse-related thoughts and difficulties. Parents may be reminded repeatedly that by coping more effectively, they not only will be enhancing their personal healing but also will be serving as better coping models for their children. The example in Box 5.1 illustrates how a therapist might introduce the concept of cognitive coping skills training to a parent. Note that the therapist highlights

---

BOX 5.1

Case Example: Introducing Cognitive Coping Skills

Here's how a therapist might introduce the concept of cognitive coping to a parent.

Therapist: Typically, people do not receive even general parenting information before having children. And certainly, most parents have not been trained in how to cope with a problem such as child sexual abuse. In fact, discovering that your child has been sexually abused is often shocking and very upsetting for parents just as the abusive experience is for children.

Mother: It certainly has been tough for everyone in our house.

Therapist: Unfortunately, parents' needs may be unintentionally ignored throughout the investigation that follows the report of child abuse, because the investigation focuses on the child. This is unfortunate, not only because parents may be suffering a great deal themselves, but also because parents may be the most important therapeutic resources for their children. In fact, research has shown that parents' responses can significantly influence children's adjustment after an experience of child sexual abuse. So one of my goals is to help you respond to this experience as effectively as possible, both to help you feel better and to enable you to help Katie as much as possible.

Mother: That sounds good to me.

Therapist: Both parents and children may experience a wide range of emotions and difficulties following an experience of child sexual abuse. We've talked about how you felt angry, sad, and even guilty about Katie's sexual abuse experience. In the next few sessions, we'll be looking at not only your specific emotions but also your general style of coping, particularly with respect to how you think and feel about problems such as this one. By helping you cope more effectively, I hope that we can help you feel less upset about the abuse, so that you can serve as an effective coping model for Katie. In fact, there is a great deal of research that demonstrates that children learn coping strategies from

---

BOX 5.1 *Continued*

their parents. Thus, if we can help you cope effectively with problems, including Katie's sexual abuse, it is likely that Katie will observe your coping style and will learn to cope successfully with problems herself.

Mother: I don't know if I can be a good model for Katie. I thought you were going to help her with this.

Therapist: Certainly, I hope I can be a good model as well in demonstrating how to cope effectively with this experience. But your ability to influence Katie is much greater than mine is. You are a much more powerful model, both because your relationship is so important to her and because you have much more time with her than I ever will.

Mother: I see. I guess I can try, but I'm not sure how I should show her to handle this situation.

Therapist: You and I will be working together to help you develop skills for being the most effective model possible. I'm sure that as we work together on your coping skills, you'll learn how to cope effectively with this experience and with other difficulties as well. We will be talking mostly about your emotional and coping responses to the discovery of Katie's sexual abuse experience; but I believe the coping methods I will be teaching you will also help you with other difficulties. The coping model we will be discussing is based on the belief that your thoughts, feelings, and behaviors all influence one another.

---

the important role nonoffending parents play in influencing the adjustment of their children.

Interrelationships Between Thoughts, Feelings, And Behaviors

The therapist may present the interaction between thoughts, feelings, and behaviors visually by presenting the triangle illustrated in Figure 5.1 Subsequently, the therapist can begin teaching the parent how thoughts can influence feelings and behaviors both negatively and positively by using examples like this one.

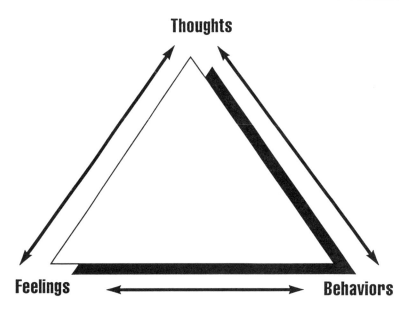

Figure 5.1. Interrelationships Between Thoughts, Feelings, and Behaviors

I'd like to describe an example that illustrates how two women may respond to the exact same situation in very different ways because they think about the situation differently. These women are at a party when each notices someone looking at them.

First Woman:
Thoughts: Why is that person staring at me? I must look really weird; I just don't fit in here.
Feelings: Sad, embarrassed, lonely.
Behavior: Leaves the party alone.

Now the second woman I'll describe is faced with the same situation, but thinks differently about it.

Second Woman:
Thoughts: I think that person staring at me is interested in me.
Feelings: Excited, curious.
Behavior: Walks over and strikes up a conversation.

As you can see, the two people in the above example had different thoughts about the situation and consequently responded with different emotions and behaviors. In fact, your style of thinking can dramatically influence your feelings and behaviors.

At this point, the therapist might ask the parent to identify a minor personal problem and trace the parent's own interactive thoughts, feelings, and behaviors. After the parent is able to successfully identify the links between his or her thoughts, feelings, and behaviors with respect to nonabuse-related problems, the therapist should help the parent apply this model to the parent's thoughts and feelings regarding the child's abusive experience. The therapist may introduce this aspect of the work as follows.

Now I'd like to use this cognitive coping model to examine your thoughts and emotions regarding your child's sexual abuse experience. In examining your coping responses to the discovery that your child may have been sexually abused, we are going to work backward from your emotional reactions to the thoughts that may be underlying those reactions. So first we will list all of the emotions you experienced in reaction to this discovery. Frequently both parents and children experience a wide range of emotions in response to an experience of child sexual abuse. In fact, parents often report experiencing seemingly opposite emotions at the same time. Although there are no emotions that are wrong, some may be so troubling that they interfere with both your daily functioning and the healing process for you and your child. Let's talk about the emotions you experienced when you learned of your child's sexual abuse experience.

IDENTIFYING ABUSE-RELATED FEELINGS
AND UNDERLYING THOUGHTS

The therapist then should help the parent record a list of emotions experienced in response to the child's abuse on a sheet of paper or on a chalkboard. Subsequently, the therapist can help the parent focus specifically on the last time he or she experienced troubling emotions related to the abuse. Next, the parent should be encouraged to identify the thoughts that seemed to be underlying those emotions. The therapist should explain that the contents of our thoughts or our style of thinking may cause us to feel even worse about a situation than is really necessary. Thus, it is important to examine thoughts underlying troubling emotions to see whether any of them are inaccurate or are particularly negative and thus are causing unnecessary distress. It is important to acknowledge that we all have frequent conversations with ourselves, but it may be difficult to bring these internal dialogues into our awareness. Therapists can help parents do this by asking them to describe the situation they were in when they experienced the identified emotions. This description may trigger the recollection of the parent's thoughts at that time. The therapist and parent should continue the process of identifying the thoughts underlying each of the distressing emotions that the parent listed.

Disputing Dysfunctional Thoughts

As the parent continues the work of identifying underlying thoughts, the therapist should emphasize that some of these thoughts may be accurate and functional whereas others may be dysfunctional. There are two general types of dysfunctional thoughts the therapist should help the parent learn to dispute or replace: thoughts that are inaccurate and thoughts that are nonproductive (regardless of whether or not they are accurate).

Inaccurate Thoughts. Thoughts that are inaccurate may be most effectively disputed by providing the parent with accurate information. Parents typically lack accurate information regarding child sexual abuse and can benefit from learning facts regarding prevalence, identities of perpetrators and the children affected, the secretive nature of sexual abuse, ways sex offenders engage children and prevent them from disclosing, and children's responses to sexual abuse. Educational materials regarding child sexual abuse are often available through child protective services and the offices of victim witness coordinators. This information may be provided to parents during sessions, or parents may be asked to read written materials for homework. Subsequently, the therapist can refer to that information in disputing inaccurate and distressing thoughts. For example, the mother of a sexually abused boy may experience unpleasant and unnecessary anxiety because she believes that all sexually abused boys grow up to be sex offenders. The therapist can help to reduce that mother's distress by providing her with the accurate information that most sexually abused children do not become offenders. The therapist should help the mother practice replacing the thoughts, "My son, David, has been sexually abused and now he is going to be a sex offender himself," with the more accurate and positive thought, "Most sexually abused children never abuse anyone else. David is getting help in coping with his abuse so there is no reason to believe he'll abuse anyone else."

Nonproductive Thoughts. The second category of dysfunctional thoughts is thoughts that are nonproductive, regardless of their accuracy. For example, a parent who is preoccupied with anger toward the perpetrator may experience repeated thoughts such as, "He's the scum of the earth. I wish he was dead." Although the parent's anger may be justified, it is not helpful. In such a case, the therapist should help the parent redirect such thoughts in a more productive way by focusing on how the parent can best help the child adjust after this experience. An example of such a replacement thought is, "I'm not going to waste time thinking about Ray anymore. I'm going to focus on helping Kathy by getting her to counseling each week and doing those homework assignments the therapist gives us."

Pessimistic Thinking. Many nonproductive thoughts are characterized by a negative style of thinking called pessimistic thinking. It is clear that many distressing emotions are driven by highly negative or pessimistic thoughts. In fact, recent research suggests that pessimistic coping styles not only lead to negative emotions but are frequently associated with poor physical health and low achievement (Seligman, 1991). Parents who are receptive to additional reading may be referred to *Learned Optimism,* by Martin E. P. Seligman (1991). He presents the coping model in a readable and interesting format. Therapists also may find it helpful to use this book as a guide to presenting the coping material. Seligman identifies three qualities that often characterize pessimistic thoughts about problems. These characteristics include viewing the problem as *permanent, pervasive,* and/or *personal.* Although problems are often thought of this way, most problems are changeable rather than permanent, specific rather than pervasive, and nonpersonal rather than personal.

Therapists may assist parents in examining their thoughts to determine if they tend to reflect any of these pessimistic qualities. When identifying negative thought characteristics, it is important that the therapist's comments not sound critical but empathic in pointing out that the parent's thoughts are in fact more harsh and negative than they need to be. The parent, in fact, deserves more kindness and comforting than the parent is giving him- or herself.

Common Areas Of Emotional Distress
And Dysfunctional Thoughts

When pursuing cognitive coping skills training with parents, the therapist should focus on the specific areas of emotional distress identified by the parent. Although the types of emotions experienced will vary from parent to parent, some of the more common areas of distress are identified below. Within the discussion of each emotion, we have included educational material and exercises designed to help the parent dispute dysfunctional thoughts that may be contributing to the parent's distress.

Responsibility/Guilt. Some parents may feel guilty for not preventing or recognizing the sexual abuse. Parents whose children were abused by a family member, such as a father or an older sibling, may be especially vulnerable to distressing feelings of responsibility. After eliciting from parents the thoughts that are underlying their feelings of responsibility, the therapist may help parents dispute their dysfunctional thoughts by providing educational information. This information can help parents *depersonalize* the problem, thereby diminishing inappropriate feelings of responsibility and/or guilt. A list of common dysfunctional thoughts and educational information that may be used to dispute them follows.

Dysfunctional thought: Of all the children in the world, why did this happen to my child?

Disputing information: The unfortunate truth is that my child is not alone. In fact, many children are affected by sexual abuse. Statistics indicate that by age 18, one of every four females and one of six males will experience some form of sexual abuse. In fact, my daughter is luckier than some because the abuse was discovered and stopped, and my daughter has caring parents who are getting help for her.

Dysfunctional thought: How could I have been such a fool? Why couldn't I see that this guy was an abuser?

Disputing information: There are no specific characteristics of sexual offenders that allow us to identify them. Even an expert in the field of sexual abuse could not pick a sexual offender out of a group of nonoffenders; thus there was no way that I could have known that this person would abuse my child. Sex offenders are generally not "dirty old men" or strangers lurking in alleys. In fact, there is nothing about their public behavior and/or appearance that distinguishes them from nonabusing individuals. Sex offenders are usually well-known and trusted by the children they victimize and frequently are members of the family such as fathers, stepfathers, grandfathers, uncles, and brothers. It is not surprising or inappropriate that we all trusted the offender. We can't go through life without trusting other people. In fact, we have to teach children to trust other people, or they will not be able to form successful relationships. All I can expect of myself is that I make myself available to help my child now. The truth is that I am doing all I can to help her.

Dysfunctional thought: I am a lousy, lousy mother. I could not even keep my son from being sexually abused. I did not even know the abuse was going on!

Disputing information: The secretive nature of sexual abuse makes it difficult to detect and to prevent. Children may be engaged in the activity by playful coaxing, and then they are pressured to keep the activity a secret. Physical evidence of abuse is present in only a small minority of cases, and even then parents are not likely to detect such evidence. So no matter what I do (short of locking my son in his room), no matter how good a parent I try to be, I cannot ensure that my child is never sexually abused. Indeed, many sensitive and caring parents, as well as professionals, are not aware that a child is being abused and cannot prevent it because the abuse is hidden and secretive.

Dysfunctional thought: I should have been looking out more for my son. I should have been supervising him all the time so I could have protected him.

> **Disputing information:** It is impossible to supervise my son at all times. In fact, it is not helpful to try to shelter my son from all possible risks or problems. An overprotected chid is often very poorly equipped to cope with life's challenges as an adult. Rather than sheltering my son, as a parent I want to teach my child to cope with negative things that happen to him because no one can avoid all of life's difficulties. I should not waste time and effort blaming myself for my son's abuse but instead focus on helping him to learn to cope with this and other problems he may face.

The educational information presented to a particular client should be tailored so that replacement thoughts can be generated that specifically address the areas of cognitive distortion that are creating distress.

In addition to helping parents generate replacement thoughts as a means of coping with dysfunctional feelings of guilt and responsibility, therapists may engage parents in role plays designed to allow them to rehearse a more effective cognitive style.

Sample Role-Play Exercise. To help parents work through their own feelings of guilt, the therapist may encourage parents to try a "best friend" role play similar to the role play described in the child intervention chapter. In this role play, the therapist should play the parent while the parent is asked to be a good friend who uses his or her compassion and knowledge about child sexual abuse to convince the guilt-ridden parent that he or she is not responsible for a daughter's abuse. In playing the parent, the therapist should express the client's previously shared guilt-ridden thoughts, while also using the Socratic method to help the "friend" evaluate the accuracy and productiveness of these thoughts.

Sadness. Many parents struggle with feelings of sadness and grief regarding their child's sexual abuse experience. Although those feelings are understandable and expected, some parents experience such overwhelming grief that their displays of emotion negatively affect their children. When working with such parents, the therapist may motivate them to examine and strengthen their coping response for the child's sake. The therapist may explain that if the parent's response to the sexual abuse communicates that a catastrophe has occurred, the child may assume that what happened to him or her is something so bad that he or she will never get over it.

Many parents experience sadness that is exacerbated by underlying thoughts that are inaccurate or dysfunctional. The dialogue in Box 5.2 demonstrates how a therapist might help a depressed parent work through the process of identifying, evaluating, and disputing inaccurate or overly pessimistic thoughts about her child's experience of sexual abuse.

Anger. Parents may experience anger at a variety of people involved in the abusive situation. For example, parents may be *angry at the child* for having participated in the abusive activities or for not telling sooner. In addition to the guilt described previously, some parents may feel *angry at themselves* for not preventing the abuse or for not helping the child to tell sooner. Most significant, parents often feel *angry at the perpetrator.* The therapist may explain that all these experiences of anger are normal and are signs that a parent cares. The therapist may further explain that it would be of greater concern if a parent was not having any strong feelings about what happened.

Anger at the Child or the Parent. When working with parents who are experiencing anger at the child for participating in the sexual activity or at themselves for not preventing it, the therapist may encourage the parents to identify ways in which they believe the child was engaged in the abuse. The therapist might list the methods generated and provide additional methods that the parent may not have previously considered. Then the therapist can use that information as illustrated below to help parents dispute the thoughts that are generating anger.

> **Dysfunctional thoughts generating anger at the child:** I don't know why Tiffany did not just hit him or come home. We've talked about how to handle situations like this, and I'm really frustrated that she let this happen.
> **Dysfunctional thoughts generating anger at self:** I'm so angry that I didn't prepare my child for this. If I had taught her how to respond to a jerk like that, she would not have been abused.

(text continued on p. 130)

BOX 5.2

Case Example: Helping a Depressed Parent
Deal With Pessimistic Thoughts

In a dialogue like the one that follows, a therapist might help a depressed parent work through the process of identifying, evaluating, and disputing inaccurate or overly pessimistic thoughts about a child's experience of sexual abuse.

Therapist: For the last couple of weeks, we've talked about how depressed you get when you think about your son having been sexually abused.

Mother: Sometimes I get so down about it I can't snap myself out of it.

Therapist: Well, let's talk about the last time you were feeling this way. I'm going to try to write down some of the thoughts you were having. Why don't you start by telling me what was happening the last time you were feeling this way?

Mother: It was just today. My son was acting really sassy. John is only 8, but sometimes he acts like he's 16. I just thought to myself, my son's childhood has been stolen. The sexual abuse has really caused him to have some problems.

Therapist: What else were you saying to yourself?

Mother: I was thinking that this is the worst thing that could have ever happened to him. It's going to ruin his life. Just like my experience with sexual abuse ruined my life.

Therapist: Those are really depressing things to say to yourself. Let's see if we can use some of the cognitive coping strategies we've been talking about to look at how accurate those thoughts are. First, you said your son's childhood was stolen. What do you think about that thought?

Mother: It's true!

Therapist: He hasn't enjoyed any aspects of his childhood?

Mother: Well, [long pause], he seems to have had lots of friends that he enjoyed doing lots of different activities with. And he's always been very close to me and his father, we've had a lot of fun vacations. But with his uncle sexually abusing him all that time, he couldn't have enjoyed life.

Therapist: Did he understand that what his uncle was doing was wrong?

BOX 5.2 *Continued*

Mother: No, I guess not at first. When he did, though, it took him a while to tell.

Therapist: How long?

Mother: A few months.

Therapist: Then maybe he did enjoy all those important childhood relationships and activities.

Mother: Maybe you're right.

Therapist: You also said that John has some problems as a result of the sexual abuse. I guess that's a pretty accurate and healthy thought. If you didn't recognize that he had problems, you wouldn't be here getting him the help he needs.

Mother: Exactly.

Therapist: But what about some of these other thoughts. Like this is the worst thing that could have ever happened to him. Are you sure there's nothing else that could have been worse?

Mother: You mean like getting hit by a car or something more permanent. I guess he could have even kept this to himself for a longer period of time and maybe he could have even been infected with the HIV virus.

Therapist: Maybe when you have these thoughts, you could remind yourself that although John has some problems as a result of the abuse, they are not necessarily permanent problems. We believe he can overcome these difficulties with your help and counseling.

Mother: That makes sense. But I still worry that he's going to just have all the problems that I had as a result of my sexual abuse.

Therapist: Well, let's list the ways in which the experience of sexual abuse and its aftermath may have been different for you as compared to your son.

The dialogue continues with the therapist helping the mother acknowledge that her experience of sexual abuse at the hands of her father was in certain respects more severe in nature and longer lasting; as a child, she did not get the support from her mother that she and her husband are providing for her son, John. In addition, the mother was able to acknowledge that she never received any kind of counseling and had a great deal of difficulty coping with the experience on her own.

> **Disputing information:** Perpetrators often identify and capitalize on children's vulnerabilities in order to engage them in sexual activity. My child's offender may have taken advantage of my child's vulnerabilities in many ways. (Using the list in Box 5.3, the therapist should help parents identify and list those vulnerabilities most applicable to their child's specific experience).

Some parents may be angry at their children for not disclosing the abuse sooner or at themselves for not having elicited a disclosure from the child sooner. When working with such a parent, the therapist may explain that in the child's mind, there may be many, many reasons not to tell, and relatively few good reasons to tell. Then the therapist may encourage the parent to list reasons children may not tell. If it is necessary, the therapist may assist the parent in generating that list of reasons by using the information in Box 5.4.

In most cases, the therapist may point out that the child has told, despite all of these reasons. The therapist may encourage the parent to use the list of reasons provided in Box 5.4 to practice disputing his or her thoughts that are anger producing. An example of that process follows.

> **Dysfunctional thought:** Why did she have to wait so long to tell? If only she had told when it first started happening, the abuse never would have gone so far!
> **Disputing information:** She was so scared that he would hurt her or would hurt me, that there was no way she could tell. That's not a realistic expectation. I'm just glad that I know about the abuse now and that we've stopped it.

The therapist may summarize the work regarding the parent's anger at the child and at the parent him- or herself with the following comments:

> When you feel angry at your child or at yourself regarding the abuse, consider all of the circumstances we listed that led to your child's sexual abuse and that prevented her from telling. Rather than focusing on the fact that your child was abused and did not tell earlier, focus on the fact that your child's sexual abuse has been discovered and stopped. Although you cannot erase the experience, you as a parent are in the best position to help your child adjust successfully and cope with future difficulties effectively.

BOX 5.3

Some Ways Perpetrators Engage Children

- The offender took advantage of my child's natural curiosity about sexuality.
- The offender encouraged my child to think that the activity was OK by presenting it as a game.
- The offender maintained my child's cooperation by making her feel good physically and emotionally.
- The offender took advantage of the fact that my child believed the sexual activity was an appropriate expression of affection or love.
- The offender took advantage of my child's eagerness to please an adult (particularly applicable when the perpetrator is a father, favorite uncle, etc.).
- The offender took advantage of my child's natural responsiveness to authority.
- The offender used my child's fears, threatening her with repeated abuse, as well as physical injury to her and to me.

Anger at the Perpetrator. Parental anger toward the perpetrator is certainly understandable and very common. However, if parents focus excessively on their anger, that preoccupation may prevent them from focusing on how best to adjust, and help their child adjust, after the sexual abuse. Therapists working with parents who are consumed by anger should help them think through to the consequences of that anger. For example, some parents feel so angry at the perpetrator that they want to seek revenge. Even after the abuse has been reported to the authorities and stopped, some parents are convinced that revenge against the perpetrator is the only way to make things right for their child. When working with such parents, therapists might pose the following questions to help parents realistically assess the impact and consequences of their anger-producing thoughts and plans for revenge.

BOX 5.4

Reasons Children May Not Tell
That They Are Being Abused

- They do not have the language to do so (i.e., developmental ability and/or words to describe sexual acts, sexual organs, etc.).
- They do not recognize the inappropriateness of the activity.
- After discovering the inappropriateness of the activity, they are too embarrassed.
- They fear they will get in trouble.
- They do not want to get the perpetrator in trouble.
- They do not want to disrupt their relationship with the perpetrator and other family members.
- Their parents will be angry.
- They want to protect their parents from being hurt emotionally.
- They are afraid the perpetrator will carry out his or her threats.

- How will murdering the offender benefit you and your child in the long run?
- What would happen to you if you did kill the offender?
- What impact would this murder have on your child?

If the parent has difficulty realistically assessing the outcome of an act of revenge, the therapist may help by providing the following information.

If you were to seek revenge against the perpetrator in a violent way, it is likely that you would be the first suspect considered. Furthermore, you may be arrested and put in jail. Then your child would have to live not only with the experience of being abused, but also with the loss of a parent.

Also, that loss would be compounded by the fact that the loss was preventable. It is likely that your child would always feel guilty for your arrest and jail sentence. If you successfully killed the perpetrator, your child also would likely feel responsible for that person's death. That is a very heavy burden to leave with your child. You are to be commended for reporting the abuse and cooperating with the legal investigation, but further revenge against the perpetrator is not going to benefit your child. In fact, it may harm your child if you focus all of your energy and attention on the perpetrator rather than focusing on how you can best help your child.

Although you may feel angry enough to seek revenge, the parents who seem to do best after this experience are those who cope effectively with their anger, and who direct their energy toward obtaining help for themselves and their child. By seeking therapy, you have already demonstrated that you have been able to direct your strong feelings in this way, and that is a very positive sign for your child.

After parents recognize the negative consequences of their plan for revenge, the therapist can help them practice replacing specific anger-generating thoughts with more adaptive replacement thoughts.

> **Dysfunctional thought:** That scumbag does not deserve to live. I'd like to blow his head off so he can never hurt anyone again.
>
> **Disputing information:** Just speaking this way may be frightening to Andy. It's not going to help him if I hurt the offender and I end up in jail myself. I'm going to concentrate on getting Andy the counseling he needs.

When working with a parent who is discussing plans for revenge, the therapist should carefully assess the parent's intent and his or her development of a true plan. Depending on the laws of the state, the therapist may have a legal obligation to inform both law enforcement officials and the intended victim if the parent acknowledges an intent to actually harm the perpetrator. The therapist should learn the relevant state laws regarding a therapist's "duty to warn" an intended victim of a crime. If the therapist is bound by such a law, he or she should inform all parents of that obligation when discussing the limits of confidentiality at the initiation of therapy and should again remind them of this obligation when issues of revenge and anger are raised in the course of therapy.

Other parents may also focus excessively on their anger, although they are not actively formulating a plan for revenge. Such parents also may be encouraged to think through the consequences of their anger in terms of its impact on their child. The therapist may ask questions such as the following:

How does your daughter feel when she sees you so angry and upset?

How does your anger help your son cope with this experience?

If a parent does not seem to recognize how significantly his or her anger influences the child, the therapist might discuss the information in Box 5.5, which describes a number of ways that children may be influenced by their parents' angry reactions to an incident of abuse.

Here's one example of how a therapist might help a parent replace anger-producing thoughts.

> **Dysfunctional thoughts:** I'm just so angry at my father for doing this to Sharon. Now we have to talk to Child Protective Services and the Prosecutor's Office and come to counseling, while nothing seems to be happening to him!

> **Replacement thoughts:** Continuing to focus on how unfair the situation is not helping Sharon or me, and it isn't making anything happen to my father. I'm going to concentrate instead on how I can best help Sharon cope with this.

Confusion. Many parents of sexually abused children report feeling confused and frustrated. They often want answers to questions such as, Why did this happen? and Why would anyone sexually abuse a child? Parents are likely to continue experiencing negative emotions as they ruminate over these questions and/or generate answers that are inaccurate or dysfunctional. Therapists can help parents break a cycle of unproductive rumination by providing some basic information, such as the material found in Box 5.6. The therapist can help

---

BOX 5.5

How Excessive Parental Anger Affects Children

- If children see their parents lose control and become over-whelmed with anger whenever the subject of the abuse comes up, the children may learn to avoid discussing the abuse in order to avoid making their parents angry.
- Young children tend to feel that they are the center of the world and that they cause what happens around them. If a child sees his or her parents get extremely upset or angry about something that has happened to them, the child may think, "Look how upset Mommy and Daddy are. I must have done something very bad."
- Children have difficulty recognizing that they have been coerced, manipulated, or bribed into taking part in the sexual activities. Thus, they may feel as blameworthy as the perpetrator for their participation.
- Children tend to imitate parental responses. Thus, if a parent exhibits extreme anger regarding the situation, the child may similarly react with apparent anger, potentially masking other emotions he or she may be experiencing.
- Children who are consistently exposed to parental anger will learn to focus exclusively on an anger response, rather than on learning to cope successfully with the sexual abuse experience.

---

parents replace confusing and/or depressing thoughts by using the information in Box 5.6 to dispute the dysfunctional aspects of their thoughts:

> **Dysfunctional thought:** I don't know why my husband did this. Maybe if I had been a more responsive sexual partner, he would not have sexually abused our daughter.

> **Replacement thought:** I'm taking too much personal responsibility for something my husband did. Maybe if he had dealt with his own experience of sexual abuse and gotten some help for his drinking, he would not have done this. Besides, even if he was dissatisfied with our sex life, he didn't have to break the law and sexually abuse our child. Many people have sexual difficulties and don't sexually abuse children.

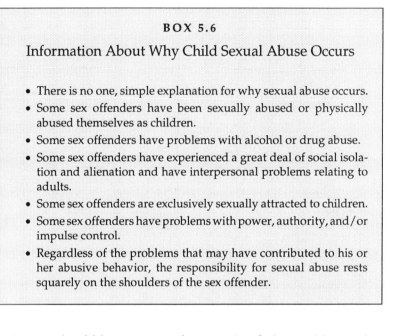

BOX 5.6

Information About Why Child Sexual Abuse Occurs

- There is no one, simple explanation for why sexual abuse occurs.
- Some sex offenders have been sexually abused or physically abused themselves as children.
- Some sex offenders have problems with alcohol or drug abuse.
- Some sex offenders have experienced a great deal of social isolation and alienation and have interpersonal problems relating to adults.
- Some sex offenders are exclusively sexually attracted to children.
- Some sex offenders have problems with power, authority, and/or impulse control.
- Regardless of the problems that may have contributed to his or her abusive behavior, the responsibility for sexual abuse rests squarely on the shoulders of the sex offender.

Parents should be encouraged to practice their cognitive coping skills for homework. They may be asked to keep a list of any distressing emotions they have experienced regarding the abuse, the thoughts underlying those distressing emotions, and the replacement thoughts they used to dispute the dysfunctional thoughts. Each week the therapist should review the homework to monitor the client's success in disputing dysfunctional thoughts and to offer suggestions for improving those skills.

❏ Gradual Exposure

This therapy component has two principle focuses: pursuing gradual exposure to help parents confront and cope with discussions about the child's abuse and training parents in how to talk with their children directly about the sexual abuse experience. We also have included training for parents in presenting sex education and personal safety skills training, as those issues may be interspersed with gradual exposure exercises. The amount of time needed to pursue gradual exposure with parents may vary dramatically from one parent to another, depending on the parent's level of distress and anxiety when confronted with thoughts of the sexual abuse.

Parents who have a personal history of child sexual abuse may experience greater distress or anxiety and require considerable gradual exposure before their distress diminishes enough that they can effectively discuss the abuse with their children. Although we do not encourage parents to focus a great deal on their own history of abuse, it is important to acknowledge that personal abusive experiences may make gradual exposure work more difficult. At the same time, however, it should be emphasized that parents who are survivors themselves can be excellent sources of support to their children. However, if parents appear to have symptoms that stem from their own history of abuse, it may be useful to share that observation and to offer a referral for adult survivor counseling. Such a referral, however, is generally best offered in the context of a well-established, trusting therapist-client relationship. The therapist, for example, might point out that the parent deserves the opportunity to work through his or her abuse experience just as much as the child does.

Other parents may be able to tolerate discussions of the abusive experience without as much difficulty. However, it is useful to pursue some gradual exposure work even with those parents who seem able to tolerate those discussions more easily in order to assess their tolerance and be certain that there are not any specific aspects of the abuse experience that are particularly distressing to them. Once parents are able to discuss the abuse experience without significant distress, the focus of therapy may shift to training them in how to participate effectively in their child's gradual exposure work.

THE PARENT'S GRADUAL EXPOSURE WORK

Gradual exposure work with parents is based on the same principles described in the earlier section on gradual exposure with children. To summarize briefly, parents will be exposed in a gradual way to thoughts and discussions of the child's abusive experiences until the parents' associated emotional distress begins to diminish.

As the distress diminishes, any existing pattern of avoiding those thoughts and related discussion will similarly diminish.

Rationale

Gradual exposure work with parents can be a crucial aspect of therapy for a number of reasons. First, gradual exposure can be useful in reducing the parent's own level of emotional distress regarding the abuse. As has been described previously, many parents experience great distress upon learning of their child's abuse experience. Parents who are highly distressed may be less available to assist their children because they are so overwhelmed with their own distress. Gradual exposure can help to reduce the level of emotional distress experienced by parents, thereby increasing their availability to their child.

Second, the parent's gradual exposure work may be crucial in enabling parents to model for their child how thoughts and discussions of the abuse can be tolerated without significant distress and need not be avoided. Early in treatment, many parents may choose to avoid abuse-related thoughts and discussion as a means of avoiding the associated emotional distress. Unfortunately, the child may then model that pattern of avoidance, which is an ineffective means of coping with the abuse experience. The therapist's progress in helping the child effectively confront and process the abuse experience will be compromised as long as the child is presented with a model of avoidance at home. In contrast, the child's progress in gradual exposure may be enhanced if both the therapist and the parents model a pattern of actively confronting and coping with memories and reminders of the abuse. Parents' own experience with gradual exposure should help them model effective coping strategies for their child.

Third, the gradual exposure process may be important in preparing parents to effectively discuss the abuse with the child, both in and outside of joint therapy sessions. Until parents are able to effectively confront and cope with their own thoughts and emotions regarding the abuse, they may not be able to participate appropriately in discussions regarding the abuse with the child. Because parental participation in those discussions is important in the child's progress, any therapeutic work, including gradual exposure, that enhances the parent's effective participation should be considered a valuable component of treatment.

The Process of Gradual Exposure With the Parent

The therapist should review the rationale for the parent's gradual exposure work before actually initiating gradual exposure exercises. The three major reasons for pursuing gradual exposure may be presented as described above. Again, it is important that parents understand the purpose of the therapeutic work, so that they can collaborate with the therapist as partners in the process of therapy. Thus, the therapist should attempt to explain the rationale fully and respond to any questions or concerns the parents have before initiating gradual exposure.

Parents may be resistant to the idea of participating in gradual exposure work for a variety of reasons. In some cases, parents are anxious about confronting their own distress-producing thoughts of the abuse. With such parents, the therapist may emphasize the fact that parents will never forget about the abuse and thus need to find ways to become more comfortable with thoughts about the abuse. Other parents may express doubts about their role in discussing the abuse with the child. With those parents, the therapist again may stress the unique opportunity the parents have, by virtue of their relationship with the child, to positively influence how the child responds to the abusive experience. It is important that the therapist identify whatever the parent's specific concerns are so that those concerns can be addressed and the parent's commitment to the therapeutic process can be enhanced. With most parents, it is appropriate for the therapist to emphasize the value of participating in gradual exposure in order to enhance the parent's emotional well-being and thus the parent's capacity to interact effectively with the child around the abuse experience.

Gradual exposure work with the nonoffending parent often follows a process that is roughly parallel to the gradual exposure process with the child. As the child progresses in individual gradual exposure sessions, the child typically provides more and more information about the abusive experiences. The therapist, in turn, may provide that information to the parent in a gradual, measured way. As the child's account of the abuse is provided, the therapist may encourage the parent to focus on the information shared, allowing him- or herself to experience all the emotions that the child's account evokes. Furthermore, parents may be encouraged to share the images that are precipitated by their children's descriptions. In this way, the parent's level of emotional distress associated with those images diminishes and the parent becomes better able to tolerate abuse-related thoughts and discussions.

If the child experienced multiple episodes of abuse, this process will need to be repeated with information about different abusive episodes and/or different types of abusive activities involved. In other cases, the child may have experienced only one abusive episode. In such a case, the gradual exposure process is likely to be much shorter. Some parents already know most of the details of the abusive episodes. Even those parents may benefit from gradual exposure as they may not have allowed themselves to experience all the emotions evoked by knowledge of the abuse. The therapist generally can judge when the work of gradual exposure is completed by the parent's emotional response. Parents should be able to discuss the abusive episodes without significant distress by the end of the gradual exposure process.

In addition to becoming more comfortable with thoughts of the abuse through gradual exposure, it is important that parents be engaged in cognitive and affective processing of their thoughts and feelings regarding the abuse. In other words, parents need to clarify their emotional responses to the abuse while identifying and disputing any dysfunctional thoughts regarding the abuse. This processing work has largely been described in the section on cognitive coping skills training for parents. However, often the gradual exposure work elicits additional thoughts and feelings that need to be processed. As was true in gradual exposure work with the child, it is preferable to first complete the gradual exposure exercises being pursued during a specific session, reserving time later in the session for cognitive and affective processing of the thoughts and feelings elicited during gradual exposure. That sequence of work is recommended to avoid interrupting the parent's gradual exposure exercises with more intellectual discussions of the parent's thoughts or feelings. Such an interruption of the gradual exposure work might allow the parent to avoid experiencing the emotions aroused by hearing the details of the child's abusive experience.

TRAINING PARENTS IN DISCUSSING
THE ABUSE WITH THE CHILD

As the parent makes progress in gradual exposure and processing of the abuse experience, the therapist may begin to focus on training the parent in communicating with the child regarding the abuse experience. As has been stated previously, parents' responses to the abuse experience can be a critically important factor in their child's post-abuse adjustment, both because children may base their perceptions of the abuse experience on the parents' responses and because children may model their style of coping with the experience on the parent's coping style. The therapist should help parents recognize the magnitude of their influence on the child and prepare parents to use their influence as positively as possible.

Opportunities for the parent to engage the child in discussions of the abuse experience may occur both during and outside of therapy sessions. In the latter stages of therapy, parents will be called upon to contribute to discussions of the abuse during joint parent-child sessions and will be encouraged to continue the gradual exposure process at home. However, even in the early stages of therapy, some children will spontaneously talk with parents about the abuse experience outside of therapy sessions. Such spontaneous conversations often are focused on the child's specific areas of concern and thus provide unique opportunities to address those concerns.

In contrast, other children may avoid any discussion of the abuse with their nonoffending parents in an effort to protect the parents from being hurt, for fear that the parents will be angry with them, or out of their own need for independence from parents. Parents of these children should be reassured that many children find it easier, especially initially, to discuss their concerns with a therapist, friend, or another relative. However, after some gradual exposure work, even those parents should be encouraged to look for opportunities to initiate conversations with their children regarding the abuse because parents are the adults who are most likely to be available on a long-term basis to help children cope with this experience.

Unfortunately, many parents are anxious about engaging in discussions of the abuse because (a) they worry that it will be distressing for themselves or for the child, (b) they are concerned that they may break down and inappropriately show their emotional distress, and/or (c) they fear they will not have the knowledge to respond effectively to the child. Effectively preparing parents for discussions of the abuse experience with the child can reduce parents' level of anxiety, increase their feelings of competence and confidence, and maximize the benefits of any such discussions for the child.

Open Lines of Communication

The therapist can begin preparing parents to discuss the abuse experience with the child by teaching them some basic skills that will help to develop or maintain open lines of communication with the child. For further information regarding effective parent-child communication, readers are referred to *How to Talk So Kids Will Listen and Listen So Kids Will Talk,* by Faber and Mazlish (1980). These skills are applicable to communication about any topic. Indeed, the skills initially may be used in discussions of topics other than the sexual abuse, particularly if either the parent or the child is highly anxious about discussing the abuse. As the parent and child become more adept at communicating and less anxious about the topic of sexual abuse, the skills may be focused more specifically on the topic of sexual abuse. The therapist might initiate this communication skills training by providing the following rationale:

> Sexually abused children may process their sexually abusive experience over the course of many years. As children develop and gain a greater understanding of interpersonal relationships and sexuality, they may begin to think of their abusive experiences in a different way and may have more questions regarding the experiences. There is little doubt that such questions will arise in the mind of a sexually abused child; however, there is no guarantee that they will be asked.

As a parent of a sexually abused child, it is important to maintain open lines of communication with your child. If he (or she) has questions in the future, as we expect, you are the person who is most likely to be available to respond to those questions or concerns. Thus, we need to make sure that your child is comfortable enough talking about the abuse to be able to ask you questions and that you are comfortable enough to respond appropriately to those questions. We're going to talk about several ways you can enhance your communication with your child that will ultimately help both of you become more comfortable discussing the abuse.

The therapist then may provide training about the following strategies that should help facilitate open communication between parent and child.

Encourage Questions. Parents should be encouraged to positively reinforce their child for asking questions, regardless of whether or not the parent has the answer. It is understandable that parents may shy away from questions that they cannot answer. However, the therapist should help parents realize that by avoiding the child's questions, they are communicating to the child that they would prefer not to discuss the topic being raised. Rather than avoiding the topic, which clearly discourages further questions, parents should be encouraged to respond positively, if only to the fact that the child asked a question. Parents should not feel pressured to have the answers to all the child's questions. They should be encouraged that even without the "right answer," they may respond effectively to the child's question by praising the child for asking the question and then assisting the child in obtaining the desired information. In fact, information-seeking behavior is an important coping response for parents to model for their children. To help parents become more comfortable reinforcing children for asking questions, the therapist may engage parents in role plays with the therapist assuming the role of the child asking difficult questions. The example in Box 5.7 illustrates how a parent might respond after training by the therapist.

Reinforce the Sharing of Problems. Parents also should be encouraged to reinforce their children for sharing their problems or

---

BOX 5.7

Case Example: Parent-Child Role Play

As time goes by, sexually abused children may bring additional questions about the incident to their parents. Here's a role
play that will help parents deal with those questions, even
when they don't know the answers.

Child [played by the therapist]: Why did Mr. Jones touch me
   like that, Mommy? Why did he want to do that?
Parent: Susie, I'm so glad you asked that question. That's a
   question that lots of kids and even grown-ups ask. I've
   wondered myself why he touched you, and I'm not really
   sure of the answer. Do you have any guesses why he did
   that?
Child: Maybe because I was acting too much like a big girl.
Parent: I'm glad we can talk about this, Susie, but I don't think
   it had anything to do with you or how you were acting or
   really even who you are. It happened because of a problem
   he has. He wanted to be sexual with children even though
   he knew it was wrong. Would you like to talk to your
   therapist about this more in our next session?
Child: OK. Thanks, Mom.

---

concerns. Children are frequently reinforced for solving problems.
However, many problems are unsolvable. Thus, it becomes important to reinforce children for sharing problems whether or not the
problem is solvable. For example, parents might be encouraged to
teach their children statements such as, "Problems always seem
bigger when you keep them to yourself, and they get smaller when
you share them with someone else."

However, verbally teaching children that philosophy is not
enough; children also need to actually experience positive consequences for confronting, processing, and coping with problems as
opposed to just solving problems. When teaching a parent how to
reinforce a child for sharing problems, the therapist can help the

parent remember times when the child has shared a problem and recall how the parent reinforced that behavior. If the parent, in fact, did not reinforce the sharing of the problem, the therapist might help the parent think of what he or she might have said to encourage the child to talk about the problem. In addition, the therapist might engage the parent in role plays, with the therapist assuming the child's role in sharing a problem and the parent rehearsing how to reinforce the child. The example in Box 5.8 demonstrates a role play in which the "parent" is reinforcing a "child" for sharing an unsolvable problem.

BOX 5.8

Case Example: Reinforcing a Child for Discussing a Problem

The therapist can help a parent learn how to encourage a child to talk about a problem by role-playing the child and letting the parent rehearse how to reinforce a child for sharing an unsolvable problem.

Child [played by therapist]: Mom, can I talk to you?
Mother: Sure, what is it?
Child: It's just not fair that nothing is going to happen to Tony for what he did to me. I told you and we told the police and everybody knows what happened, but he's walking around like nothing is wrong. It's not right. Why can't they just put him in jail?
Mother: You know, that makes me upset too. The prosecuting attorney explained to me that they aren't sure they could win the case against Tony, even though they believe everything we've told them. I guess sometimes they need to have more evidence beyond just what we've said happened. They don't want to take the case to trial and make us go through that unless they think they have a pretty good chance of winning. You know what, though?

(continued)

BOX 5.8 *Continued*

I'm really glad you talked to me about this. Even though neither of us is very happy about it, I think it helps if we talk about the problem.

Child: Yeah, I guess so. But what do we do now about it?

Mother: Well, we've done our part legally. We reported the abuse, and the rest is up to the legal system to decide. I think we should concentrate now on helping you feel better about all that's happened by talking about the abuse and going to counseling. I'm really proud of you for being able to talk about Tony today! I know it used to be really hard to even say his name, and today we had a whole conversation about him. I think that the more we talk about your worries, the better you'll feel.

Encourage the Expression of Feelings in an Appropriate Manner. The therapist also should encourage parents to teach children to share their feelings in appropriate ways. Children need to know that there are no right and wrong ways to feel. Furthermore, children should be taught that it is appropriate and helpful to share their feelings with other people, particularly their parents. However, children also need to learn that there are effective and ineffective ways of expressing emotions. For example, although sexually abused children may have every right to feel angry, they need to understand that hitting and yelling at others are not effective ways of communicating their anger. Rather, they may be encouraged to express their negative emotions through spoken words, written words, poetry, song, artwork, and so on. Again, parents should be encouraged to provide children with positive reinforcement for sharing feelings appropriately. Children also may need help labeling their emotions. Parents may provide children with the vocabulary they need to express their emotions by looking at the faces in books and magazines and identifying the emotions they seem to be experiencing. With a parent who has difficulty expressing his or her own emotions appropriately, the therapist may need to do more individual work with the parent on emotional expression skills so that the parent can be a more effective model for the child.

Special Parent-Child Time. Open lines of communication may be enhanced by setting aside a special time and place that the parent and child can talk or share an activity on a predictable and consistent basis. By setting time aside when the parent will be reliably available to the child, the parent communicates the value he or she places on spending time and talking with the child. Furthermore, as the parent and child become accustomed to talking about daily events, they will be developing skills and a tolerance for communicating about more anxiety-provoking topics such as the sexual abuse. It is more important for parents to have special time with their children on a *consistent* basis than it is for the actual time to be long in duration. For example, giving the child undivided attention for just 5 to 10 minutes a day can help to maintain positive parent-child communication. The therapist may help the parent evaluate and improve the quality, consistency, and amount of time the parent currently spends in focused communication with the child. When children are troubled by confusing issues, it is helpful for them to know that there is a predictable time when they will have their parents' undivided attention.

Initiating Parent-child Communication
About Child Sexual Abuse

After the therapist feels that the parent and child are able to communicate successfully about less threatening issues, the therapist may begin training the parent in communicating more specifically about the sexual abuse experience. This training is intended to prepare the parent for spontaneous discussions of the abuse that may arise outside of therapy sessions as well as to lay the groundwork for the joint parent-child sessions. More detailed preparations for the specific work to be done in those joint sessions will be offered in the next chapter, "Joint Parent-Child Sessions."

The therapist may offer the following basic guidelines for communicating about the sexual abuse experience.

Model Open Communication. First, the therapist should teach the parent to encourage the child's discussion of the sexual abuse by having the parent model open communication concerning this issue. As has been described previously, many parents understandably avoid discussions of the abuse, either out of their own discomfort or out of concern that such discussions will be distressing to the child. The therapist should help parents realize that such avoidance will teach the child that the parent is unable or unwilling to discuss the abuse and thus will limit any communication about the abuse. There-fore, once parents are coping more effectively with their own emo-tions, it is important that they demonstrate a willingness to discuss the abuse with their child. The parent can demonstrate this by being responsive to any questions or comments the child makes about the abuse experience. The parent may offer praise to the child for dis-cussing the issue and should take the time to respond to the child in an individualized, focused manner. If it is not possible to give the child such individualized attention at the moment the topic is raised, the parent might say, "I'm glad you asked about that. I'd really like to discuss that with you when I can give you all my attention. Let's plan to discuss that some more tonight right after dinner." Then it is crucial that the parent keep the scheduled date for discussing the abuse.

Encourage Dialogue Gradually and Naturally. The therapist may reassure the parent that the investigators and attorneys are respon-sible for investigating the abuse allegations and will generally take care of obtaining details. It is not necessary or appropriate for parents to barrage the child with numerous questions about the sexually abusive interaction(s), as many other professionals will be asking those questions. Indeed, as much as possible, the child's home should be a place of peace and safety where the child can relax from the stress of the investigation. The parent should be reassured that during the joint parent-child therapy sessions, the child will be encouraged to discuss the abuse experience more specifically with the parent. It is preferable for the parent to wait for those joint sessions before probing for details of the experience to ensure that communication about those details can occur in a positive way that will encourage further dialogue regarding the abuse.

On the other hand, parents do not want to facilitate the child's avoidance and/or secrecy with regard to abuse-related or sexual issues. Certainly, parents should respond to children's spontaneous questions or concerns about the abuse in a positive way, to encourage further discussion. Indeed, it is appropriate for parents to encourage discussion of the abuse experience, as long as such discussions do not move into interrogations about the details of the experience. Parents should be encouraged to take advantage of naturally occurring events that may be reminders of the sexually abusive experiences. These are natural moments to initiate conversation, and the child may be more responsive to discussion at those times. For example, it is appropriate for a parent to inquire about how the child feels when driving past the perpetrator's home, upon hearing the perpetrator's name, or after participating in interviews with investigating professionals.

Another means of naturally initiating conversation about the sexual abuse is to use opportunities when the topic is discussed in the media. Initially, many children find it less threatening to discuss the issue of child sexual abuse in general, rather than discussing their personal experiences. Thus, parents may use opportunities to initiate a discussion of sexual abuse when the topic arises, for example, on a news show or another television show. Rather than ushering the child out of the room, the parent might explain what the reporters are talking about and ask whether the child has any questions or concerns. However, parents should be encouraged to use caution when using such opportunities to make sure that the media information does not result in additional confusion for the child. If possible, the parent should screen the presentation or television show in advance to check for its appropriateness. If it is not possible to prescreen, the parent should at least remain present while the child is watching the show or reading the material, so that the parent is available to help the child process the information being presented.

Avoid Catastrophizing. The therapist may caution parents that when talking to children about sexually abusive experiences, they should avoid oversympathizing and/or "catastrophizing." Parental overreactions can inadvertently encourage children to think in catastrophic terms. This kind of thinking can lead to self-fulfilling prophecies. The cognitive coping work described earlier can help parents avoid this potential problem by disputing any inaccurate or excessively negative perceptions the parents have about the abuse experience.

Do Not Alter Normal Expectations and Limits. Similarly, the therapist may help parents resist the temptation to relax the normal expectations and limits for behavior that have been established in the home. Often well-intentioned parents will attempt to help the child through this difficult time by not enforcing normal consequences for inappropriate behaviors or by relaxing expectations for household chores. Unfortunately, this attempt to help usually confuses the child and communicates that the sexual abuse experience must be very serious indeed. Furthermore, children often naturally take advantage of an overly sympathetic parent in order to gain inappropriate control of the house rules and consequences. This situation can often lead to child behavior problems, which ultimately create even further difficulties for the child. Thus, parents should be encouraged to maintain the types of behavior management that have previously been effective in the home. Detailed information about effective behavior management strategies will follow in this chapter.

Do Not Expect Child to Share Parents' View. Finally, the therapist should encourage parents to allow the child to have his or her own views of the perpetrator, rather than expecting the child to share the parent's view. In particular, it is important that the therapist caution parents to avoid describing the offender either as all good or as all bad. Such a one-sided depiction of the offender can be very confusing for a child, particularly when the offender is a loved member of the child's family. Indeed, many sexually abused children have mixed feelings toward the offender following the abuse. Sometimes a nonoffending parent may state his or her own views so forcefully that he or she may inadvertently pressure the child to share the parent's viewpoint. It is most appropriate to allow victimized children to develop their own thoughts and feelings about the offender. With therapeutic assistance, most children can recognize that all people exhibit good and bad behaviors. Indeed, thinking in terms of black and white or good and evil can be very dysfunctional. Even young children can separate a person from an act, and thus they can learn that the offender's abusive action was wrong, but there may be some things he did that were right. This is particularly important if the perpetrator is the child's parent or close relative. Again, therapists hope that the cognitive coping work will assist parents in disputing any cognitive distortions that they have regarding the offender and help parents reflect a more realistic view of the offender for the child.

TRAINING PARENTS IN PROVIDING
AGE-APPROPRIATE SEX EDUCATION

Age-appropriate sex education is important for all children. Unfortunately, as a society we face serious and widespread problems with teenage pregnancy, sexually transmitted diseases, and AIDS. Sex education and open parent-child communication may be our best hope for reducing the likelihood that today's children will face these difficulties as adolescents and young adults.

Sex education is particularly important for sexually abused children for a number of reasons. First, it is critical that sexually abused children receive accurate education to correct any misconceptions they may have developed concerning sex as a result of their abusive experiences. Second, sex education may help to reduce the sexually abused child's vulnerability to further abuse, premature sexual activity, and/or adult sexual dysfunction. Third, sex education may be pursued as a part of the gradual exposure process for children who have become anxious about discussions of any sexual issues because those discussions precipitate memories of the abusive experience. Finally, through discussions of sex education, adults can model for children how sexual issues can be discussed calmly, without excessive embarrassment. Children who have effective models to imitate may be much better prepared to discuss sexual issues within their own relationships as adults.

It is most helpful when parents are able to participate in providing children with developmentally appropriate sex education. In this treatment model, usually parents are involved initially in providing sex education in conjunction with the therapist during the joint parent-child sessions. As the parent and child become more comfortable, they may pursue the work of sex education more independently, in the context of therapeutic homework assignments. By providing sex education, parents not only give the child needed information regarding sexuality but also teach him or her that the parent is able and willing to communicate about sexual issues.

Having the capacity to talk openly about sexuality should serve the child and parent well, particularly when the child is grappling with sexual issues as an adolescent and young adult.

Presenting Rationale For
Sex Education To Parents

Unfortunately, parents often initially feel uncomfortable and ill prepared to talk to their children about sex. As a result, some parents seek to avoid the subject altogether. This is not surprising, given that most parents did not receive sex education in ideal ways themselves. The dialogue in Box 5.9 illustrates how a therapist might talk with a hesitant parent about the rationale for providing sex education.

Exploring Parents' Feelings About
Providing sex Education

After presenting the rationale, the next step in preparing parents to participate in providing sex education is to help them sort through their own feelings about discussing sexual issues with the child. The therapist might begin that work by asking parents to recall any sex education they received as a child from their own parents. Parents may be asked how they felt as a child at that time. If the parent expresses any dissatisfaction with the sex education that was provided, more effective means of communicating regarding sex education can be suggested by the parents and/or the therapist. Subsequently, parents may be asked how they feel now when contemplating providing sex education to their children.

When working with parents who acknowledge anxiety or other distress when anticipating providing sex education, the therapist might use the following presentation:

> It is very important to deal with your own discomfort regarding sex and sexuality in order to provide the most effective sex education to your child. Children are highly sensitive to gestures, facial expressions, and, most important, what you don't say. If you avoid talking about sexual issues, you may inadvertently convey that sex is secretive, wrong, or something about which one should be ashamed. Moreover, you may unintentionally discourage children's questions

BOX 5.9

Case Example: Rationale for Sex Education

Here's how a therapist might introduce parents to the need for providing their children with sex education.

Therapist: I believe it is important that we provide Sally with appropriate information about healthy sexuality. Unfortunately, she has already received some inappropriate and inaccurate information about sexuality as a result of her sexually abusive experiences. Thus, it's really important that we correct that misinformation and help her to develop a positive view of healthy adult sexuality.

Mother: I'm not sure. She seems pretty young to me. I don't want to put any ideas into her head.

Therapist: Well, I don't think we would be putting any new ideas into her head. Remember she had a series of sexual interactions with Tom, even though it may be uncomfortable to think of the abuse in those terms. So we won't be putting thoughts of sex into her head, we'll just be providing her with more accurate information and helping to sort out any misunderstandings she has. Actually, I believe it would be appropriate to give her this education even if she hadn't been sexually abused. She is 11 years old now, and that really isn't too young to learn accurate information about sexuality.

Mother: But if we talk to her about sex, won't that make her want to go ahead and do it?

Therapist: Actually, there is no evidence that sex education has that kind of effect.

Mother: I just don't want her to think it's OK to go around having sex just because Tom did that with her.

Therapist: I understand. It's important that you think about the values that you want to teach Sally. We don't want to give her educational information alone. We want to combine that educational information about sexuality with information about your values.

about sex. Let's begin to examine the thoughts that are underlying your feelings of anxiety and embarrassment.

Then the therapist may lead the parent in cognitive coping exercises designed to dispute or replace any dysfunctional thoughts underlying the parent's distress regarding sex education.

Guidelines For Parents In Presenting Sex Education

When the parent appears to be more comfortable with the idea of providing sex education, the therapist should offer the following general suggestions or guidelines.

Begin Sex Education Early, Using Everyday Opportunities. The earlier sex education is initiated, the easier it may be for both parent and child. Sex education can be a natural part of everyday living. For example, at an early age, children may be taught the names of their sex organs in the natural course of teaching body part names. This may be done at bath time or bedtime. Parents often have opportunities to teach children basic information about where babies come from when a family member or friend is pregnant. General information about menstruation may be provided when young children ask questions about menstrual pads or tampons found in a family bathroom.

Focus Sex Education on the Child's Developmental Level. Both the topics discussed and the manner in which they are discussed should be focused on the child's developmental level. For example, young children do not need or want highly technical explanations of conception or sexual functioning. However, simple and accurate explanations for the differences between girls and boys and where babies come from can be offered to children as young as 3 years of age. Masturbation similarly may be dealt with at an early age, as children often exhibit masturbatory behaviors during the preschool and school-age years. A natural and appropriate time to talk with children about masturbation is when parents observe them touching their genitals. Parents may want to acknowledge to their children that this may feel good and is OK to do, but they may further explain that it is something that people do in private.

Many children in the age range of 7 to 12 are interested in and ready to receive information regarding how babies are conceived and delivered. The exact age at which that information should be provided depends on the child's level of interest and maturity, the information the child already has from peers or from the sexual abuse experience, and the parent's level of comfort.

Preteens are often most interested in information regarding pubertal changes. Parents should provide information about these changes for both sexes so that the child understands what will be happening not only to his or her own body but also to the bodies of peers.

Teenagers may also appreciate information concerning pubertal changes, as well as information about sexual desires and feelings, sexual activity, birth control, and dating relationships. Parents may be surprised to know that several studies suggest that teenagers prefer to receive this information from parents as opposed to teachers or peers (Alexander & Jorgensen, 1983; Handelsman, Cabral, & Weisfeld, 1987). Some parents may hesitate to provide this sort of information to their children for fear that they may inadvertently encourage premature sexual activity. However, there is no evidence to date that this is the case. Open parent communication about sexuality does not appear to be associated with either increased or decreased adolescent sexual activity. However, among sexually active teenagers, those who communicate openly with parents are more likely to use contraception, thereby decreasing their risk of experiencing unintentional pregnancy and/or suffering sexually transmitted diseases (Handelsman et al., 1987; Kastner, 1984).

Don't Wait for Questions. There is a widespread but often inaccurate belief that children will ask questions when they are ready to learn about sexuality. That belief may hold true for children who have no anxiety or discomfort in discussing sexual issues. In reality, however, many important questions go unasked by children who perceive that their parents are uncomfortable or embarrassed with the discussion of sexual issues. Therefore, parents need not wait for their children to ask questions about sex to provide sex education. Indeed, it is more appropriate for parents to take the initiative and to begin to develop an atmosphere of openness in which questions and discussion regarding sex and sexuality are encouraged.

Approach Sex Education in a Positive Manner, With Humor. Too often, parents and educators approach the topic of sexuality in a somber, even grim manner. This tone, in and of itself, communicates that this is a serious topic, one that is difficult and perhaps unpleasant to discuss. Such a presentation will likely serve to discourage any further conversations regarding sexuality. Furthermore, discussing sexuality in such a somber manner may reinforce a sexually abused child's perception of sexuality as a negative, anxiety-laden experience. Thus, parents should be encouraged to discuss healthy adult sexuality in a positive tone. It is appropriate to describe sexual activity as a pleasant, loving, joyful, and/or playful activity that feels good within the context of the right relationship. When presenting sexual education, it is helpful to use humor to lighten the mood and lessen everyone's feelings of embarrassment and anxiety. Often children will giggle with embarrassment when presented with sexual information. Such laughter should not be viewed negatively. Instead, parents may want to laugh as well, sharing in the child's humor regarding the information being provided.

Be a Good Listener. Effectively providing sex education to children involves listening as well as teaching. Indeed, children are unlikely to be highly responsive to lecturing. Sex education may be more effectively provided through interactive discussion. Children as well as parents have difficulty talking about sex and sexuality. Thus, parents may need to listen carefully in order to identify specific areas of underlying concerns for their children. For example, if a child seems particularly anxious or avoidant of a specific topic (e.g., pregnancy, AIDS), the parent might consider whether that issue is particularly troubling to the child for some reason. Sexually abused children sometimes harbor unexpressed fears regarding their possible exposure to the HIV virus and/or other sexually transmitted diseases. Parents can elicit and address such fears during these sex education discussions.

Use Available Sex Education Materials. A wealth of sex education material is available through books and videos. These materials can help to increase and improve parents' knowledge base, reduce their anxiety and discomfort, and provide structure for their discussions with their children. *Where Did I Come From* (Mayle, 1995) is a humorous book for young children that describes how babies are conceived and delivered. *Asking About Sex and Growing Up* (Cole, 1988) is a factual book for preteens that covers topics including puberty, conception, masturbation, contraceptive methods, and homosexuality. *How to Talk With Your Child About Sexuality* (Planned Parenthood, 1986) can be a very useful guide for parents of children of all ages.

Prepare in Advance to Discuss Difficult Sexual Issues. Therapists should help parents be prepared for some of the difficult questions and issues they may face as their children develop. In that way, parents may be better able to deal with difficult sexual questions naturally, gradually, and incidentally as they arise. For example, a child may ask a parent when the parent first became sexually active and with whom that activity occurred. The therapist may engage the parent in a role play focused on how to handle that question. Another potentially difficult situation may arise if a child engages in sexual exploration or more explicit sexual activity with another child. Again, the therapist may help the parent formulate appropriate responses to those situations and then have the parent role-play those responses. However, it is important to acknowledge that every possible sexual question or scenario cannot be anticipated. Rather, parents should practice a general response approach that sets a calm, open, and positive tone for potential parent-child interactions around complex sexual issues.

Special Obstacles Faced by Parents of Sexually Abused Children. Due to their avoidance and/or abuse-related distress, some sexually abused children may be uncomfortable receiving sex education. Sex education, however, is critical for sexually abused children, and thus neither the therapist nor the parents should accept the child's avoidance. Rather, the therapist and parents should work together to formulate a plan to present the sex education material in a gradual and less anxiety-provoking way. Indeed, with such an anxious and avoidant child, the sex education component of treatment is best conceptualized as one aspect of the overall gradual exposure process.

Personal Safety Skills. The therapist also should involve the parent in providing training to the child regarding personal safety skills. This training may be incorporated in education regarding sexuality, as the child learns to distinguish between healthy appropriate sexuality and sexual abuse. Often this training can be presented during early joint parent-child sessions. The therapist should be particularly careful to prepare the parent for any training that may focus specifically on how the child might respond to inappropriate behaviors on the part of a perpetrator who is a family member and thus may have future contact with the child. Details regarding personal safety skills training are provided in the child intervention chapter.

❑ **Behavior Management Skills:
Understanding Your Child's Behaviors**

Nonoffending parents of sexually abused children are often frightened and disturbed by the changes they see in their children's behaviors. They may fear that these behavioral changes reflect permanent scars that will damage their children's chances of having a healthy, happy adult adjustment. Clearly, the cognitive coping strategies described earlier can help parents dispute these dysfunctional thoughts. However, parents can also benefit from understanding how their children's abuse-related behavior problems developed, while learning skills that will help them to effectively respond to these difficulties.

The sections that follow conceptualize the development and maintenance of children's abuse-related symptoms and behaviors using a social learning model. This model, easily presented to parents, demystifies the development of abuse-related symptoms, such as inappropriate sexual behaviors and abuse-related fears, by placing them in the same context as more typical positive and negative child behaviors. Parents are often relieved to learn that abuse-related behaviors are learned in the same way that other child behaviors are learned and, like other problem behaviors, they can be unlearned. Most important, the therapist emphasizes that parents can play a powerful role in helping their children to develop or to increase the frequency of healthy prosocial behaviors that may replace the problematic behaviors they have developed in response to the abuse.

Although parents are often anxious for immediate solutions to their children's problem behaviors, it is important to take it step by step, presenting the social learning model from which solutions for many different problem behaviors can be derived. Simply offering parents techniques for handling the immediate problem will undermine their ability to effectively apply these methods to other current as well as future behavior problems. The sections below describe the model as it might be presented to nonoffending parents of sexually abused children. This is the foundation from which parents will learn to better understand the development of their children's problem behaviors as well as the influence parental responses may have on the maintenance and/or diminution of these problems.

ENGAGING PARENTS IN BEHAVIOR MANAGEMENT TRAINING

Resistant Parents

Parents vary considerably in their responsiveness to behavior management training. Some parents may find it difficult to accept this kind of basic parenting advice. They may point out that they use the same parenting strategies that their parents used and they turned out alright. Other parents may feel that they have more wisdom and parenting experience than the therapist does. It is important not to take this sort of criticism personally, but rather to focus on the parents' desire to help their sexually abused child. It is useful for the therapist to acknowledge and praise those things that the parent, in fact, does very well (e.g., use of praise, consistent follow-through). However, at the same time, the therapist should point out that most parents are not prepared for the discovery that their child has been sexually abused. This places the child at higher risk for developing behavioral difficulties. Thus, although they may have good solid parenting skills, they may need to sharpen these skills in order to prevent any difficulties that the sexually abused child might be prone to develop.

Parents Who Lack Confidence

Parents who feel insecure about their parenting abilities may not feel capable of managing their sexually abused children's behaviors and serving as a therapeutic resource for their children. For these parents it may be very reassuring to know that the therapist is meeting with their children for individual sessions as well. Interestingly, we have found that some parents greatly underestimate their skills. In fact, they may use many appropriate behavioral methods but tend to be inconsistent because of their lack of confidence. When these parents begin to absorb social learning principles that support their natural parenting instincts, their confidence and consistency often improve dramatically. Thus, even when parents seem to be effective in managing their children's behaviors, it never hurts to help them develop a parenting philosophy that will build their confidence and guide their practices in the future.

Establishing Reasonable Expectations for Parents

It also is important to recognize that many parenting habits stem from childhood experiences with our own parents, and, therefore, may be quite ingrained. Thus, it is important to encourage all parents to have reasonable expectations for themselves. They should not expect to break ingrained parenting habits overnight. These are habits that may be as difficult to break as smoking and nail biting. Parents should be encouraged to take pride in their willingness to critically examine their current parenting responses. Indeed, when parents are able to consider alternative and more effective responses to children's behaviors, they are on their way to making significant parenting changes.

Responding to Abuse-Related Behavior Problems

Many nonoffending parents feel very protective and sympathetic toward their children following a disclosure of sexual abuse. Although these feelings are natural, they may interfere with parents' abilities to effectively respond to their children's behavioral difficulties. In fact, when parents attribute problem behaviors (e.g., angry outbursts, fears, sexualized behaviors) specifically to the sexual abuse, they may be more tolerant of these behaviors and also may inadvertently reinforce their maintenance over time. It is, therefore, important to emphasize that although a behavior may have developed in response to the sexual abuse, there may not be a direct link to the abuse each and every time the problem behavior occurs. Often the consequences experienced by children in the present best explain why they continue to exhibit abuse-related difficulties long after the abuse has ended. Furthermore, the therapist should communicate to parents that not all behavioral problems in abused children are necessarily related to the abuse. Many children develop behavior problems that are independent of any abuse experiences they may have had.

Formats for Presenting Behavior Management Training

When parent training is initiated, we often recommend that parents simultaneously begin reading a basic parent training book such as *Families: Applications of Social Learning to Family Life*, by Gerald Patterson (1975), or *SOS! Help for Parents*, by Lynn Clark (1985). The skills reviewed in these books are derived from the social learning model, are supported by empirical research, and are applicable to all children, abused or nonabused. Parenting skills may best be presented in an interactive format rather than a lecture mode. Thus, it helps to pose frequent questions, while also eliciting detailed examples of parent-child interactions. This will allow the therapist to tailor the information to the clients' particular circumstances. Parents may be most responsive if principles are presented using the examples they provide. Throughout this section, suggestions are offered for questions and exercises that might encourage a collaborative approach. In general, it is advisable to teach the basic parenting skills before jumping ahead to tackling the child's most serious abuse-related difficulties. Described below are some of the essential parenting concepts therapists will want to convey to nonoffending parents in the early stages of parent training.

INTRODUCING PARENTS TO BEHAVIOR MANAGEMENT

Children learn from all of their experiences; good experiences, bad experiences, even sexually abusive experiences. Many child behaviors, both the ones we like and the ones we do not like, are the result of learning. Children learn behavior in various places and from various people, including, perhaps, the perpetrator of the abuse. Learned behaviors that are problematic, however, can be unlearned and replaced with more positive behaviors. Fortunately, children are learning and changing constantly, and as a result they are often quite resilient following traumatic events.

It is important for the therapist to emphasize that parents cannot shield their children from all of life's difficulties, nor would they want to. In fact, an overprotected child may not experience many significant childhood difficulties but may be fearful nonetheless due to lack of confidence in coping with problems. Such a child would be poorly prepared to deal with the struggles we all face as adults. Clearly, every parent would prefer that their children not experience sexual abuse. However, most individuals experience some significant traumas during childhood, and those traumas cannot be erased. In fact, efforts to do that, to forget or suppress childhood traumas, seem to result in less successful adjustment in the long run. Thus, the sexual abuse crisis may represent an important opportunity for parents to help their children learn invaluable coping skills for the future.

Parents generally have more influence than anyone in shaping their children's behaviors. Children's behaviors are most significantly influenced by their parents' current behaviors and responses. Without realizing it, parents are constantly teaching their children. Sometimes the teaching is deliberate, for example, teaching a child to ride a bicycle; other times, it may be inadvertent. In actuality, children are constantly learning from the interactions they have with others, especially parents.

Therapists may best help parents respond to their children's behavior problems effectively by offering a model for understanding how children learn both adaptive and maladaptive behaviors. This model not only will provide parents with an understanding of how abuse-related behaviors are learned but also will offer them hope that these problem behaviors can be unlearned and replaced with more adaptive behaviors.

MECHANISMS OF LEARNING

The therapist may introduce the social learning model by describing three mechanisms of learning: observation, association, and consequences. It is important to emphasize that these three mechanisms explain not only the development of abuse-related behaviors but also how children learn both positive and negative behaviors in general. Thus, when describing how each of these learning mechanisms work, it is useful to provide examples of both abuse-related and nonabuse-related behaviors.

Observation

Observational learning is a process that goes on almost continuously in the lives of children. However, parents are often unaware of the degree to which their children are observing and imitating parental behavior. The therapist may help parents recognize how much children learn through observing parents by posing the following questions.

What kinds of helpful, friendly, or positive behaviors has your child learned from observing you?

What kinds of negative or inappropriate behaviors has your child learned from observing you?

These questions often lead to amusing and sometimes very revealing discussions that are intended to help parents recognize how natural it is for children to imitate what they observe.

> *Example:* A 4-year-old child is drawing in preschool class when the teacher points out that he has accidentally drawn off the paper and on the table. Imitating his father's language, the child responds, "Shoot, I'm off my game today." The child goes on to explain, "That's what my dad says when he messes up while he is playing golf."

After realizing how readily children imitate behaviors, parents may find it less frightening to acknowledge that sexually abused children learn behaviors and language as a result of their observations during the abusive interactions as well. At this point, parents may be encouraged to identify behaviors that they think their child learned from observing the perpetrator of the abuse.

It is also important to point out to parents that in addition to behaviors, children learn cognitive and affective coping styles through observation. Parents, in fact, may be reminded that they have been encouraged to work on their own coping skills so that they can model more effective coping responses for their children.

Association

Association refers to learning as a result of respondent conditioning. The therapist may describe this process by offering examples of how children's behavioral reactions are sometimes prompted by the associations they have learned. From very early on, children recognize that certain things are linked or connected.

> *Example:* A very young child may learn to associate Mom putting on her coat with Mom leaving for work. A child who's experiencing separation anxiety may then become upset and have a temper tantrum each time Mom puts on her coat.

Again, it is helpful for parents to identify behaviors that their children exhibit as a result of associations they have learned. Some of these associations may lead to problem behaviors like the tantrums described above, whereas others may lead to productive behaviors. For example, a child may touch a hot stove and feel pain. As a result of learning the association between hot stoves and pain, the child may learn the adaptive behavior of avoiding hot stoves. After the parent is able to identify nonabuse-related behaviors the child learned through association, the therapist should describe how learning through association also applies to the experience of sexual abuse.

> *Example*: A child is sexually abused in the bathtub by her father. She experiences anxiety as well as physical discomfort during the abusive experiences. Over time, the child begins to associate abusive interactions with taking a bath. The mere thought of having to take a bath begins to elicit feelings of anxiety and discomfort. Thus, while it may be natural for this child to avoid having her father give her a bath, the child begins to avoid taking baths altogether because of the association between the bath and the abusive interactions.

As this example demonstrates, sexually abused children may suffer feelings of anxiety, shame, embarrassment, anger, or pain during an abusive experience. These feelings often do not go away after the abuse and may generalize to things associated with the sexual abuse that are not in themselves harmful, such as bathtubs, darkness, men, and talking about the abuse. The therapist can help parents to identify any maladaptive associations the child formed as a result of the abuse by asking about any new fears the child is experiencing or activities or objects the child has begun avoiding since the abusive experience. If the parent identifies areas of fear or avoidance, the therapist and parent should work together to try to identify the specific abuse-related stimuli associated with the child's emotional distress. Subsequently, the therapist and parents can help the child to disconnect these associations by gently exposing the child to the harmless things he or she fears, such as bathing, darkness, trustworthy men, and calm discussions of the abuse. Furthermore, sexually abused children can learn to replace global fears that are not helpful, with specific and realistic warning signals of potential abuse, such as not-OK touch and/or inappropriate sexual remarks.

Consequences

The consequences that follow a behavior influence whether or not the behavior is likely to happen again through the learning process of operant conditioning. When parents respond to children's positive behaviors with praise, children are likely to repeat those behaviors. However, parents sometimes inadvertently encourage children's negative behaviors with reinforcing consequences such as negative attention.

> *Example:* A parent is supermarket shopping when her child begins to yell for candy. The parent initially hesitates but eventually responds by giving the child candy in order to quiet him. This parent has inadvertently taught the child that if you yell loud and long enough, you will get candy. As a result of the child's success in obtaining candy, he is likely to yell for candy again.

After offering several examples of how children learn from both positive and negative consequences, the therapist may ask the parents to share examples of how they have encouraged positive behaviors and how they may have inadvertently reinforced negative behaviors. The therapist should describe how abuse-related behaviors that may have been learned through observation or association may subsequently be maintained by the reinforcing consequences they achieve in the child's current environment.

> *Example*: A child learned to expose his penis to others by observing the perpetrator. After the abuse is discovered and the child no longer has contact with the perpetrator, he continues to expose himself. Each time he does this, his parents get excited and lecture him at length about his behavior. The parents are, in fact, inadvertently encouraging the repetition of the behavior by providing reinforcing consequences in the form of increased parental attention.

Consequences That Motivate Child Behaviors. Many different consequences encourage and maintain children's positive and negative behaviors. The consequences that children aim to achieve when engaging in problem behaviors are generally reasonable ones. It is their means of achieving these consequences that are sometimes problematic. Therefore, it is important for children to learn healthy

prosocial means of satisfying their natural desires for these consequences. Once the consequences children desire are identified,
parents can be assisted in developing a plan that will discourage
negative means and encourage more positive means of achieving the
desired consequences.

The therapist may assist parents in identifying the consequences
their children desire by reviewing the types of consequences children
typically seek. Knowing what motivates a negative behavior will
enable the parent to alter the reinforcing consequences as well as to
identify an appropriate positive behavior that may replace the negative behavior. What follows is one way to view the types of things
that motivate many child behaviors and is based on the work of
Durand (1990). Therapists may draw from the following information
to describe the four types of motivating consequences for parents.

1. *Attention* may be the consequence a child is seeking when
   engaging in entertaining behaviors as well as acting out behaviors. Children particularly want parental attention because
   they love their parents so much. Indeed, parents are the most
   important people in children's lives. Moreover, children seem
   to prefer negative attention (i.e., yelling, lecturing, etc.) to no
   attention or unpredictable attention. In fact, parental attention
   is probably the most powerful motivator and reinforcer of a
   young child's behavior. It is therefore important to teach
   children healthy ways to predictably obtain positive parental
   attention.

2. *Escape* is the consequence children are often motivated by when
   they engage in avoidance behaviors. When children fear
   the dark, school, certain people, or other stimuli, they may
   engage in a variety of behaviors that allow them to escape
   contact with those anxiety-provoking stimuli. The child is
   motivated to avoid the negative feelings associated with these
   stimuli. By exposing the child to the feared stimuli in a safe
   environment, the child learns to tolerate and cope with these
   feelings. For example, a child is most likely to overcome a fear
   of dogs through gradual but repeated exposures to friendly
   dogs. In a similar way, sexually abused children may overcome

their fears of talking about the abuse through their participation in gradual exposure to calm discussions of the abuse. With repeated exposures to discussions of the abuse, children's distress levels diminish (i.e., the feared discussion elicits less and less distress).

3. *Feeling good* is a commonly desired consequence that motivates many positive behaviors, such as hugging a friend, as well as negative behaviors, such as sniffing glue. Masturbation is another behavior that is often motivated by the desire to feel good. However, sexually abused children who masturbate in public may be motivated not only by feeling good but by the attention they receive. Compulsive masturbation, on the other hand, may be motivated by a desire to escape the disturbing thoughts and memories sexually abused children experience. Thus, it is very important to examine the quality and pattern of the behavior in order to determine the motivation underlying it.

4. *Control* is a consequence that children desire from a surprisingly early age. Control may be achieved through negative behaviors such as noncompliant behaviors, as well as positive independent behaviors. Following a disclosure, abused children may experience a heightened desire to have things "their way," in order to regain the control that was denied them during the abuse. Parents can encourage children to achieve a sense of control by giving them opportunities to make choices, exercise independence, and take on responsibilities that are age appropriate. These positive independent behaviors can replace negative child behaviors that are also motivated by a desire for control or independence.

Antecedents, Behaviors, and Consequences. It is natural for children to seek any one of the above consequences. Thus, we cannot expect a child to give up a negative behavior that achieves a desired consequence until we have taught him another, more positive, and equally predictable means of achieving that consequence. The particular function a problem behavior serves for the child can best be understood by examining the child's behavior patterns in the setting in which it occurs. This may be done by having the parent describe in detail the *antecedents, behaviors, and consequences* of the behavior as it happens in the context of real life. The therapist should explain that *antecedents* refers to environmental events that may increase the potential for problem behaviors to occur (e.g., child is overtired; parent is arguing with spouse, etc.). *Behaviors* refers to the problem behaviors being examined. *Consequences* refers to events that follow the problem behavior, particularly parental responses (e.g., hitting, scolding, discussions). The therapist may use the antecedents, behaviors, and consequences (ABC) format to record examples the parents have generated on a chalkboard or sheet of paper. In this way, the parents and therapist can examine different episodes of the same problem behaviors to identify the patterns of antecedents and consequences that contribute to the child's behavior. An example of how this is done is described in Box 5.10.

ENCOURAGING ADAPTIVE BEHAVIORS

Parents are often unaware of the many subtle consequences that influence their children's behaviors. Most parents think of rewards in terms of tangible items such as money, prizes, and ice cream, and punishment in terms of scolding, yelling, and spanking. These consequences often do not have the intended effects, nor are they as powerful as consequences that are social in nature. Social consequences such as parental attention, smiles, hugs, and/or involvement tend to be much less expensive and more available than tangible rewards, and they are much more pleasant to use than coercive methods such as threats and demands. It is, therefore, useful to help parents become more aware and deliberate regarding their use of social consequences in encouraging positive adaptive behaviors.

Inadequate Attention for Positive Behaviors

Attention may be the most powerful consequence parents can use in influencing their children's behaviors. Children seek and enjoy attention. For some children, however, the most predictable way for them to get attention is to engage in negative behaviors, which parents respond to with excited, angry, negative attention. Unfor-

---

BOX 5.10

Case Example: Using the ABC Format
to Analyze Behaviors

When working with a mother who complained that her 5-year-old son, Michael, constantly interrupted her when she talked on the phone, the therapist encouraged her to use the ABC format to analyze the behavior pattern by writing antecedents, behaviors, and consequences on a piece of paper, as follows:

Antecedents	Behaviors	Consequences
Mother begins talking on telephone	Interrupting telephone conversations	Mother frequently stops talking on telephone to scold Michael, finally hanging up in frustration to yell at Michael

After analyzing the behavior pattern, the mother was able to see that by stopping to scold Michael and getting off the phone, she was giving him the consequence he desired, her attention, and thus was inadvertently maintaining his negative behavior. Moreover, she realized that she never praised Michael when he did not interrupt her on the phone. She was, in fact, ignoring the positive behavior and attending to the negative behavior.

---

tunately, positive behaviors may not get attention from parents in a predictable and/or consistent manner. Many parents today are preoccupied with numerous external stressors and use the time when children are engaged in positive behaviors to take care of business (e.g., chores, phone calls, job related duties). As a result, parents may inadvertently ignore positive child behaviors. Even when a parent does acknowledge a child's positive behavior with praise, often the parent's positive response is much less dramatic and exciting than the negative parental response the child receives following an inappropriate behavior.

The tendency to ignore children's appropriate behaviors may be exacerbated in the aftermath of a child sexual abuse discovery, when nonoffending parents may be preoccupied with the many pressing concerns raised by an abuse investigation (e.g., protection, shelter, separation, legal proceedings). This may inadvertently lead children to act out in order to regain their parents' attention. Other nonoffending parents may become overly attentive to and protective of their sexually abused children. Out of concern, they may find themselves focusing on and inadvertently reinforcing their children's abuse-related behavioral difficulties.

It is not unusual for parents to be focused on their children's problem behaviors, particularly when they are seeking help for those problems. However, it is important to remind parents that sexual abuse does not completely transform children and eliminate all of their positive qualities. Their children's positive qualities may simply be overshadowed by the abuse-related difficulties they are experiencing.

Refocusing Attention on Positive Behaviors

Due to the natural parental tendency to focus on children's problem behaviors, it is often useful to begin behavior management training with a skill that requires parents to refocus their attention on more positive behaviors. Learning to effectively use praise or positive attention is an important skill, particularly for parents who rely heavily on negative methods (e.g., threats, scolding, spanking, evoking guilt) to influence their children's behaviors. In addition, when parents develop skills in using positive social attention, they often see immediate increases in positive child behaviors. This not only helps parents gain a greater awareness of their potential influence on their children, but it often inspires greater confidence in the treatment approach in general.

Praise essentially helps children learn how to get what they want (i.e., attention, control, escape, good feelings) through positive behaviors. When children learn there are things they can do to predictably receive positive attention, they are likely to engage in those behaviors more frequently. This in turn leads them to be less reliant on negative behaviors to predictably get parental attention.

Most parents can benefit from learning to use positive attention and praise more effectively. Even parents who report that they give their children a great deal of attention may not be doing so in a way that leads to increases in positive behaviors. For example, the parental attention and praise may be given inconsistently, rather than being contingent on the child's behavior. These parents may be encouraged; for them, training will simply be a process of learning the most effective ways and times to provide positive attention, while identifying and minimizing their tendencies to provide negative attention. Other parents may be more resistant to using praise. Some parents report that praise seems artificial and too simplistic to counteract their child's significant difficulties. Other parents insist that *their* parents used strict discipline to get them to behave. Those parents may have received little praise themselves during childhood. For these parents, learning to praise may be a difficult process that will require the therapist to shape and model this parenting skill.

Assessing Parents' Use of Praise

To assess parents' current use of praise and positive attention, the therapist may ask parents to do one of the following exercises:

- List as many positive behaviors exhibited by their child as possible
- Estimate the number of times they praised their child today
- Describe the last time they praised their child in as much detail as possible

This information may help the therapist to identify particular "praising errors," while also gauging the degree to which these skills will need to be developed and practiced before moving on to further skill development. Some parents will need some help in identifying small positive things that their children are already doing. No matter how troubled a child is, the therapist should be able to elicit from the parent a positive behavior already in the child's repertoire that may be encouraged.

Guidelines for Using Praise

To help parents develop greater skill in the use of contingent positive attention, the therapist can outline several important guidelines to follow when offering positive attention in the form of praise.

- Praise the desired behavior *immediately* after it occurs. Positive reinforcement tends to be more powerful the closer the temporal relationship is between the behavior and the positive consequences.
- Praise the desired behavior as *predictably* as possible. When first attempting to increase the desired behavior, it is best to offer predictable praise each and every time the behavior occurs. After some time, however, praise for well-established behavior need only be intermittent.
- Praise the desired behavior using *specific* language. When shaping a desired behavior, parents should be taught to be as direct and as clear as possible regarding the behavior they would like to encourage. For example, "Johnny, I like how you shared your toys" is preferable to "Good boy, Johnny."
- Praise should be *purely positive*. Encourage parents to avoid the use of negative tags, such as, "You played so quietly when I was on the phone, why don't you do that all the time?" The negative tag, "Why don't you do that all the time?" inadvertently focuses on the problem behavior, thereby reducing the effectiveness of the praise and potentially reinforcing the negative behavior rather than the positive behavior.
- Praise the desired behavior as *enthusiastically* as possible. Parents often inadvertently reinforce negative behaviors with loud, exaggerated responses. Parents should be encouraged to respond to positive behaviors with similarly loud and exaggerated displays of positive attention.

Building Parents' Skills in Using Praise

The skill-building process begins when the therapist encourages the parent to role-play or practice the praising skills in vivo with the child in the waiting room. For example, the parent may be encouraged to praise the child for picking up the toys in the waiting room as requested. This exercise allows the therapist to provide parents with some constructive feedback before parents practice praising the agreed-upon child behavior at home. The therapist may also model how to praise by offering the child specific, purely positive, and highly enthusiastic praise for a positive behavior exhibited.

For homework, parents should be encouraged to identify one simple positive behavior that they would like to see their child engage in more frequently. The behavior chosen should be exhibited by the child occasionally and should reflect appropriate expectations for the child's age. It is preferable to begin with simple positive behaviors, such as playing quietly, sharing toys, or helping with dishes. Throughout the week, parents should actively look for the agreed-upon behavior. This is a shaping process that requires parents to praise approximations of the desired behavior. Parents should not wait for the behavior to be performed to perfection. For example, it is useful to praise efforts to set the table rather than waiting until the table is set perfectly. Each time the behavior occurs, parents should be encouraged to offer praise that is immediate, predictable, specific, purely positive, and highly enthusiastic. When reviewing homework the following week, the ABC format may be used to discuss instances when the desired behavior occurred. Parents can then critique their own efforts to praise using the guidelines offered above. Through the process of "shaping," parents will ultimately learn to encourage more complex behaviors such as getting good grades, cleaning the bedroom, and resolving conflicts with siblings effectively. These complex behaviors will need to be broken down into small steps so that parents can learn to reinforce each small step the child makes toward the development of complicated behaviors.

ALTERING CHILDREN'S MALADAPTIVE BEHAVIORS

Once parents have begun to see increases in their children's positive behaviors as a result of their deliberate efforts to use praise and other social consequences (e.g., hugs, smiles, conversation), parents will be ready to focus on children's maladaptive behaviors. In order to gain parental confidence in the process, it helps to tackle relatively minor behavior problems first, before taking on more serious difficulties. When parents experience some success in eliminating minor behavioral difficulties (e.g., whining, yelling, mild temper tantrums), they will be motivated to apply the same skills to more difficult problems.

The Application Of Differential Attention To Angry Outbursts

The next few sections will outline the use of differential attention As It Applies To The Treatment Of Angry Outbursts Or Temper Tantrums In Sexually Abused children. The skills and principles discussed, however, are applicable to a wide range of behavioral difficulties exhibited by both abused and nonabused children. Thus, it is important for the therapist to emphasize that the goal of this work is to provide parents with skills to effectively manage not only current behavior problems exhibited by the sexually abused child but also any future behavior problems that the abused child or siblings may display.

Angry Outbursts. Many parents respond ineffectively to their children's angry outbursts. This may be particularly true of parents who believe that their child's anger is linked to the experience of sexual abuse. Understandably, parents of sexually abused children may feel that their child's angry outbursts are justified given the abusive experience. Parents may believe that by throwing angry temper tantrums, the child is releasing pent-up emotions associated with the abuse. Not surprisingly, parents who link the angry outbursts to the abuse in these ways may find it difficult to discipline their child for this type of behavior.

Although the therapist may validate the parents' view that their child's angry outbursts may be linked to the abuse and thus be justifiable, it is important to stress that the child's current means of expressing anger is maladaptive. In fact, it is likely that a child who exhibits repeated angry outbursts and temper tantrums will develop significant difficulties with respect to social interactions, family relationships, and school performance. Moreover, there is considerable evidence that those who cope with anger by lashing out may not only suffer psychosocial difficulties but may increase their risk of developing significant physical health problems (e.g., high blood pressure, cardiac difficulties, and other stress-related ill-nesses).

In general, behavior that is violent in nature, even if it is symbolic, should not be encouraged. There is no evidence that punching a pillow or a bobo doll reduces anyone's anger. In fact, the reverse appears to be true. When children are encouraged to act out their anger in these ways, these violent behaviors tend to increase and may generalize from hitting pillows to hitting walls to hitting other children. In light of this information, parents may be more receptive to teaching their children healthier methods of expressing anger, while minimizing their children's reliance on dysfunctional means of expressing anger (e.g., tantrums, hitting). It is important to be clear from the start that the objective of therapy is not to suppress the child's anger. Rather, parents may be reminded that their child will be learning to label and express his or her negative emotions more effectively during individual sessions.

Differential Attention: Positive Reinforcement and Active Ignoring. Therapists should encourage parents to model, shape, and reinforce appropriate expressions of anger. Some parents will first need to learn more effective anger control and coping skills themselves before they can be effective models. Once parents are successful in expressing and managing their own anger effectively, they should be taught to use differential attention to encourage their child's adaptive means of expressing anger while discouraging maladaptive means.

Positive Reinforcement for Appropriate Expression of Anger. The first step in teaching parents to use differential attention to shape ap-propriate expressions of anger is to teach parents to identify and reinforce children's attempts to express anger and other emotions in productive ways. This may simply mean encouraging their children to share their feelings. Interestingly, although a parent may be con-vinced that his or her child is constantly angry, that same parent may never have heard the child simply state, "I'm feeling really mad or frustrated because . . . " In fact, parents who have their hands full coping with their children's acting out or angry behaviors often spend hours talking to their children about these maladaptive be-haviors, while more appropriate expressions of emotions are inad-vertently ignored or given minimal attention. This pattern will need to be reversed before any strategies for diminishing the angry outbursts can be effectively implemented.

Many children do not know how to express anger appropriately. With such children, the therapist and parents should work together to teach them a new repertoire of mechanisms for coping with anger and other negative emotions. These strategies may include talking about their feelings; writing a letter or story expressing their emotions; drawing a picture; or engaging in activities such as exercising, relaxation, or breathing techniques. Parents should reinforce such behaviors by empathizing and offering immediate, specific, purely positive, and enthusiastic praise for healthy responses to anger-provoking situations.

Identifying Consequences Motivating Maladaptive Expressions of Anger. Next, parents should be asked to examine the patterns associated with their child's maladaptive expressions of anger, using the antecedents, behaviors, and consequences approach described earlier. Starting with the most recent episode, it is useful to examine several episodes of angry outbursts so that the consequence(s) the child achieves through these outbursts may be identified. As with any other behavior problem, it is important to determine whether the consequences achieved by the outbursts provide the child with attention, control, escape, and/or good feelings. This information will help the parent identify a replacement behavior that will allow the child to achieve the desired consequences in more socially appropriate ways.

Angry tantrums, in fact, may be motivated by several different types of consequences. For some sexually abused children, angry outbursts may achieve the consequence of escaping from situations in which they are reminded of the abuse (e.g., therapy sessions, going to bed, taking a bath). Such outbursts may be best addressed by encouraging children to develop other means of expressing negative feelings. In addition, children's participation in the gradual exposure and processing sessions may help them overcome the fear that may be underlying their escape-motivated tantrums.

Angry outbursts also are frequently motivated by social consequences such as parental attention. Parents of sexually abused children may inadvertently reinforce angry outbursts by responding with a great deal of sympathetic attention in the form of "encounter discussions," comforting hugs, and so on. Other parents may become exasperated with the repetitiveness and the seemingly unprovoked nature of the angry outbursts and respond with a great deal of negative attention in the form of yelling or stern lectures. Attention, whether it is positive or negative, is reinforcing to young children, especially when the attention is provided by parents or other primary caretakers. Children quickly learn which behaviors receive attention most predictably, and they repeat those behaviors. Although children would not necessarily report that their parents' yelling is pleasing to them, their behavior patterns reveal that if negative attention (e.g., yelling) is more predictably achieved than positive attention, they will work for negative attention.

A third consequence that may motivate angry outbursts is the sense of control the child may achieve from the outburst. If the child is able to use the angry outburst to elicit a certain response from the parent (e.g., yelling or giving in to the child's request), the child may achieve a sense of control through the tantrum. Furthermore, if the parent responds to the child's outburst in a dramatic way, the parent may inadvertently encourage the child to feel he or she is in control because the parent appears so out of control.

Positive or negative attention is reinforcing to young children.

Parents may find it difficult to believe they are inadvertently encouraging tantrums or outbursts. They may believe that scolding or yelling, for example, is effective because the outburst or tantrum stops for the moment. However, it is important to point out that yelling does not stop children from repeating the behavior in the future. Therapists may help parents recognize this problem by asking them if they find themselves yelling about the same problem behaviors over and over again. This provides parents with evidence that yelling is not working to eliminate the problem behavior. Yelling, in fact, often provides two consequences children are motivated to achieve: attention and control. Parental yelling also tends to be a powerful reinforcer because in many cases it is so predictable. Indeed, when a parent says, "My child really knows how to push my buttons," the parent is indicating that the child really knows how to predictably get negative attention from the parent. Unfortunately, this same child may not know how to predictably obtain positive parental attention with adaptive behaviors. Thus, it is extremely important to provide consistent and predictable attention for the desired adaptive behaviors that will replace the maladaptive ones.

Active Ignoring. The next step in using differential attention to reduce children's angry outbursts is to implement active ignoring. This process requires parents to withdraw the reinforcing consequences that their child is experiencing following a temper tantrum or outburst by actively ignoring the outburst. It is important to acknowledge that this process will be difficult as it requires parents to break ingrained habits (e.g., yelling) and/or withdraw attention (e.g., comforting hugs) that they believe their child needs and deserves. Thus, the therapist will need to emphasize that by learning to actively ignore the child's maladaptive behaviors and praising a positive replacement behavior, parents will be teaching their child a more adaptive means of expressing needs.

It is important to emphasize that active ignoring will not work alone but should be used in combination with positive reinforcement. In addition, parents should be warned that the targeted problem behavior often increases temporarily when active ignoring is initiated. This temporary increase is often referred to as an "extinction burst." It is important for parents to continue to actively ignore through the extinction burst to avoid inadvertently reinforcing a more exaggerated version of the original problem behavior. The potential for an extinction burst should be discussed in advance, as parents may question the soundness of the therapeutic suggestions if they experience unexpected increases in their child's problem behaviors. Active ignoring should not be attempted if parents believe the tantrum behavior has the potential to become violent. In such cases, other intervention strategies, such as time out combined with predictable positive consequences, may be more appropriate. Guidelines for time out will be described in the sections to follow.

Here's how a therapist might present an example of an extinction burst.

Your child is used to getting negative attention from you for having a temper tantrum. When you begin to actively ignore the tantrums, he will get louder and louder at first, trying to get you to respond in your usual way. Your child may not understand the change in your response and may wonder if your eyesight or hearing has gone bad. However, if you can continue to ignore the tantrums, he will learn that it does not get him the negative attention any more, and the behavior will decrease.

To build their skills using differential attention, parents may be given the following homework assignment:

- Shape and reinforce the adaptive replacement behavior agreed upon (e.g., appropriate expression of feelings).
- Wait for the identified maladaptive behavior to occur and actively ignore it.
- Recognize and be prepared to discuss their interactions with their child using the ABC format.

This homework may need to be repeated over several sessions until parents master the use of differential attention.

Giving Effective Instructions

Although differential attention is a powerful parenting tool, there are many problem behaviors for which it is neither effective nor appropriate. For example, as indicated earlier, active ignoring should not be used with problem behaviors that have the potential to escalate into dangerous behaviors during the extinction burst. Nor should active ignoring be used with noncompliance, as such a response may only serve to reinforce noncompliant behavior. For these and other problems, parents may be encouraged to use effective instructions combined with mild punishment techniques such as time out. When parents learn to communicate with their children more effectively, they are likely to increase their children's cooperative behaviors and decrease their maladaptive behaviors.

Learning to give effective instructions may be particularly important for parents whose sexually abused children are exhibiting a great deal of noncompliance. Some sexually abused children, in an effort to regain control over their lives, exhibit increased rates of noncompliant behaviors. During the course of the sexual abuse, offenders often use guilt, bribes, threats, and/or physical force to maintain control over their victims. As a result, many sexually abused children feel they lack control over access to their own bodies, as well as over decisions about how and with whom they spend their time. However, after disclosing the abuse, the children may experience a sudden surge in their ability and desire to exert control over their environment. For some children, this need is expressed in the form of increased demanding and/or noncompliant behavior.

It is important for parents to recognize that this change may be natural and expected given the circumstances. Parents, in fact, may be encouraged to offer their children more opportunities to make choices and to engage in independent behaviors in order to encourage adaptive means of experiencing feelings of control. However, it is not healthy or reasonable for children to believe that they can be in complete control all the time. Although children's influence and control over events in their lives will increase as they grow older, even when they are adults they will have only limited control over many aspects of their lives. Thus, it is important for parents to help their children identify when it is appropriate to assert control and express their independence and when it is necessary for them to accept certain circumstances and/or comply with instructions. In order to help children distinguish between those situations, parents must develop skill and clarity in their methods of giving instructions to their children.

The effectiveness of parental communication styles, particularly with respect to their methods of giving their children instructions, may also be assessed using the ABC format. Parents may be encouraged to describe in as much detail as possible the last several times they gave their children instructions. These examples are likely to reveal some instances in which parents were successful and others in which they were unsuccessful in gaining their children's cooperation.

Using the guidelines offered in Box 5.11, parents may be encouraged to critique their own performances and identify particular areas for improvement in terms of their personal styles of communicating instructions.

After providing educational information regarding effective instructions, the therapist may describe a parent-child scenario that would compel parents to give an instruction. The parent can then role-play giving an instruction, while the therapist responds as the child might. When the parent inadvertently makes one of the errors discussed, the therapist, acting as the child, may respond negatively (e.g., taking advantage of the parent who gives instructions in the form of a question). As always, when critiquing the role play, offer positive feedback as well as some suggestions for improvement.

For homework, in addition to continuing their work with differential attention, parents may be asked to do the following:

- Examine the frequency and quality of the instructions they give their children.
- Give children effective instructions to do things parents think they would like to do (e.g., "Billy, please sit down and draw a picture with me").
- Offer effective praise for children's efforts to comply (e.g., "Billy, I really liked how you followed my instructions to sit down and draw a picture with me").

Parents are shaping compliant behavior by starting with instructions with which children are likely to comply. It is then easier in future homework assignments to move on to instructions that are less appealing.

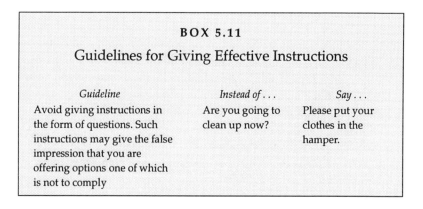

BOX 5.11

Guidelines for Giving Effective Instructions

Guideline	Instead of . . .	Say . . .
Avoid giving instructions in the form of questions. Such instructions may give the false impression that you are offering options one of which is not to comply	Are you going to clean up now?	Please put your clothes in the hamper.

BOX 5.11 *Continued*

Guideline	*Instead of . . .*	*Say . . .*
Avoid instructions that are vague and indirect. Don't expect children to read your mind.	I think you know what you're expected to do.	I expect you to finish your homework now, before you go outside to play.
Avoid guilt-inducing instructions. Such instructions are more likely to encourage your child to feel anxious/depressed than they are to lead to compliant behaviors.	If you don't clean up this mess, I'm going to have a breakdown.	Please put your paints and playthings away.
Do not expect children to stop on a dime. Like adults, children respond better if they are given a reasonable time frame (e.g., 2 to 5 minutes) within which to respond.	Go to bed right now.	After 3 more minutes of playing, it will be time to go to bed.
Keep instructions brief. For younger children, include only one behavior per instruction rather than a string of behaviors.	Pick up your toys, go finish your homework, put on your pajamas, brush your teeth, and go to bed.	Please pick up your toys. [Add other instructions later.]
When possible, instead of giving instructions to stop an inappropriate behavior, instruct your child to pursue an appropriate behavior that is incompatible with the behavior you want to stop.	Stop changing the TV channel.	Please help set the table.
Move close to child; say his or her name; maintain eye contact, using firm, positive tone of voice.	(calling from another room) Did you hear me? Are you washing your hands yet?	(walking to stand near child, making eye contact) Johnny, please wash your hands.
Do not make empty threats; rather, back up your instructions with consequences.	If you don't stop hitting your sister, you can forget your birthday party!	If you hit your sister, you will go to time out.

Time Out

Many behavior problems can be dealt with successfully using positive reinforcement, ignoring, and effective instructions. However, as we noted earlier, some negative behaviors should not be ignored, and sometimes children do not respond to instructions. In these instances, parents may need to use mild punishment techniques.

Some nonoffending parents of sexually abused children, however, abandon all forms of discipline after discovering that their child was abused. For some parents, this may stem from a belief that their child has endured enough punishment already. For others, feelings of guilt or responsibility for the abuse may interfere with their ability to discipline effectively. These issues as well as general attitudes regarding punishment should be explored before encouraging the use of the time-out procedure.

Time out from positive reinforcement is a procedure that is extremely effective for noncompliant behavior as well as other problem behaviors that cannot be ignored. It simply involves removing the child from an environment where reinforcement is available and placing the child in a designated place where no attention or gratification may be obtained. Time out is given for a short period of time (2 to 10 minutes) contingent upon the occurrence of a specified problem behavior. It is preferable to use time out initially with one repetitive problem behavior that has been identified in advance.

Because it may be difficult for some parents to use even mild forms of punishment again, it is often useful to review the advantages of using time out as opposed to other discipline practices. This review is also important for parents who continue to rely on less effective forms of discipline such as scolding, yelling, hitting, and criticizing. Box 5.12 provides an overview of the reasons for using time out.

Teaching Parents the Steps for Using Time Out. Once parents understand and have accepted the concept of time out, the steps for implementing the procedure may be outlined as follows.

1. Be positive when explaining how time out works. Tell children it is intended to help them remember a particular rule: For example, "We love you and we want to help you to remember the rule about no hitting. If you forget the rule and hit your brother, you will go to time out. You will sit in this time-out chair until you hear this timer ring."

BOX 5.12

Advantages of Time Out

The time-out procedure:

May be presented as a teaching method rather than a punishment.

Provides a response to a problem behavior that generally may be implemented immediately.

Requires only a brief amount of parent's time and minimal monitoring.

Does not require parents to think of a punishment when they are emotionally upset.

Does not require any expression of negative emotion or criticism.

Does not model unhealthy behavior as is the case with physical punishment techniques.

Does not negatively affect children's self-esteem as does the repeated use of scolding or criticism.

When implemented correctly, is more effective than punishments that are seemingly more severe.

Has been tested by scientific research and found effective.

---

2. Role-play or use dolls to show the child how time out works.

3. Start by using time out for one problem behavior or one important rule (e.g., no hitting others). Describe the problem behavior in clear, specific terms.

4. Choose a boring place for time out.

5. Every time the chosen problem behavior occurs, call time out for the problem behavior in a calm, unemotional manner.

6. Do not yell or offer additional comments when giving time out.

7. Do not yank or grip the child's arm too tightly or use force to put the child in time out.

8. Set the portable timer for 2 to 10 minutes depending on the child's age (use shorter intervals for younger or overactive children).

9. Actively ignore and withdraw all privileges from the child until he or she goes to and completes time out. When necessary, repeat a simple phrase like, "Not until you do your time out."

10. During time out, remove all attention from the child. Do not give reassurance or make eye contact. If you must check on the child, look briefly his or her way without making eye contact.

11. Do not lecture the child following time out. After the child completes time out, wait for the child to engage in the positive replacement behavior and offer specific, purely positive praise.

Do not use time out for the following behaviors: sulking, pouting, compulsive masturbation in private, fearfulness, passiveness, and restless inattentiveness. These behaviors may reflect anxious/depressive states that may not be responsive to time out.

Time out is useful for stopping behavior, not for starting behavior. Parents can use it when a child disobeys a command, but the behavior they will influence is the disobeying, not the positive behavior they had wanted the child to engage in. For example, if a child verbally refuses to put on his or her coat, the parent could place the child in time out, saying, "Time out for not following my instructions to put on your coat." To get the child to put on a coat more often when it is time to go outdoors, parents need to positively reinforce the child when he or she does so.

> *Time out is useful for stopping behavior, not for starting it.*

As is true with active ignoring, time out must be combined with the positive reinforcement of a positive behavior that can replace the problem behavior.

Potential Problems in Implementing Time Out. Because parents may have some difficulty implementing time out, it is helpful to anticipate this by outlining some of the potential problems they may encounter. Here's some language therapists might use in describing time-out problems and suggesting solutions.

> *Delays:* Tell your child that you expect him or her to go to time out immediately after you give that instruction. This rule is so important that all privileges will be denied until the child goes to time out (e.g., no TV, no snacks, no discussion). When a child refuses or delays going to time out, actively ignore him or her and/or respond to requests for privileges with a brief statement such as, "Not until you do time out."
>
> *Making noise in time out:* Ignore it and expect it to get louder before it gets quieter.
>
> *Making a mess in time out:* Tell your child that he or she will have to clean up any messes before time out is over. Then follow through and require him or her to stay until the mess is cleaned up.

Escaping time out: Place the child back in time out for the remainder of the time, but do not turn it into a game of tag or a physical struggle. If your child will not return to time out without a physical struggle, inform the child that he or she will have no privileges until he or she returns and completes the time out. As was described above for the problem of delays, if the child refuses to return to time out, actively ignore the child and withhold privileges such as television, outdoor play, snacks, and conversations for a period of 10 minutes. If at the end of the 10 minutes the child has not returned to time out, give the child a choice of completing the time out or accepting a more severe consequence, such as the loss of television for the rest of the day or the cancellation of a planned outing or activity.

Not leaving time out after the bell rings: This is equivalent to sulking after time out. The child's motivation is often to make the parent feel guilty and offer the child special attention. It is important in all cases after time out to give the child no more or no less attention than usual. As soon as the bell rings, your attention-giving behavior should return to normal with positive attention provided contingent upon the occurrence of positive behaviors.

For homework, parents may begin by spending a week offering consistent, specific, immediate, and purely positive praise for the positive behavior that has been identified as a replacement for the problem behavior. Simultaneously, the parents should eliminate any reinforcing consequences (e.g., yelling, lectures) that the child has been receiving for the problem behavior. Next, parents may present or review the time-out procedure with their child, emphasizing that initially it will be used for only one target behavior. The target, however, may be a class of behaviors such as not following parents' instructions. It is important that the parents be clear and specific in defining the target behavior for the child. For example, if the target behavior is not following parental instructions, the parent should explain to the child, "Whenever I say to you, 'I'm giving you an instruction now,' that is a signal to you that you must follow my instruction. If you do not follow the instruction, you will go to time out to help you remember that rule the next time." Parents may then implement time out, making every effort to follow the steps outlined in session, while noting errors made along the way.

When problem behaviors occur that are not identified time-out behaviors, parents may use differential attention if possible or other negative consequences as described below.

Alternative Negative Consequences

In several situations, other types of negative consequences may be used effectively. For example, if an inappropriate behavior occurs that cannot be ignored but that has not been identified as a target behavior for time out, then alternative negative consequences may be used. In addition, parents of older children (i.e., 10 years and older) who have never previously used time out may find it easier to initiate the use of alternative consequences rather than time out. As is true with time out, any negative consequences should be applied as soon as possible following the inappropriate behavior and should be limited in duration (typically lasting no longer than a day, at most). Parents should be reminded that negative consequences are administered as a means to change behaviors, not as punishment. Several types of negative consequences are described in the section that follows.

Natural Consequences. Natural consequences are those consequences the child would experience naturally following a problem behavior, without the parent needing to artificially create or impose the consequences. For example, the natural consequence of a child not eating dinner is that the child will be hungry late in the evening. Well-meaning parents often protect their child from experiencing the natural consequences of behavior, thus inadvertently preventing the child from learning why that behavior is not appropriate or effective. Many times, simply allowing the child to experience the natural consequence of his or her behavior is sufficient to change the problem behavior. However, there are times when it is not appropriate or possible to allow the child to experience natural consequences. For example, the natural consequence for running into the street after a ball is that the child may be hit by a car or truck. Obviously, the child cannot be allowed to experience that natural consequence. Thus, the parent must be encouraged to consider other types of consequences, described below.

Logical Consequences. When it is not possible to use natural consequences, parents should be encouraged to use logical consequences,
that is, negative consequences that are logically linked to the problem
behavior. For example, if a boy rides his bicycle outside the area
permitted by his parents, a logical consequence would be to prohibit
him from riding his bike for the rest of the day (or the next day, if the
problem behavior occurs late in the day). Logical consequences can
be described as *punishment that fits the crime.*

Behavior Penalties. Parents should be taught to consider using
behavior penalties in situations in which natural and logical consequences are not possible or appropriate. Behavior penalties are negative consequences that are not inherently related to the inappropriate
behavior. There are two primary types of behavior penalties. The first
type, work chores, are household chores that can be completed in a
brief period of time, about 5 minutes. Parents may give an older child
a work chore to complete as a consequence for an inappropriate
behavior. Patterson and Forgatch (1987) describe work chores in
detail in *Parents and Adolescents Living Together, Part 1: The Basics.*

The second type of behavior penalty is a loss of privileges, such as
using the telephone, listening to the television, stereo, or radio, riding
a bike, participating in extracurricular or social activities, and so on.
Typically, parents should be encouraged to take away only one
privilege and to take it away for a limited period of time, typically
no longer than one evening or one day. However, if a work chore is
given initially as a negative consequence and the child refuses to
complete the work chore, the parent may take away multiple
privileges until the child completes the work chore (Patterson &
Forgatch, 1987).

Reviewing Weekly Progress With Parents

In general, throughout the parenting sessions, it is important to
focus on parents' behavior changes rather than children's behaviors
from week to week. This emphasizes for parents that the expectation
is for them to make parenting changes prior to seeing any changes in
their children's behaviors. Thus, the therapist may initiate the review
of homework by asking parents to describe their efforts toward

changing their parenting style using the behavior management skills. In fact, the therapist might emphasize that children's behavioral changes generally reflect the consistency of their parents' efforts. Parents should be prepared to expect gradual improvements as well as occasional setbacks. These setbacks often can be explained by factors in the environment that influence both parent and child behaviors. For example, when parents are suddenly under a great deal of stress or are experiencing an illness, they are likely to provide less positive attention and thus children may engage in negative behaviors once again. These setbacks are generally short-lived if parents are able to return to using behavior management techniques more consistently once the stressors pass. Parents may be encouraged to view setbacks as a normal part of recovery and as opportunities to explore the antecedents and consequences that may be influencing the reoccurrence of problem behaviors.

It also is important to remind parents that the critical impact of therapy occurs not in session but at home. Parents are certainly in the best position to see that these changes are implemented at home. Finally, it may be helpful to remind parents of the wealth of research supporting the effectiveness of these techniques when they are implemented correctly. In general, it is important for therapists to be modeling the behaviors they are endorsing by shaping, praising, and focusing attention on parents' small efforts toward positive change.

SLEEPING DIFFICULTIES

Sexually abused children often suffer sleeping difficulties such as sleep refusal, frequent nighttime awakenings, fear of sleeping alone or in the dark, and/or repetitive nightmares. As readers are undoubtedly aware, many nonabused children experience these types of sleep difficulties as well. Thus, sleep problems exhibited by sexually abused children should not automatically be attributed to abuse experiences. Indeed, sleep problems are one of the most common behavioral problems with which parents of young children struggle. However, parents of sexually abused children may have particular difficulty deciding how to respond to sleep problems appropriately.

Assessment Of Sleeping Difficulties

The first step in addressing these difficulties should be to carefully assess the child's sleeping problems in terms of their nature, duration, and relationship to the sexual abuse. The therapist, together with the parents, should attempt to assess whether or not the child's sleep problem is a result of a negative association between abuse factors and the sleeping situation. For example, a child who was abused in the dark may learn to fear sleeping in the dark. Similarly, a child abused in the bedroom or during sleep in any location may then link the abusive experience with sleep. Even without such a direct association, a sexually abused child may experience increased anxiety at night regarding any concerns the child has about the abuse, such as any threats the perpetrator made. Children who have such negative associations between sleeping and abuse-related thoughts may then attempt to avoid the anxiety experienced at bedtime by altering the sleeping arrangements. For example, many children who experience anxiety about the sleep situation will develop the habit of sleeping with a nonoffending parent. Although that arrangement does temporarily alleviate the child's anxiety about sleeping, it ultimately may create further problems, because both the child and the parent may experience disrupted sleep. In such situations, the child's negative association between sleep and abuse-related thoughts must be broken in order to reduce the child's anxiety or fear regarding sleep.

Helping The Child Learn To Sleep Alone

In order to break the association between sleep and abuse-related thoughts, the therapist and parents should engage the child in cognitive coping exercises focused on disputing the thoughts producing the anxiety. For example, a child who fears sleeping alone may be thinking, "It's going to happen again. He's going to come and touch me again." The therapist and the parents can help the child to dispute that thought with a more accurate thought such as, "He's in jail now, he can't hurt me," or "My mom and the police know what happened, and they won't let him near me anymore."

Even after disputing any negative or inaccurate thoughts, some children may continue to fear sleeping alone or in the dark because their avoidance of that situation prevents them from learning that their fears are unnecessary. In such cases, the child must learn to break the maladaptive associations between anxiety and sleeping alone through behavioral means. The child must learn through experience that sleeping alone need not be feared or avoided. Other children continue to insist on sleeping with their parents long after their fears have subsided, due to the reinforcing consequences derived from cuddling with parents at night. For these children as well as more avoidant children, parents should be encouraged to use a plan developed by Ferber (1985) that applies differential attention to the treatment of sleep difficulties. It is often useful to use the ABC format to help parents examine their interactions with their child immediately prior to bedtime and in response to sleep difficulties. When parent-child interaction patterns are examined, it often becomes apparent that the child is receiving a great deal of reinforcement for fearful and/or noncompliant bedtime behavior. The following treatment approach essentially aims to turn this pattern around by providing reinforcing consequences for brave and/or compliant bedtime behavior.

Parents should explain that they will be helping the child learn to sleep in his or her bed alone. Some parents may offer the promise of a small reward (e.g., stickers) in the morning when the child sleeps in his or her bed throughout the night. Then parents should put the child to bed, saying, "I will come back to check on you. I want to see what a great job you can do of staying in your bed all by yourself." Then a parent should return in a limited, predetermined amount of time, anywhere from 2 to 10 minutes, depending on the child's level of anxiety and the parent's level of comfort in implementing this plan. Upon returning to the child's room, the parent should lavishly but briefly praise the child for staying in bed and leave the room again, promising to return in a few minutes. Subsequently, the parent should return in a somewhat longer time interval and again praise the child. This pattern should continue, with longer time intervals between the parent checks on the child, until the child falls asleep during one of the periods when the parent is out of the room. It is crucial that the child fall asleep alone in the room so that he or she forms new, more positive associations with the experience of sleeping alone.

If the child cries or calls out during this process, parents should actively ignore and stick to the plan of going into the child's room at the predetermined time intervals. Parents should be forewarned that actively ignoring their child's calls is the most difficult aspect of the plan. In addition, parents should be encouraged to praise the child excessively for staying in bed alone, perhaps providing a small reward or a breakfast celebration in the morning. It has been our experience that even sexually abused children who have slept in their parent's bed for a long period of time respond quickly and successfully to this program. Readers are referred to *Solving Your Child's Sleep Problems* (Ferber, 1985) for additional details regarding this treatment plan for sleep difficulties. The example in Box 5.13 illustrates how this treatment plan might be implemented.

Nightmares and Sleep Terrors

Another type of sleep disturbance may be exhibited by children who go to sleep alone without great difficulty, only to have their anxiety or distress regarding the sexual abuse experience disrupt their sleep with nightmares. When working with parents of such children, it is important to help the parents distinguish between nightmares and sleep terrors. Unlike nightmares, which generally occur during REM sleep in the second half of the night, sleep terrors usually occur in the first few hours after the child goes to sleep during partial awakenings from non-REM sleep. Sleep terrors are characterized by extended periods of crying, moaning, sobbing, thrashing, and screaming during which children are generally nonresponsive to parental comforting.

Not surprisingly, parents of sexually abused children often confuse sleep terrors with nightmares and assume that they are extreme reactions to the trauma of sexual abuse. However, before the age of 5 or 6, these episodes are believed to reflect the normal maturation of a child's sleep stages rather than physical or emotional problems (Ferber, 1985). When they occur after age 5 or 6, these sudden partial

wakings may be reflective of emotional struggles, and thus therapeutic work focused on helping the child cope with the underlying
anxieties should be pursued.

However, regardless of the underlying causes, children's sleep
terrors, as well as other partial arousal states (e.g., sleepwalking), are
often more troubling to parents than they are to the children. In fact,
children generally have no memory of these partial arousal states and
are often quite relaxed and able to quickly return to sleep once the
episode is over. Parents, however, may need some guidance in
managing these disruptive nighttime episodes. As a general rule, it
helps for parents to ensure that their children get sufficient sleep by
establishing bedtime and daily schedules that are as consistent as
possible. Because children are not fully awake when these episodes
occur, parents' efforts to comfort the child or extract information
about his or her dream may be unsuccessful and inappropriate.
Rather, parents should simply supervise the child until the episode
passes, so that the child does not harm himself or herself.

BOX 5.13

**Case Example: Cognitive Coping and Behavioral
Techniques Used to Treat Sleep Problems**

David is a 5-year-old boy who was sexually abused by a
neighbor. The neighbor threatened David that if he ever told
about the abuse, he would be hurt or even killed. After the
abuse began, David started experiencing sleep problems. Because of his strong resistance to going to bed, David's parents
began allowing him to sleep in their bed. When they eventually
learned of the abuse, they continued the policy, feeling that they
should provide comfort and support for David. A year later,
the perpetrator had been arrested and incarcerated. However,
David still refused to sleep alone. His parents were no longer
certain how they should best respond to this problem.

Upon hearing of this difficulty, the therapist first helped
David identify the thoughts underlying his feelings of anxiety.
David was able to say quite clearly that he was afraid that the
perpetrator would get him if he were alone in his room. The

BOX 5.13 *Continued*

therapist and David's parents helped David formulate some more helpful statements David could use to replace that anxiety-provoking thoughts. With practice, David began to replace the thought, "He'll get me if I'm alone," with the thought, "He's in jail and he can't hurt me again." Although David reported that he felt better when he said that, he still refused to sleep alone.

Subsequently the therapist began working with the parents to formulate a strategy for helping David learn to sleep in his own bed. The therapist explained to the parents that David had to actually fall asleep in his own bed in order to learn that there was nothing to fear from sleeping alone. Although his parents expressed concern about David becoming overly distraught, they were willing to commit to the treatment plan. They implemented the following plan.

The first night, they explained that both they and David would sleep better if they slept in their own beds. They stated that they wanted to help him learn to sleep in his own room and that they were sure he would do a great job. They went on to say that they were so confident of his success that they had bought him a matchbox car (which he loved) that he would receive in the morning if he slept in his bed all night. Then they left the room, saying that they would be back to check on him in a few minutes. As they left, David began crying, but his parents remained firm and left the room. David's mother returned in 5 minutes (the predetermined length of time), briefly praised David for staying in his bed, and said she would return in a few more minutes. As she left, David began crying louder; however, after a few minutes, his crying became somewhat quieter. In 10 minutes (again, the predetermined length of time), David's mother returned again. David pleaded with her not to leave, however, she simply said she was really proud of him for staying in his bed and then she left, saying she would return shortly. Again, David increased his crying as she left and continued to cry during the next 15-minute interval. At the end of that time period, his mother returned again to praise David. David sobbed loudly as she left; however, after about 10

(continued)

BOX 5.13 *Continued*

minutes the sound of his crying diminished until it was no longer audible. When his mother went to check on him at the end of the 20-minute time interval, David had fallen asleep. The next morning, David's parents praised him extravagantly and proudly presented him with his matchbox car.

The same process was followed for the next 3 nights. Each night David cried for briefer time periods and fell asleep more quickly. Simultaneously, his parents lengthened the time intervals between their return trips to his room. By the end of the fourth night, David fell asleep before his parents returned for the first check-in. They continued to praise him each morning for some time after that, and David continued to sleep alone successfully.

Repetitive nightmares, on the other hand, are generally believed to reflect emotional conflicts. However, nightmares are experienced by most individuals at some point during childhood (Ferber, 1985). As children grow, they naturally confront developmental conflicts. During these periods of conflict, some children may experience frightening dreams that reflect the emotional struggles they are experiencing during the day. Nightmares seem to be particularly common among preschoolers, as they naturally confront conflicts around separation, toilet training, and aggressive impulses. Interestingly, frequent nightmares seem to be less common between 7 and 11 years of age but tend to reappear during puberty when significant new anxieties arise. In most instances, nightmares associated with developmental stressors will subside without professional intervention over a short period of time, as children naturally resolve the conflicts they are facing. In general, it is important for parents of sexually abused children to recognize that the occurrence of sleep terrors and/or the appearance of transient nightmares in young children may be a reflection of a normal developmental process rather than a traumatic reaction to the abuse.

However, when sleep terrors continue or appear beyond 6 years of age, or when repetitive nightmares persist for more than a couple of months, these difficulties may reflect emotional conflicts that children are unable to resolve on their own. Sexual abuse is certainly a conflict that most children are not prepared to confront. Thus, it is not unusual for sexually abused children to continue to suffer disturbing abuse-related dreams long after they disclose the abuse. These repetitive dreams seem to reflect unsuccessful efforts to make sense of confusing and frightening abuse experiences. It is, therefore, important to encourage children to confront and process abuse-related memories and fears in the light of day when educational and therapeutic feedback can be provided by the therapist or the nonoffending parent. However, parents should be forewarned that nightmares as well as other symptoms may appear to worsen during the initial stages of gradual exposure and processing. Children who have been actively avoiding abuse-related thoughts, feelings, and reminders prior to the initiation of therapy may be particularly prone to this type of temporary symptom exacerbation. Parents may take comfort in knowing that such symptom exacerbations may be a positive sign indicating that for the first time their child may be acknowledging rather than avoiding troubling thoughts and feelings related to the abuse. Moreover, it is expected that repetitive nightmares and problematic sleep terrors, as well as other forms of reexperiencing symptoms, will diminish as children make progress in the gradual exposure and processing sessions.

INAPPROPRIATE SEXUAL BEHAVIORS

Nonoffending parents of sexually abused children frequently find sexualized behaviors to be the most difficult abuse-related symptoms with which to cope. As Friedrich (1990) points out, therapists, as well as parents who otherwise appear to be highly skilled in managing children's behaviors, may become quite disoriented and ineffective when it comes to sexually inappropriate behaviors. As a society, we do not openly and comfortably discuss issues relating to either adult or childhood sexuality. Thus it is not surprising that many parents are ill prepared to respond to their children's sexual behaviors and concerns. Therapists can use the steps outlined below to help parents respond effectively to inappropriate sexual behaviors.

Training Parents To Respond Effectively To
Inappropriate Sexual Behaviors

1. Assess parental experiences, attitudes, and knowledge regarding childhood sexuality.
2. Assess the inappropriateness of the child's sexualized behavior(s).
3. Help parents cope with the anxiety elicited by children's sexual behaviors and questions.
4. Demystify the development and maintenance of inappropriate sexual behaviors.
5. Examine the antecedents and consequences associated with the inappropriate sexual behaviors.
6. Discourage inadvertent reinforcement of the problem behavior.
7. Identify and reinforce positive replacement behavior.
8. Help the child emotionally and cognitively process the abuse.

Parental Attitudes and Knowledge About Childhood Sexuality. Parents of sexually abused children exhibit a wide range of responses to the sexualized behavior and talk exhibited by their abused children. By exploring parental experiences and attitudes regarding sexuality, the therapist will be better equipped to collaborate effectively with parents in the development and implementation of intervention strategies that are consistent with parents' views. Depending on the circumstances of the case, the therapist may want to explore the parents' histories of child sexual abuse, their understanding of normative sexual development, and their attitudes toward sex education, masturbation, adolescent sexuality, contraception, premarital sex, and homosexuality.

A parental history of sexual abuse often is a particularly important variable contributing to a parent's level of comfort or distress regarding a child's sexual abuse and sexualized behaviors. Indeed, empirical evidence indicates that parents who report a personal history of childhood or adult sexual assault suffer higher levels of distress upon discovery that their child has been sexually abused than those without such a history (Deblinger et al., 1993). Moreover, those parents who use denial and avoidance as primary mechanisms for coping with their own sexual abuse memories may find it particularly difficult to cope with their children's sexualized behaviors, as these are blatant reminders of the abuse both they and their children endured. It should be noted, however, that a history of child sexual abuse does not disqualify parents from being effective therapeutic resources for their children. As noted earlier, enhancing parental awareness of how their personal history may be affecting their responses to their sexually abused child may be particularly useful in motivating parents to alter their responses and/or to pursue abuse-focused therapy for themselves.

Educating Parents Regarding Typical Childhood Sexual Development. Parents' understanding of normative sexual development may also significantly influence their responses to their children's sexual behaviors. Not surprisingly, parents of sexually abused children may view any sexual behavior exhibited by their child as a reaction to the abuse. One parent, for example, was convinced that her preschooler's desire to show off her body was a reaction to the abuse and would ultimately lead to promiscuity. Other parents have viewed any type of masturbatory behavior exhibited by their children as a traumatic reaction to the abuse. Unfortunately, these types of fears and misconceptions can lead parents to overreact and inadvertently reinforce the exaggeration and/or increased frequency of these normative sexual behaviors. The overreaction sets up a cycle in which parents become increasingly concerned that their children's sexualized behaviors are not only deviant but are becoming more severe over time.

A recent investigation conducted by Friedrich, Grambsch, Broughton, Keuiper, and Beilke (1991) offered statistics on the rates of specific sexualized behaviors exhibited by nonabused boys and girls of different age groups. Therapists may use this type of information to reassure parents that some of the sexual behaviors exhibited by their children are, in fact, normal. Parents are often surprised to learn that behaviors such as being shy with men, walking around in underwear, scratching one's crotch, touching one's own sex parts at home, walking around nude, and undressing in front of others are exhibited by more than 40% of nonabused children (Friedrich et al., 1991). This information is critical in order to help parents differentiate between healthy expressions of childhood sexuality and age-inappropriate or abusive sexual behaviors.

Training Parents to Respond Calmly to Children's Sexual Questions and Behaviors. Interestingly, parents often need some assistance in modifying their reactions to normative sexual behaviors and questions. As noted earlier, overreacting to normal sexual behaviors may lead to an exaggeration of these behaviors and/or a disruption of the normal process of sexual development. It is, therefore, important to help parents develop or regain a degree of comfort with their children's emerging sexuality and curiosity. This may start by encouraging parents to practice calm and accepting reactions to their children's sexual questions and behaviors. In addition, the therapist may help parents role-play the initiation of sex education discussions with their children. Ideas for engaging children in such discussions are offered in a previous section of this chapter.

Demystifying Inappropriate Sexual Behaviors. Some abused children do exhibit sexualized behaviors that are age inappropriate and/or abusive in nature (Deblinger et al., 1989; Kolko, Moser, & Weldy, 1988). Adultlike sexual behaviors, such as inserting one's tongue in the mouth of another person, touching another person's sexual body parts, imitating intercourse, engaging in oral-genital contact, and inserting objects in the vagina and/or anus, appear to be associated with experiences of childhood sexual abuse (Friedrich et al., 1992). Parents are often frightened by these sexualized behaviors. They may fear that these behaviors reflect a loss of innocence suffered by their child as a result of the abuse. Other parents may worry that inappropriate sexual behaviors reflect damage to their child's developing sexual identity and may lead to promiscuity, prostitution, sex-role confusion, and/or sexual offending. Cognitive coping exercises described earlier may be used to help parents develop a more optimistic view of their child's future. In addition, these concerns may be allayed by demystifying the development and maintenance of inappropriate sexual behaviors in children. Parents are often surprised to find that social learning principles apply to inappropriate sexual behaviors in the same way that they apply to other child behaviors. By reviewing the basic learning mechanisms, including observation, association, and consequences, parents will begin to see that the process by which most children learn inappropriate sexual behaviors is neither mysterious nor complex.

As noted earlier, many child behaviors are learned through observation. Children essentially imitate much of what they see and hear. Unfortunately, children are not very selective in the behaviors they imitate, particularly young children, whose understanding of the meaning of the imitated behaviors may be quite limited. Viewed in this context, the development of inappropriate sexual behaviors may seem less mysterious to parents. Children exposed to or engaged in adult sexual behavior will sometimes imitate it, just as they repeat many other behaviors observed. In fact, given the extent to which children engage in imitation, it is almost surprising that inappropriate sexual behaviors are not exhibited by all sexually abused children. Moreover, in some cases, it is fortunate that the child imitates the inappropriate sexual interaction as this may be the only clue provided that the child is experiencing sexual abuse.

In addition to observational learning, children may exhibit inappropriate sexual behaviors as a result of the offenders' deliberate efforts to shape and reinforce specific sexual behaviors. This process, referred to as "grooming," has been described from both the victim's and offender's perspective in several recent articles (Berliner & Conte, 1990; Conte, Wolf, & Smith, 1989). The offender, for example, may introduce and reinforce simple touching behaviors before encouraging more complex sexual interactions such as oral-genital or genital-genital contact. In order to repeatedly engage the child in increasingly sexual interactions, offenders may use a variety of reinforcers including attention, affection, and play, as well as concrete rewards and bribes. Negative reinforcers are also commonly used in the form of threats (e.g., "I will not kill your mother if you engage in this sexual behavior and keep it a secret"). By developing an understanding of how their child learned the inappropriate sexual behaviors exhibited, parents can begin to view these behaviors as a reflection of basic learning mechanisms rather than frightening symbolic representations of a loss of innocence or disturbed psychosexual developments. This understanding also allows parents to explore the underlying learning mechanisms that may be inadvertently maintaining the inappropriate sexual behaviors even after the abusive episodes have ceased.

Using Behavior Management Techniques To Decrease Inappropriate Sexual Behaviors. At this point, parents may begin to examine the current patterns associated with their children's inappropriate sexual behaviors, just as they would for any other behavior problems. By examining the antecedents and consequences associated with sexualized behaviors, parents can begin to determine what consequences their children are seeking when engaging in these behaviors. As we have seen with other problem behaviors, sexually inappropriate behaviors are often inadvertently reinforced by the consequences they achieve. When this is the case, the therapist may help the parents:

- Learn to communicate more openly and clearly about both appropriate and inappropriate sexual behavior.
- Identify the consequences that may be motivating inappropriate sexual behaviors by examining the behavioral patterns.
- Alter parental responses by establishing a negative consequence, such as time out, for the inappropriate sexual behavior.
- Identify and shape positive replacement behaviors (e.g., healthy affectionate behaviors) that will afford the child a means of achieving the desired consequence in a socially appropriate manner.

The case example in Box 5.14 illustrates how these behavior management techniques can be used effectively to reduce a child's inappropriate sexual behaviors.

Masturbation

Parents of sexually abused children also often become quite concerned about masturbatory behavior. This sexualized behavior can be particularly difficult to treat because it may serve different functions for different children. In most cases, the therapeutic goal should not be to eliminate the behavior completely. For example, in some instances, an examination of the behavioral pattern suggests that the child achieves the "feels good" consequence when engaging in masturbation on an occasional basis in private. Such a pattern suggests that there may be no reason to intervene. It is important, however, to recognize that some parents will consider any type of masturbatory behavior morally wrong. While one needs to respect this view, the therapist may offer parents some information about the normative and widespread nature of the behavior and the potential pitfalls of attempting to eliminate it. In fact, although such parents are not likely to change their views, they should recognize that their responses to the behavior may inadvertently lead to more frequent, secretive, and/or problematic masturbatory behavior. This may motivate these parents to modify their responses to some degree.

In other cases, however, masturbatory behaviors may be maladaptive. This may be true, for example, when the behavioral pattern suggests that the child not only derives pleasurable sensations through masturbation but seems to engage in the behavior when others are present in order to obtain attention. Clearly, public masturbation is a problem behavior that can create difficulties at home, at school, and in other social settings. Masturbation in private also may be maladaptive if it appears to be compulsive; that is, if it occurs so frequently that it interferes with the child's participation in age-appropriate activities. The sudden appearance of compulsive masturbation may be just as disconcerting to parents as public masturbation. Interestingly, although both public and compulsive masturbatory behaviors are problematic, they may be maintained by different consequences. Public masturbation, for example, is frequently inadvertently reinforced by the negative attention it elicits from parents, teachers, and others. Not knowing how to react,

(text continued on p. 206)

BOX 5.14

Case Example: Decreasing Inappropriate Sexual Behaviors With Behavior Management Techniques

The following example illustrates how 6-year-old Jessica's inappropriate behaviors were reduced by use of behavior management techniques.

Six-year-old Jessica was placed in foster care as a result of her mother's neglect due to substance abuse difficulties. During Jessica's most recent foster placement, she suffered repeated sexual abuse perpetrated by older foster boys. When therapy was initiated, Jessica had been in the care of her maternal great aunt, Mary, and her great uncle, Jim, for approximately 6 months. Although they were older, Mary and Jim were considering adopting Jessica, but they were concerned about her behavioral difficulties, particularly the inappropriate sexual behavior she exhibited.

Jessica was preoccupied with sexual matters and was very aggressive toward her Uncle Jim. She frequently attempted to French-kiss him, and she grabbed at his genitals on several occasions. Upon examining the patterns of interaction between Jessica and her uncle, it was apparent that after his long work day, Jim rarely gave Jessica much positive attention. However, Jim's responses to Jessica's inappropriate sexual behaviors tended to be highly emotional and long-winded. Not only would he yell at Jessica, but he would draw his wife into family discussions with the child about ladylike behavior and the dangers of sexual promiscuity.

Jim and Mary were quick to acknowledge that the content of these discussions may have been beyond 6-year-old Jessica's comprehension. Moreover, they recognized that they were probably inadvertently reinforcing Jessica's behavior with lots of highly emotional negative attention. Thus, they were responsive to using time out for inappropriate sexual behavior as it would require much less energy and effort and would minimize the attention Jessica would receive. However, Mary and Jim

---

BOX 5.14 *Continued*

found it very difficult to identify and agree on positive replacement behaviors for which Jessica could receive positive attention and affection. Jim was very concerned about encouraging
any affectionate behaviors, as he feared Jessica would get "carried away" and somehow he might be accused of sexual abuse.
However, after some discussion and debate, Jim was able to
identify several behaviors (e.g., a kiss on the cheek and sitting
with arms around one another on the couch) that he would be
comfortable encouraging and praising.

OK and not-OK touching was reviewed with Jessica in a
family session (see chapter on joint parent-child sessions). It is
important to note that such discussion should not follow a
problem episode. Much of the discussion with Jessica revolved
around giving and receiving OK touches, particularly those
that Mary and Jim had agreed to praise on a consistent basis. In
addition, time out was presented as a way of reminding Jessica
which types of touching behaviors were not OK. These not-OK
behaviors were described clearly and calmly by Jessica's aunt
and uncle.

Jessica showed significant improvement in response to this
program. She was clearly very fond of her aunt and uncle and
was only now learning how to express these feelings in socially
appropriate ways. It should be noted, however, that during a
particularly stressful period for the family, Jessica got into her
uncle's bed and touched him inappropriately. Startled by the
sudden reappearance of this behavior, Jim did not respond
appropriately with time out. However, the family was able to
recognize that Jessica was probably feeling desperate for attention as they were highly distracted by other family stressors.
Thus, they had been giving Jessica little positive attention. After
some convincing, Jim and Mary were able to view the incident
as a temporary and predictable setback and thus agreed to
reinstate the program outlined. They were encouraged to focus
on reinforcing appropriate affection and behaviors, while also
involving Jessica in age-appropriate discussions about the
stressors the family was facing.

parents and others often provide attention in the form of yelling, lecturing, and/or highly emotional discussions following episodes of public masturbation. On the other hand, when sexually abused children engage in compulsive masturbation in private, they may not be seeking attention but rather may be using the behavior to achieve the consequence of escape. The sexually abused child may be using this behavior to cope with and/or escape from abuse-related anxieties, as well as the stressors associated with the aftermath of disclosure.

Treating Problematic Masturbation

The guidelines outlined earlier for inappropriate sexual behaviors may be used to treat public and/or compulsive masturbation as well. It should be emphasized; however, that parents often need a great deal of practice talking about masturbation in a calm and positive manner before participating in joint sessions with their children. It is often difficult for parents to discuss the behavior in a positive manner because of the stress it has created. Thus, the therapist will need to strongly encourage parents to focus initially on the positive aspects of masturbation while also normalizing the behavior. After spending some time talking about masturbation in a positive, lighthearted manner, parents may introduce the rules about masturbation with respect to appropriate times and places. The consequences for breaking these rules also should be discussed during this session. The negative consequences chosen should be based on the behavioral patterns associated with the particular inappropriate sexual behavior. For example, although time out may be used effectively to minimize the attention associated with public masturbation, compulsive masturbation is not likely to respond to this procedure because attention is not motivating the behavior in the first place. If a child is engaging in compulsive masturbation just for the escape it provides, parents may identify other response cost procedures such as withdrawing television or highly desirable play privileges that may be used as negative consequences when the child engages in compulsive masturbation at times other than the designated times and places. In addition, because compulsive masturbation is often motivated by abuse-related anxiety, it is particularly important to shape and reinforce other more effective coping strategies while also encouraging the child to participate in gradual exposure and cognitive processing exercises.

Precocious Sexual Activities With Peers

Another type of sexualized behavior that can be troubling for parents is precocious sexual activity with peers. Indeed, many parents are aghast to learn that their child is engaging another child in sexual activities. The parents may leap to the conclusion that their child will become a sexual abuser him- or herself. The first step in dealing with such a problem is to help the parent dispute any dysfunctional thoughts about the child's behavior. For example, the fact that a child is engaging another child in sexual activities does not mean that the child will grow up to be a sexual offender.

The next step in coping with this problem is to analyze the child's motivation for the sexual behavior. The therapist should educate the parent about the fact that many nonabused children also participate in sexual exploration and play based upon curiosity about their bodies. When working with a child for whom curiosity seems to be the motivator, the therapist should work with parents to satisfy the child's curiosity by providing appropriate education regarding sexuality and to set limits regarding appropriate versus inappropriate touches. Often those two steps are sufficient to reduce the child's problematic sexual behaviors.

For other children, the motivation to engage peers in sexualized behaviors may be focused on their unresolved thoughts and feelings regarding their own abuse experiences. For example, children who did not understand and are not coping effectively with their own experience of abuse may attempt to gain a better understanding and to master that experience by reenacting it with another child. Children who were left feeling powerless and out of control by the abuse experience may engage other children in sexual activities in an effort to gain control of their lives. With children whose sexual behaviors are driven by the troubling thoughts and feelings generated by their own abuse experiences, it is anticipated that the gradual exposure and processing work will help them to cope more effectively with those thoughts and emotions. As they are coping more successfully, we expect to see the sexualized behaviors diminish. Again, however, firm limits should be established and consistently enforced regarding appropriate versus inappropriate touches.

A third motivator of inappropriate sexual behaviors among children who lack well-developed social skills may be a desire to engage peers in relationships. During the course of their own sexual abuse experiences, children may learn that sexual behaviors are a means of engaging people in relationships. Children who have well-developed social skills are not likely to rely on sexual interactions as a means of forming relationships; however, children who lack adequate social skills may fall back on the sexual behaviors they have learned to engage peers in relationships. With such children, it is important to provide appropriate social skills training as well as to provide the necessary limits regarding inappropriate sexual behaviors.

Finally, some children may pursue sexual activity with peers or younger children based upon their own sexual drives and interests. With these children, as is true for all sexually abused children, it is very important to provide education regarding sexuality. Depending on the child's age, it may be appropriate to include information regarding the physical and emotional risks of precocious sexual activity. In addition, the therapist may explore with the parent the possibility of suggesting private masturbation as an alternative means of satisfying the child's sexual drive.

In general, after carefully assessing the pattern of inappropriate and/or abusive sexual behaviors, the therapist should (a) foster clear, open, and positive parent-child communication about sexuality and (b) encourage the use of basic behavior management techniques to reduce the occurrence of inappropriate sexual behaviors and to enhance the child's ability to express his or her sexuality and affection in healthy ways. Discussions regarding sexual development and behavior will likely need to be revisited as the child enters different developmental phases. With guidance and preparation, some parents may feel comfortable engaging their children in such discussions as they get older, whereas others may prefer to recontact the therapist for assistance in the future.

6

Joint Parent-Child Sessions

PARENT SERVING AS ROLE MODEL
IN COPING WITH CHILD SEXUAL ABUSE

In most cases involving child sexual abuse, the culmination of treatment should include joint sessions involving both the child and the nonoffending parents. These sessions are important for a number of reasons. Initially, these sessions provide an opportunity for the parent to serve as a positive role model for the child, particularly in terms of how to cope effectively with the sexual abuse experience. It must be acknowledged that parents typically serve as much more powerful role models for children than a therapist ever can, due to both the nature of the parent-child relationship and the amount of time parents spend with their children.

Thus, whether or not parents are involved in joint sessions with the child, their response to the abuse undoubtedly will influence the child's response. Unfortunately, the parent's initial response to a child's disclosure of sexual abuse may not demonstrate effective coping for the child. Well-meaning parents may initially respond to a disclosure of sexual abuse in a manner that may frighten the child, discourage further discussion of the abuse, and/or encourage avoidance of such discussions. The joint parent-child sessions then offer another opportunity for the parent to model more effective coping strategies for the child.

Therefore, the therapist should plan carefully how to involve parents in joint sessions in order to maximize the positive influence they may have as a role model in coping with the sexual abuse. Parents can model several effective coping strategies for the child. For example, parents can teach the child by example how it is possible to discuss the sexual abuse experience calmly, without avoidance or extreme distress. Similarly, parents can model how to express emotions effectively by simply verbalizing their own emotions during sessions. Parents also may demonstrate effective cognitive coping skills by discussing the abuse in rational ways, without catastrophizing or dramatizing the situation or the aftereffects.

FACILITATING OPEN COMMUNICATION
REGARDING THE ABUSE

The joint parent-child sessions also are important as they provide an opportunity for the parent and child to learn to communicate openly regarding the abuse. When parents do not participate in therapy, the child may successfully learn to discuss the abuse with the therapist, only to have all such communication stop when therapy sessions end. To be able to continue such effective communication with another caring adult after therapy ends is important for the child. The joint parent-child sessions allow the parent and child to develop such communication skills. Furthermore, in communicating about the abuse, the parent and child are able to clarify any points of confusion or misunderstanding that may exist between them. For example, many children are left with some misunderstanding following their parents' response to the initial disclosure. If parents respond with great anger toward the perpetrator, children may misunderstand and perceive the parents as being angry with them. Without any further communication regarding that situation, children may never have that misperception corrected. However, in learning to communicate openly regarding the abuse, such points of confusion can be clarified.

CONTINUING THE GRADUAL EXPOSURE PROCESS

The joint sessions also allow for the continuation of the gradual exposure process. Even after becoming relatively comfortable discussing details of the abuse with the therapist, many children are anxious when asked to discuss those facts with a parent. By providing an opportunity for children to do that, the joint sessions allow them to further reduce their anxiety regarding memories of the abuse. In addition, the joint gradual exposure sessions allow children to see that their parents are not disgusted, ashamed, or uncomfortable hearing about what happened.

Joint sessions help the child reduce anxiety about memories of the abuse.

TRAINING PARENTS AND CHILD TO
CONTINUE THERAPEUTIC WORK AT HOME

The joint sessions also can be crucial in preparing the parent and child to continue discussing the sexual abuse on their own, after formal therapy sessions have ended. During the individual parent sessions, therapists will have taught parents many of the skills they need to work with their children regarding the sexual abuse experience. The joint sessions allow parents to practice those skills under the tutelage of a therapist. As the joint sessions continue and the parents' skills progress, the therapists should assume a more passive role, allowing the parents to become more and more active in talking with their children about the therapeutic issues. Thus, the transition to ending formal counseling sessions and continuing the therapeutic work at home will be a gradual and natural one.

FACILITATING COMMUNICATION REGARDING SEX EDUCATION
AND PERSONAL SAFETY SKILLS

Finally, joint parent-child sessions allow parents and children to become comfortable discussing issues of healthy sexuality and personal safety skills. Having the ability to openly and clearly discuss these issues allows parents to provide accurate information, impart their own values regarding sexual issues, and assist their children in problem solving around sexual concerns or difficulties. In addition, teaching children to discuss issues of sexuality and personal safety openly with their parents may increase the likelihood that the children will be able to disclose to parents any future experiences of inappropriate or confusing touch. The need to involve parents in providing this type of education is underscored by research suggesting that such involvement may enhance children's retention and/or use of personal safety skills (Finkelhor et al., 1995; Wurtele et al., 1992).

❏ Assessing Parental Readiness for Joint Sessions

The determination of when to initiate joint parent-child sessions depends upon an assessment of readiness of the parent and the child. It is crucial that the parent be ready, both in terms of emotional state and level of skills, before initiating joint sessions. A parent who is not emotionally ready or is not adequately trained not only may fail to facilitate the child's progress but may actually hinder the therapeutic progress. For example, if a child who has been progressing nicely in gradual exposure during individual sessions observes a parent break down and sob dramatically during the initial joint session, the child may be discouraged from any further disclosures to that parent. Thus, during the individual parent sessions, the therapist should be constantly monitoring the parent's progress, in an attempt to determine parental readiness for joint sessions. In a few cases, parents may simply be unable to participate effectively in joint sessions due to their own psychological issues. In such cases, it is preferable to forgo joint intervention rather than to risk highly counterproductive sessions. However, in most cases, parents are able to participate, at least to some degree, in joint sessions following adequate individual preparation.

PARENT'S EMOTIONAL REACTION TO
DISCUSSIONS OF THE CHILD'S ABUSE

The initial assessment of parental readiness will consist of the therapist's evaluation of the parent's emotional reaction to the topic of the child's sexual abuse. During the individual parent sessions focused on cognitive coping and gradual exposure, the therapist can assess the parent's emotional reaction. It is anticipated that many parents will initially react to such discussions with emotional distress of some type. However, with the development of effective coping skills and the experience of gradual exposure, the level of distress should diminish. As the parent is able to dispute distressing thoughts effectively and tolerate gradual exposure sessions comfortably, it is time to consider initiating joint sessions.

PARENT'S ABILITY TO ACTIVELY SUPPORT CHILD

A second issue to consider when assessing parental readiness for joint sessions is the parent's ability to take an active and supportive role in these sessions. Typically, this ability will develop concurrent with the emotional readiness just discussed. Parents must move beyond their own emotional response to the abuse to be able to assess what they can say that will be most helpful and supportive to the child. As was noted previously, it should be recognized that evidence indicates mothers who have a history of sexual assault themselves tend to be more distraught when confronted with their child's abuse experience (Deblinger et al., 1993). Thus, therapists working with such women may want to allow them more time and preparatory work before initiating joint parent-child sessions.

PARENT'S ABILITY TO PROVIDE SEX EDUCATION

Similarly, the therapist should assess whether or not the parent will be able to effectively discuss sex education with the child. Sex education will be included as a component of the joint sessions; thus, it is important that the parent be able to discuss the topic positively, without great embarrassment. Some parents may need to process their thoughts regarding sexuality or finish cognitive coping work (focused on disputing dysfunctional thoughts underlying any feelings of embarrassment or anxiety) before being able to effectively provide sex education for their child.

PARENT'S ANXIETIES OR CONCERNS

Finally, when assessing parental readiness for joint sessions, it is important that the therapist talk with the parent about any specific anxieties or concerns she or he may have about the joint sessions. Often parents do have particular worries, such as fear that the child is angry with the parent for allowing the abuse to occur, concern about becoming tearful during the joint sessions, or anxiety regarding hearing the details of the abuse from the child. Having parents discuss their worries allows the therapist to deal with those concerns directly and to plan whatever preparatory work (such as role plays or education) is needed to prepare parents and reduce their anxiety. It should be noted that joint sessions may be initiated before parents are ready to discuss all the topics outlined above, as long as the joint sessions are limited to those topics that the parent and child are comfortable discussing. For example, joint sessions may be initiated with a focus on sex education prior to parents being comfortable discussing the details of the sexual abuse. The order of topics to be discussed in joint sessions may be determined based upon the needs of specific clients.

> *Parents must be able to help and support their child.*

❏ **Preparing Parents for Joint Sessions**

Parents should have been introduced to the idea of joint parent-child sessions at the beginning of treatment, when the therapist presented the overall treatment rationale. By presenting the idea early in treatment and making periodic references to the joint sessions to come, the therapist helps parents become comfortable with the idea of participating in joint sessions. However, as the time approaches to actually begin the joint sessions, the therapist should begin some more specific preparatory work with the parent. Some parents may need a great number of sessions to prepare, whereas others can begin participation in joint sessions quite early.

PRESENTING RATIONALE FOR JOINT SESSIONS

Initially, the therapist should review the rationale for the joint sessions that was presented briefly earlier in treatment. The key points to emphasize in presenting the rationale are as follows. The joint sessions offer the parent an opportunity to serve as a positive role model, demonstrating how to cope effectively with the sexual abuse experience. Joint sessions allow for the continuation of the child's gradual exposure process. The sessions can facilitate communication between the parent and the child regarding the sexual abuse, providing an opportunity for the clarification of any points of confusion or misunderstanding. Finally, during joint sessions, the parent can assume a more active role in helping the child process the abuse experience, developing patterns that will allow the therapeutic process to continue long after formal therapy sessions are over.

TRAINING THE PARENT IN HOW TO RESPOND APPROPRIATELY TO THE CHILD

After presenting the rationale, the therapist should train the parent in how to most effectively respond to the child during the joint sessions. Much of that training can occur in the context of role plays. Initially, it may be useful to have the parent assume the role of the child while the therapist assumes the parent's role and demonstrates alternative means of giving support and encouragement to the child. Subsequently, as the parent grows more confident, the parent can retain his or her own role with the therapist playing the role of the child.

Praising the Child

Often it is appropriate to focus the initial role plays on communication skills, because that topic is less threatening for many parents than is gradual exposure or sex education. The therapist may begin with a review of how to effectively praise the child, a topic that may have already been discussed in sessions focused on behavior management skills. At this point in therapy, role plays may focus specifically on providing praise for the child's courage and hard work in disclosing the abuse and in participating in treatment.

Asking Nonthreatening, Open-Ended Questions

A second area of communication to rehearse with parents is asking nonthreatening, open-ended questions that might encourage discussion of the sexual abuse. Together, the therapist and parent might brainstorm a list of such questions. For example, the parent might ask the child questions about what he or she was thinking or feeling when specific episodes of abuse occurred. Or the parent might ask questions regarding specific details, such as what the offender said before or after the abusive interactions occurred. The parent should be cautioned against asking questions the child might interpret as being critical in any way. For example, the parent should be discouraged from asking questions such as "Why didn't you tell me earlier what was happening?" or "Why didn't you scream for help when he touched you?" If a parent desires some specific information, the therapist might help the parent formulate a question in a non-critical way. For example, to a parent who is questioning why the child did not disclose the abuse earlier, a therapist might suggest posing the question in this way: "There are lots of reasons children don't tell about abuse. Some children never tell. I'm so proud that you did tell. I wonder if you can tell me some of the reasons you had for not telling at first."

Rehearsing Responses to Information Regarding the Sexual Abuse

After rehearsing those two general types of communication skills, the therapist and the parent may pursue role plays using the specific materials generated by the child during his or her individual gradual exposure sessions. For example, the child's book or poems regarding the sexual abuse experience may be incorporated into the role plays so that the parent feels comfortable responding to those specific materials. Having the therapist assume the role of the child in reading those materials, the parent may practice giving praise; asking empathetic, open-ended, nonjudgmental questions; and expressing his or her own thoughts and feelings.

Preparing to Discuss Points of Confusion or Concern

The therapist also should prepare the parent to discuss any points of confusion or concern for the child. From individual sessions with the child, the therapist will be aware of any specific issues related to the parent-child relationship that are concerning to the child. The therapist then can share that awareness with the parent so they can plan how the parent can best address those concerns. Examples of such concerns for children include worry that a parent is upset with the child for disclosing, concern that a parent is angry that the child did not disclose earlier, and anger with the parent for not being aware that the abuse was going on and stopping it. Such issues can be addressed effectively in joint sessions if the therapist prepares effectively by encouraging the child during individual sessions to raise the issue in the joint session and by using role plays to rehearse with the parent how to best respond to the child's concern.

Preparing for Sex Education

Another focus of preparation for the joint sessions should be sex education. The therapist may introduce this topic by describing the dual goals of presenting sex education during joint sessions. The initial goal is to provide children with age-appropriate information about healthy sexuality, thus eliminating any confusion they have regarding sexuality and helping them to develop a positive view of sexuality. Second, but equally important, is the goal of increasing communication between parent and child regarding the topic of sexuality. The thought of discussing sexuality with their children is anxiety-provoking for many parents. Without adequate preparation, that anxiety may be communicated to children, which may discourage them from discussing sexual issues with the parent. Thus, it is important to prepare parents for joint sessions focusing on sex education by discussing with them what their thoughts and/or concerns are regarding providing this information to the child. With parents who are hesitant to discuss sexuality with their children, the therapist may discuss the goal of helping children develop a positive view of sexuality so that they eventually can have a positive adult relationship. It may be noted that the child unfortunately has already had a negative sexual experience, which may predispose him or her to experience greater anxiety around sexual issues and to suffer sexual dissatisfactions as an adult (Cohen, 1995; Finkelhor et al., 1989). Thus, positive discussions and education concerning healthy expressions of adult sexuality are important in countering that negative experience.

Discussion of healthy adult sexuality is important.

In preparing parents to present sex education, the therapist may want to help parents choose developmentally appropriate reading material regarding sexuality. The use of such materials can help to structure the presentation of the material and reduce the parent's anxiety about how to approach the task. Depending on the child's age, the parent and therapist may choose to focus on one or more of a variety of topics such as how a baby grows prenatally and is delivered (for young children), how a child is conceived, puberty, dating relationships, adolescent sexuality, and contraceptive methods. In addition to preparing to present the factual information, the therapist may encourage parents to think about what values they want to communicate to the child. After deciding on appropriate topics for the child, the therapist and parent may engage in role plays using the educational materials. As was mentioned previously, the therapist may initially assume the role of the parent, in order to demonstrate how to effectively present the educational material. After the parent becomes more comfortable, the therapist may assume the role of the child. In that role, the therapist may ask the parent increasingly difficult and perhaps embarrassing questions. In this way, the parent becomes more comfortable discussing sexual topics and has the opportunity to think through his or her responses to such questions.

Finally, the therapist may review with parents information about any education that will be provided in joint sessions regarding OK versus not-OK touches and personal safety skills. This educational information was discussed in some detail in the chapter entitled, "Child Intervention: Therapeutic Components."

❏ Assessing the Child's Readiness and Preparing for Joint Sessions

The assessment of the child's readiness for joint sessions should focus on issues similar to those outlined in assessment of parental readiness. Initially, the therapist should assess the child's progress in gradual exposure. Typically, children should have progressed in the gradual exposure process to the point at which they can discuss the sexual abuse with the therapist with relatively little distress before beginning joint sessions focused on gradual exposure.

During individual sessions, the therapist will have explained to the child that an eventual goal will be to include the parent in discussions of the child's sexual abuse experiences. As the time approaches for joint sessions to begin, the therapist will want to present the rationale for the joint sessions in more detail. The therapist should emphasize that the joint sessions will provide an opportunity for the parent and child to become closer as they discuss the details of the sexual abuse experience. Many children are proud to share with a parent any "creative products" they have worked on in therapy. However, if children are hesitant to share such "products" or to share the details of the sexual abuse experience, the therapist may explain that it is important that there not be any remaining secrets that can build walls between child and parent.

The therapist may point out that the parent also is attending sessions so that he or she can learn how to best help the child.

Furthermore, the therapist may emphasize that the parent loves the child and wants to provide support. If children have experienced any confusion or discomfort in their relationship with parents around the issue of the sexual abuse, the therapist can identify the joint sessions as an opportunity to clarify that confusion. Finally, the therapist may talk with the child about the fact that the joint sessions allow the parent and child to become accustomed to discussing difficult issues such as the sexual abuse, so that they can continue the therapeutic work at home on their own.

After presenting a rationale for the joint sessions, the therapist will want to outline the contents of those sessions for the child. With younger children, it may only be necessary to say,

> We are going to have your parent join us so that you can show him (or her) what you have been working on and tell him (or her) what we have been discussing.

With older children, it is useful to provide more detail about the gradual exposure and sexual education activities that will occur in joint sessions.

In preparing children for joint sessions, the therapist will want to talk with them about what they have worked on in individual sessions that they can share with the parent. In most cases, the child will have produced something (e.g., a book, poem, song, drawings) that communicates something about the sexual abuse experience. After identifying the work to be shared, the therapist may want to prepare the child further by initiating role plays in which the child shares the product with the therapist who is playing the role of the parent. Additional role plays may be necessary to give the child practice disclosing further information about the sexual abuse. Similarly, the therapist may encourage the child to rehearse discussions of any concerning or confusing issues with the parent. Although fairly anxious children may benefit from multiple role plays devoted to preparing for joint sessions, other children may not need such specific preparatory work before initiating the joint sessions.

❏ Contents of Joint Sessions

The order of the topics covered in joint sessions should be determined based upon the needs and level of comfort of both children and parents. The initial joint sessions should be satisfying and not overwhelmingly anxiety provoking for either. In some cases, children are so proud of the product they created in individual gradual exposure sessions that it is natural to share that product and begin the joint sessions with gradual exposure. In other situations, discussing the sexual abuse experience is highly anxiety provoking and should be delayed until the parent and child have achieved some level of comfort discussing other issues such as sexual education or personal safety skills. In such a case, it may be appropriate initially to have the parent and child read the sexual education materials together. Regardless of the order in which they are presented, the following topics generally should be included in the joint parent-child sessions.

CONTINUATION OF GRADUAL EXPOSURE PROCESS

The topic of perhaps greatest importance in the joint sessions is continued gradual exposure. The goals of this work are encouraging open communication between parents and children regarding the sexual abuse and decreasing anxiety and avoidance of the topic. As was mentioned previously, the child may have created something during individual gradual exposure sessions that provides information about the sexual abuse experience. Sharing such a product can be a relatively easy way to begin gradual exposure in joint sessions; it provides some structure for the session, allows the child to exhibit work of which he or she is proud, and gives the parent an opportunity to provide lots of positive reinforcement for the child. However, the presentation of that finished product alone is not sufficient to achieve the goal of increased communication regarding the sexual abuse. For children and parents to feel more comfortable discussing the abuse, they need to have some dialogue. Thus, the parent should be encouraged to comment on and ask questions about the child's project. Then, using that product as a starting point, the parent and child should be encouraged to discuss other aspects of the abuse experience.

DISCUSSION OF AREAS OF CONFUSION OR CONCERN

Another focus of the joint sessions should be to address any specific points of confusion or concern the child has. As has been described previously, the therapist will have already worked individually with the child to identify any such issues and with the parent to practice appropriate responses. Thus, during the joint session, both parent and child should be adequately prepared to address those issues. This is an important use of joint sessions; specific problems within the parent-child relationship may be addressed in this context that otherwise would never have been addressed.

One common issue is the anger some children experience toward the nonoffending parent for not being aware of and/or not stopping the abuse. In order to resolve that anger appropriately, children need to verbalize their feelings as well as the beliefs underlying the anger. For example, a child who is very angry at her nonoffending mother may be able to explain that she is angry because, "I told you I didn't want to stay at home alone with Joe, that he wasn't nice to me, but you made me anyway." With further questioning, it may become clear that the child believes her comments should have been adequate to communicate to her mother that she was being abused. It is important that the child's inaccurate belief (that her mother knew of her abuse) be corrected and that her anger be processed effectively in order to prevent the possibility of long-term difficulties in the mother-child relationship.

The mother may help the child to replace her inaccurate and anger-producing thought by describing the mother's own thoughts and understanding of the situation at the time the child made that initial disclosure. For example, the mother might explain that she genuinely did not understand what was happening at the time and that she is sorry she was not able to intervene then. Furthermore, the child might be helped to recognize that the mother did intervene to stop the abuse and protect the child once she really understood that the child was being abused.

In other cases, the child's perception may be accurate: He or she did disclose clearly, but the mother failed to respond in an appropriately protective way. In such a case, during the mother's individual sessions, the therapist should help the mother prepare to explain to the child why she responded to the child's disclosure as she did and to apologize for failing to protect the child. For example, the mother might explain,

> Samantha, I'm so sorry. I know you told me that John was hurting your bottom, and I should have really listened and helped you then. I just didn't want to believe that I could have married a man who would abuse my daughter. It was easier for me to believe that it was an accident or that you were confused about what happened. I made a mistake, a big mistake, but I understand now, and I want to do whatever I can to help you get through this.

The case example in Box 6.1 illustrates how joint parent-child sessions might be used to effectively clarify and process a point of confusion or concern in the parent-child relationship.

BOX 6.1

Case Example: Clarification of Points of Confusion During a Joint Parent-Child Session

A 12-year-old victim of sexual abuse believes that her mother must be angry with her for having seduced her father (a belief that was encouraged by her father, the perpetrator). Although the therapist has attempted to deal with this erroneous belief through cognitive coping skills, the girl needs to hear from her mother that in fact she is not angry with her daughter. After spending part of the joint session engaged in gradual exposure exercises, the therapist encourages the daughter, Tracey, to raise this issue. Her mother has been prepared through prior role plays with the therapist to respond to her daughter's concern effectively.

> **BOX 6.1** *Continued*
>
> **Therapist:** Tracey, I think there was something else we agreed that you would talk about with your mother tonight.
>
> **Tracey:** Do you mean now? Do I have to?
>
> **Therapist:** I think that the only way for you to feel OK about all of this is to discuss it. You know your mom really wants to help you, but she can't if you don't share your worries with her.
>
> **Mother:** Tracey, I hope you can talk to me about whatever is bothering you. I'd really like to help.
>
> **Tracey:** Well, it's not such a big deal. I guess I was just wondering if you were really a little mad at me. I mean, I know you said you weren't. But Dad said that I started everything by walking around in short shorts and bathing suits and stuff; he said that I'd seduced him. And he said that if you knew that I'd teased him like that, you'd be really mad at me and that it would break up your marriage. And now you guys have broken up, so I just wondered . . .
>
> **Mother:** Oh, Tracey, I'm so sorry that you were worried about that. I'm not mad at you about anything.
>
> **Tracey:** But when I first told you what was happening, you started screaming at me. You seemed really mad.
>
> **Mother:** Well, I was very upset. I'm really angry with your father for all that he did. And it makes me angry that he made you even think that any of this could be your fault. Nothing that happened was your fault. You were only 10 when it started. There is no way that a 10-year-old could seduce a 40-year-old man if she wanted to. And Tracey, you don't ever need to feel badly about our getting a divorce. I'm so glad that I know now what was going on. I don't want a marriage where there are all these secrets and my own child is being abused.
>
> **Tracey:** [Begins crying] You're really not mad at me?
>
> **Mother:** [Embraces Tracey] No, honey, I'm not mad at you at all. I'm so glad that you were able to tell me what you were worried about.

SEX EDUCATION AND PERSONAL SAFETY SKILLS TRAINING

Another topic to be covered in the joint sessions is sex education. In general, it is helpful to use humor to keep the discussions regarding sex education positive and even lighthearted. As was described earlier, it is often useful to begin discussions of sex education with the use of developmentally appropriate reading materials. With very young children, a portion of a joint session may be devoted to having the parent (or therapist, if parent is too uncomfortable) read the material to the child. With older children, the child may be encouraged to read the material or take turns reading with the adults who are present. As the material is being read, the adults should pause at times to solicit comments or questions regarding the material, in an attempt to encourage open dialogue. If the first joint session(s) focused on providing sex education in this way go well, the therapist may ask the parent and child to continue reading and discussing the material at home, as a homework assignment. They should be cautioned against each reading the material independently because that will not serve to enhance communication between the parent and child.

With older children, the presentation of sex education material may serve as a springboard for discussions of issues such as dating, adolescent sexuality, and even contraceptive methods. During a joint session, the therapist may facilitate such discussions by asking general questions such as the following:

Do many students in your grade have boyfriends or girlfriends?
What does it mean if you are "going together"?
What do you look for in a boyfriend or girlfriend?
What happens physically between boyfriends and girlfriends?
How do you know when it is appropriate to have a sexual relationship with someone?

By having the parent and child begin to discuss these issues in session, the therapist is encouraging an open atmosphere in which they can continue discussions of sexual issues on their own.

Personal safety skills often may be discussed in joint sessions in conjunction with the provision of sexual education. With older children whose sex education discussions include a focus on dating relationships, discussions of personal safety skills should incorporate the issue of sexual aggression in dating relationships. With younger children, the discussion of personal safety skills may be more limited to issues such as OK versus not-OK touches, body ownership, the right to say no, getting away, and telling someone. Again, for many clients this is a relatively nonthreatening topic that may be covered in part during homework assignments completed on their own. Written materials such as *It's My Body* (Freeman, 1982) and *My Very Own Book about Me* (Stowel & Dietzel, 1982) are available outlining basic personal safety skills. Clients may be asked to take such materials home to complete for homework.

❑ **Including Siblings in Joint Sessions**

In many cases, the siblings of the victimized child should be evaluated to assess the possibility that they may have been sexually abused by the perpetrator as well. Only if it is clear that the siblings have not had contact with the perpetrator is it appropriate to forgo that type of assessment. Even in situations in which there is no concern that siblings have been abused, it is appropriate at the time of the initial evaluation to screen for symptoms of emotional distress or behavioral problems that the siblings might have developed in response to the overall family distress. That screening may consist of interviewing the parent regarding the siblings' symptomatology, having the parent complete the CBCL for each sibling, and if possible interviewing the sibling. If it is discovered that a sibling was abused as well, that sibling should be seen in psychotherapy conducted in coordination with the psychotherapy provided for the originally identified child. Often it is possible for the same therapist to see the siblings in concurrent individual sessions. In other cases, it may be more appropriate for the children to have different therapists, if it appears that the children would benefit from having their own individual relationships with therapists.

In a number of different types of situations, it is helpful to include siblings in some of the later joint sessions. Sessions involving siblings are particularly important if both siblings were victims of abuse, the sibling was aware of the abuse as it was ongoing, or the sibling has been significantly affected by the identified client's abusive experience in some way. When deciding whether or not to include siblings in joint sessions, the therapist should carefully assess the purpose(s) of such work. One common goal is to improve communication and increase understanding of the sexual abuse experience among all family members. For example, in some families, younger siblings have not been told why the perpetrator, who was a family member, had to leave the home. The therapist may help the parent and the victimized child decide how to share that information during the joint session. We believe that in most cases, it is useful for siblings to be informed of the basic information that the victimized child was sexually abused. Usually, it will be important to provide some education about sexual abuse. However, it typically is not necessary, and sometimes it is not appropriate, to give siblings explicit details of what happened during the sexual abuse. By fostering open communication among all family members, including siblings, the therapist can help the family to lift the veil of secrecy that was created within the family by the abuse. Even in families in which multiple siblings were abused, the siblings may never communicate clearly with each other about their experience without some therapeutic intervention.

Another reason to include siblings is to correct any misconceptions or misunderstandings the siblings may have. To expand upon the previous example, if a father who is the alleged perpetrator has left the home, an unaware sibling may blame the victimized child for somehow making Daddy so angry that he left. It would be important to clarify that misunderstanding in an attempt to avoid long-term conflict between those siblings. In other situations, the nonabused siblings sometimes feel inappropriately guilty about the abuse because they failed to protect the abused sibling, they failed to stop the abuse, or simply because they were not abused themselves. Again, those siblings need to be educated about the dynamics of sexual abuse and the reality of this particular situation in order to alleviate their feelings of guilt.

The therapist can help the family lift the veil of secrecy.

Another benefit of including siblings is that sex education can be provided to the siblings as well to the identified client. It should be recognized that when one child is taught about sexuality, he or she often will share that information with siblings, although not necessarily accurately. Thus, it may be useful to delay sex education with the identified client, so that the therapist and parent can simultaneously provide the information to the identified client and his or her siblings, particularly if they are close in age. If there is a wide age discrepancy, then any sex education provided for siblings must be geared to their developmental level and often may be done outside the therapy sessions. In cases in which siblings are preadolescents or adolescents, sessions including siblings can produce some useful and wide-ranging discussions of sexuality that serve to facilitate communication throughout the family.

In most cases, it appears beneficial to wait until the identified client and the parent have achieved most of the goals previously outlined for their joint sessions before including siblings. In addition, it is important that the therapist prepare the identified client well in advance for the siblings' participation. The identified client and the parent should be encouraged to provide input regarding the structure of the joint sessions with siblings. By this time in the course of therapy, parents and children can offer many ideas in terms of exercises to do and issues they think it would be useful to discuss with siblings. Some parents and children may wish to avoid discussing certain topics such as the intimate details of some abusive experiences. The therapist generally should honor these suggested limits. In more extreme cases, the identified client may strongly resist having siblings participate at all in joint sessions. If the therapist believes the siblings' participation would be valuable, the therapist might discuss with the child the possibility of having the siblings participate in short, time-limited sessions focused on a specific, nonthreatening topic, with the goal of gradually broadening the topics allowed for discussion. If the victimized child continues to resist the inclusion of siblings in joint sessions, it is the authors' feeling that the therapist should not push the issue further at that time.

Whenever siblings are included, the therapist should be clear that the siblings' participation in the joint sessions will not substitute for their participation in individual therapy. Thus, a sibling who is experiencing significant distress should see a therapist individually. In that case, any joint sessions including siblings should be carefully coordinated between therapists and may eventually include the parent(s), both siblings, and both therapists for the siblings.

The preparation for joint sessions including siblings would be essentially the same as the preparation for the joint parent-child sessions described earlier. After deciding upon the specific topics to be addressed, the identified client and the parent may participate in role plays with the therapist designed to increase their skills and their comfort level in discussions with the sibling. For example, in some cases the parent and child will rehearse, with the therapist's help, how to tell a sibling that the identified client was sexually abused.

The exact contents of the joint sessions involving siblings will vary from case to case but typically include the following components. The largest component usually consists of an exchange of information regarding all family members' thoughts and feelings about the sexual abuse experience. As was mentioned earlier, the exact information to be provided regarding the abusive experience and the specificity of that information should be determined in advance with the identified client and the parent. In conjunction with that exchange of information, the therapist may want to include education regarding child sexual abuse in general and discussions regarding any specific points of concern for the identified client or the siblings. In particular, these joint sessions can be used effectively to work on any difficulties in the sibling relationships that have arisen as a consequence of the abusive experience. Another frequent component of these joint sessions is sex education, as was described earlier. Finally, joint sessions including siblings often include a component on personal safety skills. If the offender was a family member or a friend whom the children may encounter again, the therapist may include role plays that focus on possible future interactions between that perpetrator and the children. It is helpful for all children to have information regarding how to respond to any inappropriate touches.

❑ Family Reunification

The issue of reunification of the family when the offender is a family member is a complex topic beyond the scope of this text. However, because family reunification is a common issue with which therapists and families struggle, some points to consider are provided. First, we believe that no moves toward reunification should be made while legal action against the perpetrator is pending. The legal outcome may powerfully influence the family's situation; thus, it is almost impossible to plan effectively for the future until that outcome is clear.

In addition, we believe that it is not appropriate to begin or even consider the possibility of reunification until the victimized child has had an opportunity to complete his or her own course of therapy regarding the sexual abuse experience. To pursue reunification prior to that point jeopardizes the child's progress in therapy, because the presence of the perpetrator in the home may influence the extent to which the child can explore or express his or her own true feelings. Furthermore, when the perpetrator is the mother's husband or boyfriend, it is crucial that the mother have an opportunity to explore her own thoughts and feelings and strengthen her own independent living skills before embarking on a course of reunification. If the mother does eventually choose to reunite with the offender, she then can make that decision from a position of strength, knowing that reunification is truly best for both herself and her child. If she rushes into reunification prematurely, she may be doing so for less appropriate reasons, such as fear that she cannot survive and provide for her family without the perpetrator.

Finally, reunification is not advised until the offender openly acknowledges the abuse and has participated successfully in a course of treatment specifically designed for sex offenders. In general, the process of reunification is a complicated process that entails considerable risk for all family members involved. Thus, all parties deserve the right to carefully consider whether the risks are worth the benefits to be obtained.

Reunification should be pursued only with the help of the therapists working with the child, the siblings, the nonoffending parent, and the offending family member. Furthermore, all of these therapists should be highly skilled and educated regarding the dynamics of child sexual abuse and the process of reunification. For further information regarding the reunification process in cases of child sexual abuse, readers are referred to O'Connell (1986) and Patton (1991).

❏ **Termination**

The process of termination should occur fairly naturally based upon this treatment model. The therapist should begin considering termination when clients are approaching the following goals:

- Diminished anxiety, avoidance, and distress when confronted with thoughts and memories of the sexual abuse experience
- Decreased child behavior problems
- Successful acquisition of relevant coping skills, such as cognitive coping skills or relaxation skills
- The completion of education regarding sexual abuse, sexuality in general, and personal safety skills
- Enhanced communication among family members regarding the sexual abuse experience

The client's progress in reaching these goals should be evaluated periodically throughout the therapy process, both through appropriate paper-and-pencil measures and through clinical observation. These interim evaluations will help the therapist determine areas in which the clients need continued work as well as when it is appropriate to consider termination. The clients' therapeutic progress should be applauded during therapy sessions in order to enhance the client's recognition of progress. When the treatment plan and goals have been clearly identified and the clients' progress toward those goals is recognized, termination will come as a natural culmination of treatment.

In some cases, the identified treatment goals largely have been reached, but the child still has other difficulties, unrelated to the sexual abuse experience, which might be addressed in treatment. Then the therapist must make a decision with the clients as to whether or not further treatment shall be pursued to address those other issues. If the decision is reached to continue treatment focused on the other issues, the therapist should clearly communicate that shift in focus and present a new treatment plan to the clients. If the therapist feels that the clients would be better served by a referral to a different therapist with expertise in the other issues to be addressed, that plan should be presented to the clients at this time.

When the decision is made to move toward termination, the therapist, in collaboration with the parent, should formulate a plan outlining the number of sessions to be completed and the activities involved in those sessions. Then this plan should be presented to the child. It will vary from case to case as to how far in advance children should be given a formal termination date. Typically, it is sufficient to tell clients of a termination date when there are two to three sessions remaining. Often younger children will require a shorter time period between notification of a termination date and the final session. Conversely, clients who have been involved in a longer course of treatment or who have a particularly strong attachment to the therapist may benefit from a longer time frame for the termination process.

When possible it is often useful to phase out the therapy process gradually, with increasing time intervals between the final therapy sessions. For example, with clients who have been seen for weekly therapy sessions, it may be advisable to space out the final two or three therapy sessions with 2 or even 3 weeks between sessions. In that way, termination occurs more naturally and gradually. It also may be useful to plan one or more booster sessions spaced 2 to 3 months after the final therapy session, at which time the skills acquired can be reviewed.

The contents of the final therapy sessions should consist largely of a review of skills acquired, education provided, and progress achieved. In addition, the clients should be given some suggestions as to how to maintain the gains achieved in treatment on their own. For example, clients should be encouraged to discuss the sexual abuse experience at home whenever an opportunity arises to do so naturally, that is, when a TV show is on regarding sexual abuse or personal safety skills are presented at school. Parents also may be instructed in how to continue to provide sex education at home. When young children are involved, the therapist may help the parent anticipate and plan how to present sex education information that will be needed later but is not appropriate at the child's current developmental level.

In addition, parents should be provided with suggestions as to how they may judge whether additional treatment becomes necessary at some future time. In general, if the child is experiencing a reoccurrence of previously treated difficulties, parents should be encouraged to apply the techniques they learned in therapy to address the problem. If parents do not then see a reduction in the problem behaviors, they should be encouraged to contact the therapist. For example, if the child again begins to exhibit inappropriate sexual behaviors, parents should be encouraged to apply the same behavior management techniques they used before successfully with those problems. If parents are not able to reduce the behaviors with those techniques, then they should consider returning to treatment. Furthermore, high-stress events such as court proceedings or possible family reunification may be identified as times when some children benefit from additional treatment. If the therapist continues to be available in the same facility, the clients may benefit from simply knowing that they may call the therapist to discuss issues of concern and for help in deciding whether or not further treatment is required in the future.

It is fun and beneficial to structure the final therapy session largely as a celebration of the client's achievement in treatment. A celebratory party may be planned with snacks. Or a "graduation" party may be held with a graduation hat or a certificate noting the child's successful completion of treatment. The therapist should focus on ending therapy on a positive note, recognizing the strengths of the parents and child in coping with this experience and applauding their accomplishments in therapy.

7

Conclusion

In this text, we have focused specifically on the presentation of the treatment model and have not attempted to address a number of other relevant issues due to limitations in the scope and length of this book. However, we would like to draw the reader's attention to several of those issues now and encourage readers to pursue further information regarding these topics.

First, it is important to recognize the importance of being sensitive to cultural issues in applying this treatment model. Researchers have suggested that among the most critical factors in effective treatment of minority groups are the therapist's ability to demonstrate cultural sensitivity and cultural competence. In other words, therapists should have knowledge about cultural variables that may affect treatment and then should use that knowledge to provide treatment effectively (Paniagua, 1994). Furthermore, it is important that therapists communicate credibly, demonstrating that they have something of value to provide to the client (Sue & Sue, 1990).

We believe the treatment approach described here can be useful with clients from a number of minority groups. It has been suggested that minority groups, including African Americans, Native Americans, Hispanics, and Asian Americans, prefer therapy approaches that are directive, that are structured, and that allow the client to assume an active role (Sue & Sue, 1990). Those characteristics are all applicable to the treatment approach described here. Readers are referred to *Assessing and Treating Culturally Diverse Clients: A Practical Guide* (Paniagua, 1994) as a valuable source of further information about the importance of cultural considerations in clinical treatment.

Similarly, we want to emphasize the importance of recognizing and responding to developmental issues when applying this treatment model. We believe that the basic principles of treatment described are applicable to children in a relatively wide age range. However, there are clearly vast differences in the cognitive abilities of children at various ages, as well as the clinical issues of greatest concern for them. For example, preschool children may understand little about the sexual nature of their abusive experience and may focus primarily on the fact that the experience was painful. In contrast, preadolescents may have great concerns about the sexual implications of their experience, with worries such as whether or not they are still virgins. These children will need help in processing their experiences in dramatically different ways.

Similarly, the dynamics of involving parents in the child's treatment will vary depending upon the child's developmental level. Although we believe it is appropriate to involve parents whenever possible in the treatment of their children, the nature and timing of that involvement may vary. For example, with a young child, it may be natural to involve the parent from the beginning of treatment, at least to some extent, as the child has not yet achieved much independence from the parent. However, with an older child who is more independent, both the child and parent may have more anxiety regarding the involvement of the parent, and thus that involvement may need to be achieved in a more gradual fashion. It is not possible to discuss all the variations that may be made in this treatment model based upon developmental issues. However, readers are asked to carefully consider the child's developmental level when planning how to implement this treatment model.

Finally, we would like to draw the reader's attention to the issue of motivating clients effectively. The proposed treatment approach requires a strong commitment by clients if it is to be optimally effective. Clients must be motivated to participate in sometimes difficult exercises during sessions, as well as to complete homework assignments as requested. All therapists will at times struggle with the issue of how to motivate a resistant client. Rather than accept the rationalization that the client was not ready for change or did not want to change, it is more helpful for therapists to understand the basis and function of the client's resistance. Based upon that understanding, therapists can plan appropriate interventions designed to cope effectively with the resistance and motivate the client's active participation in treatment. Readers are referred to an excellent article by Newman (1994), which outlines methods for enhancing the client's level of motivation.

We have attempted to outline in this book a time-limited, cognitive behavioral approach to the treatment of sexually abused children and their nonoffending parents. We are well aware that many other modes of treatment are used with this population as well. In fact, we strongly recommend several books that offer excellent additional reading on the treatment of sexually abused children, as well as several books that further elaborate on the general cognitive behavioral interventions described in this book. These include several books by William Friedrich (1990, 1991, 1995), as well as a book by Eliana Gil (1991) that offers useful ideas concerning the use of play in the treatment of abused children. Recommended books regarding general cognitive behavioral interventions include works by Dobson (1988), Kendall (1991), and Reinecke, Dattilio, and Freeman (1996). It should also be noted that we make numerous references throughout the book to articles and resources that may be useful to therapists in the field.

In summary, this book offers a concise, practical guide to a treatment approach that addresses the diverse needs of sexually abused children and their families. We believe this approach has many strengths. First, the therapist engages the clients as partners in this therapeutic process, explaining the process to them and requesting their collaboration. This approach encourages clients to have considerable input and control over the work of therapy and to claim credit for their progress. Second, the therapist using this approach communicates to clients that their thoughts and emotions regarding the abuse are understandable responses to the sexual abuse experience, rather than mysterious manifestations of some underlying psychological problems. Such an approach helps to normalize the clients' experience while enhancing clients' self-confidence in their abilities to cope with this experience. Third, the fact that it is time limited is an advantage, not only from a managed care perspective but also because this therapy approach is less likely to encourage the client's dependence on the therapist. Finally, in this treatment approach, the therapist focuses on providing clients with skills that will serve both to enable clients to continue this therapeutic work after therapy ends and to allow clients to more effectively cope with other life problems. In that way, we hope clients will continue to reap the rewards of this therapeutic work long after the formal therapy sessions have ended.

References

Achenbach, T. M. (1991a). *Manual for the Child Behavior Checklist/4-18 and 1991 Profile.* Burlington: University of Vermont, Department of Psychiatry.

Achenbach, T. M. (1991b). *Manual for the Teacher's Report Form and 1991 Profile.* Burlington: University of Vermont, Department of Psychiatry.

Adams-Tucker, C. (1981). A socioclinical overview of 28 sex-abused children. *Child Abuse and Neglect, 5,* 361-367.

Alexander, S. J., & Jorgensen, S. R. (1983). Sex education for early adolescents: A study of parents and students. *Journal of Early Adolescence, 3*(4), 315-325.

American Professional Society on the Abuse of Children. (1995). *Practice guidelines: Psychosocial evaluation of suspected sexual abuse of young children.* Chicago: Author.

American Psychiatric Association. (1994). *Diagnostic and statistical manual of mental disorders* (4th ed.). Washington, DC: Author.

Anderson, S. C., Bach, C. M., & Griffith, S. (1981). *Psychosocial sequelae in interfamilial victims of sexual assault and abuse.* Paper presented at the Third International Conference on Child Abuse and Neglect, Amsterdam, The Netherlands.

Beck, A. T., Rush, A. J., Shaw, B. F., & Emery, G. (1979). *Cognitive therapy of depression.* New York: Guilford.

Beck, J. S. (1995). *Cognitive therapy.* New York: Guilford.

Beitchman, J. H., Zucker, K. J., Hood, J. E., daCosta, G. A., & Akman, D. (1992). A review of the short-term effects of child sexual abuse. *Child Abuse and Neglect, 15,* 537-556.

Berliner, L., & Conte, J. R. (1990). The process of victimization: The victim's perspective. *Child Abuse and Neglect, 14*(1), 29-40.

Berliner, L., & Wheeler, J. R. (1987). Treating the effects of sexual abuse on children. *Journal of Interpersonal Violence, 2,* 415-434.

Browne, A., & Finkelhor, D. (1986). Impact of child sexual abuse: A review of the research. *Psychological Bulletin, 99,* 66-77.

Cautela, J. R., & Groden, J. (1978). *Relaxation: A comprehensive manual for adults, children, and children with special needs.* Champaign, IL: Research Press.

Clark, L. (1985). *SOS! Help for parents.* Bowling Green, KY: Parent Press.

Cohen, J. (1995). *Understanding the thoughts and feelings of sexually abused and nonabused children.* Unpublished doctoral dissertation, Yeshiva University, New York.

Cohen, J., & Mannarino, A. P. (1996). A treatment outcome study for sexually abused preschoolers: Initial findings. *Journal of the American Academy of Child and Adolescent Psychiatry, 35*(1), 42-50.

Cole, J. (1988). *Asking about sex and growing up.* New York: William Morrow.

Conlin, S., & Levine Friedman, S. (1989). *Let's talk about feelings: Ellie's day.* Seattle, WA: Parenting Press.

Conte, J. R., & Berliner, L. (1988). The impact of sexual abuse on children: Empirical findings. In L. E. Walker (Ed.), *Handbook on sexual abuse of children* (pp. 72-93). New York: Springer.

Conte, J. R., & Schuerman, J. R. (1987). Factors associated with an increased impact of child sexual abuse. *Child Abuse and Neglect, 11,* 201-211.

Conte, J. R., Wolf, S., & Smith, T. (1989). What sexual offenders tell us about prevention strategies. *Child Abuse and Neglect, 13*(2), 293-301.

Cormier, B. M., Kennedy, M., & Sangowicz, J. (1962). Psychodynamics of father daughter incest. *Canadian Psychiatric Association Journal, 7,* 203-217.

Deblinger, E., Hathaway, C. R., Lippmann, J., & Steer, R. (1993). Psychosocial characteristics and correlates of symptom distress in nonoffending mothers of sexually abused children. *Journal of Interpersonal Violence, 8,* 155-168.

Deblinger, E., & Heflin, A. (1994). Child sexual abuse. In F. Dattilio & A. Freeman (Eds.), *Cognitive-behavioral strategies in crisis intervention* (pp. 177-199). New York: Guilford.

Deblinger, E., Lippman, J., & Steer, R. (in press). Sexually abused children suffering post-traumatic stress symptoms: Initial treatment outcome findings. *Child Maltreatment.*

Deblinger, E., McLeer, S. V., Atkins, M., Ralphe, D., & Foa, E. (1989). Post-traumatic stress in sexually abused, physically abused, and nonabused children. *International Journal of Child Abuse and Neglect, 13,* 403-408.

Deblinger, E., McLeer, S. V., & Henry, D. (1990). Cognitive behavioral treatment for sexually abused children suffering post-traumatic stress: Preliminary findings. *Journal of the American Academy of Child and Adolescent Psychiatry, 29,* 747-752.

Dobson, K. S. (1988). *Handbook of cognitive-behavioral therapies.* New York: Guilford.

Durand, V. M. (1990). *Severe behavior problems: A functional communication training approach.* New York: Guilford.

Everson, M. D., Hunter, W. M., Runyon, D. K., Edelson, G. A., & Coulter, M. L. (1989). Maternal support following disclosure of incest. *American Journal of Orthopsychiatry, 59*(2), 197-207.

Faber, A., & Mazlish, E. (1980). *How to talk so kids will listen & listen so kids will talk.* New York: Avon.

Fairbank, J. A., & Keane, T. M. (1982). Flooding for combat-related stress disorders. Assessment of anxiety reduction across traumatic memories. *Behavior Therapy, 13,* 499-510.

Faller, K. (1996). *Evaluating children suspected of having been sexually abused.* Thousand Oaks, CA: Sage.

Ferber, R. (1985). *Solve your child's sleep problems.* New York: Simon & Schuster.

Finkelhor, D. (1994). The international epidemiology of child sexual abuse. *Child Abuse and Neglect, 18*(5), 409-417.

Finkelhor, D., Asdigian, N., & Dziuba-Leatherman, J. (1995). The effectiveness of victimization prevention instruction: An evaluation of children's responses to actual threats and assaults. *Child Abuse and Neglect, 19*(2), 141-153.

Finkelhor, D., Hotaling, G. T., Lewis, I. A., & Smith, C. (1989). Sexual abuse and its relationship to later sexual satisfaction, marital status, religion, and attitudes. *Journal of Interpersonal Violence, 4,* 379-399.

Finkelhor, D., Hotaling, G., Lewis, I., & Smith, C. (1990). Sexual abuse in a national survey of men and women: Prevalence, characteristics, and risk factors. *Child Abuse and Neglect, 14,* 19-28.

Foa, E., Rothbaum, B. O., & Ette, G. S. (1993). Treatment of rape victims. *Journal of Interpersonal Violence, 8,* 156-276.

Foa, E. B., Rothbaum, B. O., Riggs, D. S., & Murdock, T. (1991). Treatment of PTSD in rape victims: A comparison between cognitive behavioral procedures and counseling. *Journal of Counseling and Consulting Psychology, 59,* 715-723.

Freeman, L. (1982). *It's my body, a book to teach young children how to resist uncomfortable touch.* Seattle, WA: Parenting Press.

Friedrich, W. N. (1990). *Psychotherapy of sexually abused children and their families.* New York: Norton.

Friedrich, W. N. (1991). *Casebook of sexual abuse treatment.* New York: Norton.

Friedrich, W. N. (1995). *Psychotherapy with sexually abused boys: An integrated approach.* Thousand Oaks, CA: Sage.

Friedrich, W. N., Grambsch, P., Broughton, D., Kuiper, K., & Beilke, R. L. (1991). Normative sexual behavior in children. *Pediatrics, 88,* 456-464.

Friedrich, W. N., Grambsch, P., Damon, L., Hewitt, S., Koverola, C., Lang, R., & Wolfe, V. (1992). The Child Sexual Behavior Inventory: Normative and clinical comparisons. *Psychological Assessment, 4,* 303-311.

Friedrich, W. N., Urquiza, A. J., & Beilke, R. (1986). Behavior problems in sexually abused young children. *Journal of Pediatric Psychology, 11,* 47-57.

Gil, E. (1991). *The healing power of play.* New York: Guilford.

Goodman, G. S., Bottoms, B. L., Schwartz-Kenney, B. M., & Rudy, L. (1991). Children's testimony about a stressful event: Improving children's reports. *Journal of Narrative & Life History, 1*(1), 69-99.

Goodwin, J. (1988). Post-traumatic symptoms in abused children. *Journal of Traumatic Stress, 1*(4), 475-488.

Handelsman, C. D., Cabral, R. J., & Weisfeld, G. E. (1987). Sources of information and adolescent sexual knowledge and behavior. *Journal of Adolescent Research, 2*(4), 455-463.

Hindman, J. (1985). *A very touching book.* Oregon: McClure-Hindman Associates.

Janoff-Bulman, R. (1986). The aftermath of victimization: Rebuilding shattered assumptions. In C. Figley (Ed.), *Trauma and its wake: Study and treatment of post-traumatic stress disorder* (pp. 15-36). New York: Brunner/Mazel.

Kastner, L. S. (1984). Ecological factors predicting adolescent contraceptive use: Implications for intervention. *Journal of Adolescent Health, 5,* 79-86.

Kelley, S. J. (1990). Parental stress response to sexual abuse and ritualistic abuse of children in day care centers. *Nursing Research, 39*(1), 25-29.

Kendall, P. C. (1985). Toward a cognitive-behavioral model of child psychopathology and a critique of related interventions. *Journal of Abnormal Child Psychology, 13,* 357-372.

Kendall, P. C. (1991). *Child and adolescent therapy: Cognitive behavioral procedures.* New York: Guilford.

Kendall-Tackett, K. A., Williams, L. M., & Finkelhor, D. (1993). Impact of sexual abuse on children: A review and synthesis of recent empirical studies. *Psychological Bulletin, 113*(1), 164-180.

Kolko, D. J., Moser, J. T., & Weldy, S. R. (1988). Behavioral emotional indicators of sexual abuse in child psychiatric inpatients: A controlled comparison with physical abuse. *Child Abuse and Neglect, 12,* 529-541.

Kovacs, M. (1985). The Children's Depression Inventory (CDI). *Psychopharmacology Bulletin, 21,* 995-998.

Kumar, G., Steer, R. A., & Deblinger, E. (1995). *Lack of differentiation in sexually abused and nonabused adolescent psychiatric inpatients for self-reported anxiety, depression, internalization, and externalization.* Manuscript submitted for publication, University of Medicine and Dentistry of New Jersey-SOM.

Lanktree C., & Briere, J. (1992). *The Trauma Symptom Checklist for children.* Paper presented at the San Diego Conference on Responding to Child Maltreatment, San Diego, CA.

Lanktree, C., Briere, J., & Zaidi, L. (1991). Incidence and impact of sexual abuse in a child outpatient sample: The role of direct inquiry. *Child Abuse & Neglect, 15,* 447-453.

Leitenberg, H., Greenwald, E., & Cado, S. (1992). A retrospective study of long-term methods of coping with having been sexually abused during childhood. *Child Abuse and Neglect, 16,* 399-407.

Lyons, J. A. (1987). Post-traumatic stress disorder in children and adolescents: A review of the literature. *Developmental and Behavioral Pediatrics, 8,* 349-356.

Mannarino, A., Cohen, J., & Berman, S. (in press). The children's attribution and perception scale: A new measure of sexual abuse-related factors. *Journal of Clinical Child Psychology.*

Martin, J., Anderson, J., Romans, S., Mullen, P., & O'Shea, M. (1993). Asking about child sexual abuse: Methodological implications of a two-stage survey. *Child Abuse & Neglect, 17*(3), 383-392.

Mayle, P. (1995). *Where did I come from?* New York: Carol.

McLeer, S. V., Deblinger, E., Atkins, M. S., Foa, E. B., & Ralphe, D. L. (1988). Post-traumatic stress disorder in sexually abused children: A prospective study. *Journal of the American Academy of Child and Adolescent Psychiatry, 138,* 119-125.

McLeer, S. V., Deblinger, E., Henry, D. & Orvaschel, H. (1992). Sexually abused children at high risk for PTSD. *Journal of the American Academy of Child and Adolescent Psychiatry, 31*(5), 875-879.

Morrow, K. B. (1991). Attributions of female adolescent incest victims regarding their molestation. *Child Abuse & Neglect, 15*(4), 477-483.

Mowrer, O. H. (1939). A stimulus response analysis of anxiety and its role as a reinforcing agent. *Psychological Review, 46,* 553-565.

Newman, C. (1994). Understanding client resistance: Methods for enhancing motivation to change. *Cognitive and Behavioral Practice, 1,* 47-69.

O'Connell, M. A. (1986). Reuniting incest offenders with their families. *Journal of Interpersonal Violence, 1*(3), 374-386.

Paniagua, F. (1994). *Assessing and treating culturally diverse clients: A practical guide.* Thousand Oaks, CA: Sage.

Patterson, G., & Forgatch, M. (1987). *Parents and adolescents living together, Part I: The basics.* Eugene, OR: Castalia.

Patterson, G. R. (1975). *Families: Applications of social learning to family life.* Champaign, IL: Research Press.

Patton, M. Q. (1991). *Family sexual abuse.* Newbury Park, CA: Sage.

Planned Parenthood. (1986). *How to talk with your child about sexuality.* New York: Doubleday.

Polland, B. K. (1975). *Feelings: Inside you and outloud too.* Berkeley, CA: Celestial Arts.

Reinecke, M. A., Dattilio, F. M., & Freeman, A. (1996). *Cognitive therapy with children and adolescents.* New York: Guilford.

Rohsenow, D. J., Corbett, R., & Devine, D. (1988). Molested as children: A hidden contribution to substance abuse. *Journal of Substance Abuse Treatment, 5*(1), 13-18.

Russell, D. (1983). The incidence and prevalence of intrafamilial and extrafamilial sexual abuse of female children. *Child Abuse and Neglect, 7,* 133-146.

Sanford, D. (1986). *I can't talk about it.* Oregon: Multnomah Press.

Sanford, D. (1993). *Something must be wrong with me.* Sisters, OR: Gold'n'Honey Books.

Sansonnet-Hayden, H., Haley, G., Marriage, K., & Fine, S. (1987). Sexual abuse and psychopathology in hospitalized adolescents. *Journal of American Academy of Childhood and Adolescent Psychiatry, 26*(5), 753-757.

Sarles, R. M. (1975). Incest. *Pediatric Clinics of North America, 22,* 633-642.

Seligman, M. E. P. (1991). *Learned optimism.* New York: Knopf.

Seligman, M., Peterson, C., Kaslow, N., Tanenbaum, R., Alloy, L., & Abramson, L. (1984). Attributional style and depressive symptoms among children. *Journal of Abnormal Psychology, 93,* 235-238.

Seligman, M., Reivich, K., Jaycox, L., & Gillham, J. (1995). *The optimistic child.* New York: Houghton Mifflin.

Sgroi, S. M., & Dana, N. T. (1982). Individual and group treatment of mothers of incest victims. In S. M. Sgroi (Ed.), *Handbook of clinical interventions in child sexual abuse* (pp. 191-214). Lexington, MA: Lexington Books.

Silver, R. L., Boon, C., & Stones, M. H. (1983). Searching for meaning in misfortune: Making sense of incest. *Journal of Social Issues, 39*(2), 81-101.

Sirles, E., & Franke, P. (1989). Factors influencing mothers' reactions to intrafamilial sexual abuse. *Child Abuse & Neglect, 13,* 131-139.

Spielberger, C. D. (1973). *Preliminary manual for the State-Trait Anxiety Inventory for Children.* Palo Alto, CA: Consulting Psychologists.

Stauffer, L., & Deblinger, E. (1996). Cognitive behavioral groups for nonoffending mothers and their young sexually abused children: A preliminary treatment outcome study. *Child Maltreatment, 1*(1), 65-76.

Stowell, J., & Dietzel, M. (1982). *My very own book about me!* Spokane: Lutheran Social Services of Washington.

Sue, D. W., & Sue, D. (1990). *Counseling the culturally different: Theory and practice* (2nd ed.). New York: John Wiley.

Tavris, C. (1989). *Anger: The misunderstood emotion.* New York: Simon & Schuster.

Tufts New England Medical Center, Division of Child Psychiatry. (1984). *Sexually exploited children: Service and research project* (Final report for the Office of Juvenile Justice and Delinquency Prevention). Washington, DC: U.S. Department of Justice.

van der Kolk, B. A. (1988). The trauma spectrum: The interaction of biological and social events in the genesis of the trauma response. *Journal of Traumatic Stress, 1,* 273-290.

Wolfe, V. V., Gentile, C., & Wolfe, D. A. (1989). The impact of sexual abuse on children: A PTSD formulation. *Behavior Therapy, 20,* 215-228.

Wurtele, S. K., Kast, L. A., & Melzer, A. M. (1992). Sexual abuse prevention education for young children: A comparison of teachers and parents as instructors. *Child Abuse & Neglect, 16*(6), 865-876.

Wurtele, S. K., Marrs, S. R., & Miller-Perrin, C. L. (1987). Practice makes perfect? The role of participant modeling in sexual abuse prevention programs. *Journal of Consulting & Clinical Psychology, 55*(4), 599-602.

Wurtele, S. K., Saslawski, E. A., Miller, C. L., Marrs, S. R., & Britcher, J. C. (1986). Teaching personal safety skills for potential prevention of sexual abuse: A comparison of treatments. *Journal of Consulting & Clinical Psychology, 54*(5), 688-692.

Wyatt, G. E. (1985). The sexual abuse of Afro-American and White-American women in childhood. *Child Abuse and Neglect, 9*(4), 507-519.

Wyatt, G. E., & Peters, S. D. (1986). Methodological considerations in research on the prevalence of child sexual abuse. *Child Abuse & Neglect, 10,* 241-251.

Index

About the Authors

Esther Deblinger, Ph.D., is Associate Professor of Clinical Psychiatry and an Adjunct Associate Professor of Pediatrics at the University of Medicine and Dentistry of New Jersey–School of Osteopathic Medicine. In this position, she serves as the Clinical Director of the Center for Children's Support, a multidisciplinary program that provides diagnostic and therapeutic services to sexually abused children and their families, offers training to professionals in the field, and conducts cutting edge research in the area of child sexual abuse. She was previously Co-director of the Child Sexual Abuse Diagnostic and Treatment Center at the Medical College of Pennsylvania. She received her B.A. from the State University of New York at Binghamton and her M.A. and Ph.D. in clinical psychology from the State University of New York at Stony Brook.

Dr. Deblinger has been actively involved in the development of research examining the impact of child sexual abuse and the treatment of the resulting sequelae. Her research has been supported by grants from the Foundation of the University of Medicine and Dentistry of New Jersey, the National Center on Child Abuse and Neglect, and the National Institute of Mental Health. She is a frequent invited speaker and has written numerous publications in the field. She is a member of the editorial board of the journal *Child Maltreatment*, and

255

a member of the Board of Directors of the American Professional Society on the Abuse of Children (APSAC).

Anne Hope Heflin, Ph.D., is Clinical Assistant Professor of Psychiatry and Adjunct Assistant Professor of Pediatrics at the University of Medicine and Dentistry of New Jersey–School of Osteopathic Medicine. Her primary affiliation there is with the Center for Children's Support, a program devoted to the evaluation and treatment of children suspected of having been sexually abused. She received her B.A. from Meredith College. Subsequently, she earned her M.A. and Ph.D. in clinical psychology from the University of North Carolina at Chapel Hill and completed her clinical training at the University of Colorado Health Sciences Center.

Since joining the Center for Children's Support in 1991, Dr. Heflin has focused primarily on the evaluation and treatment of sexually abused children. In addition to her clinical work with these children, she lectures and writes about child sexual abuse. Her current research interests focus on associations between different aspects of cognitive styles and experiences of childhood abuse.